THE BEST
CHRISTIAN
WRITING
2001

THE BEST CHRISTIAN WRITING 2001

SERIES EDITOR
JOHN WILSON

INTRODUCED BY
LARRY WOIWODE

 HarperSanFrancisco
A Division of HarperCollinsPublishers

CONTENTS

In Denis Johnson's most recent novel, *The Name of the World*, the narrator and protagonist, whose wife and daughter were killed in a car accident several years earlier and who has been teaching history at a midwestern university, stumbles on an early evening worship service—given to hymn-singing and prayer—of "one of those Protestant sects descended from Rhineland Anabaptists, like the Mennonites or the Amish." The people are friendly, he observes, and when they begin to sing (the hymn is "Sweet Hour of Prayer") he is astonished by the harmonious fullness of their voices.

"As the hymn swayed around me like wheat in a wind," Johnson's narrator tells us,

> I found myself counting the house. Fourteen rows, about a dozen folks on each side of the aisle: nearly three hundred people, all singing beautifully. I wondered what it must sound like out in the empty green fields under the cloudless blue sky, how heartrendingly small even such a crowd of voices must sound rising up into the infinite indifference of outer space. I felt lonely for us all, and abruptly I knew there was no God.
>
> I didn't think often about that which people called God, but for some time now I'd certainly hated it, this killer, this perpetrator, in whose blank silver eyes nobody was

too insignificant, too unremarkable, too innocent and small
to be overlooked in the parceling out of tragedy. I'd felt this
all-powerful thing as a darkness and weight. Now it had
vanished. A tight winding of chains had burst. Someone
had unstuck my eyes. A huge ringing in my head had
stopped. This is what the grand and lovely multitude of
singers did to me.

This anti-testimony, which inverts the familiar narratives of
conversion and second birth, might seem grotesquely out of
place in a book called *Best Christian Writing*. But in fact, without
this voice something essential would be missing.

In his *Introduction to Christianity*, Joseph Cardinal Ratzinger
writes that "the believer is always threatened with the uncertainty which in moments of temptation can suddenly and
unexpectedly cast a piercing light on the fragility of the whole
that usually seems so self-evident." Ratzinger cites as an example St. Thérèse of Lisieux, whose writings have inspired generations of believers, Thérèse the "Little Flower" who "looks so
naive and unproblematical." After all, she "had grown up in an
atmosphere of complete religious security; her whole existence from beginning to end, and down to the smallest detail,
was so moulded by the faith of the Church that the invisible
world had become not just part of her everyday life but that
life itself." And yet, in her final illness, she recorded in her
diary "shattering admissions which her horrified sisters toned
down in her literary remains and which have only now come
to light." Where she had seen God's order and love, she was
tempted to see the abyss, the void, the great nothing—the
"infinite indifference" of which Denis Johnson writes.

But by the same token, Ratzinger reminds us,

> the non-believer is troubled by doubts about his unbelief, about the real totality of the world which he has made up his mind to explain as a self-contained whole. He can never be absolutely certain of the autonomy of what he has seen and interpreted as a whole; he remains threatened by the question whether belief is not after all the reality which it claims to be. Just as the believer knows himself to be constantly threatened by unbelief, which he must experience as a continual temptation, so for the unbeliever faith remains a temptation and a threat to his apparently closed world. In short, there is no escape from the dilemma of being a man [from the dilemma of being *human*, let us say].

Christian readers who read only "Christian writing" are trying to wall themselves off from the world—so too those non-believers who wouldn't touch anything labeled "Christian" with a ten-foot pole. This collection of Christian writing is for anyone who acknowledges the dilemma of being human. It could be subtitled "The Temptation to Believe."

What you will find in these essays is Christianity in its natural habitat, which is the whole world with all its beauty and suffering, its simplicity and complexity, its clarity and its muddle. An essay that touches on the Holocaust is followed by one on American public education. Quantum mechanics and persecuted Catholics in sixteenth- and seventeenth-century England are next-door neighbors. Converted prostitutes from the first Christian centuries and a reluctant contemporary Catholic novelist, Shakespeare's Lear and that protean historical figure no playwright or novelist could have imagined, Jean-Jacques Rousseau: they're all here, a refreshing alternative to the relentlessly narrow preoccupations of our principal media, secular and Christian alike.

This is the second number in an annual series. I would like to thank the reviewers of the first volume for their comments, both positive and negative, and the many readers who wrote in response to a particular essay or the book as a whole.

If you're the editor of a periodical that you believe should be represented in the next volume of this anthology, *Best Christian Writing* 2002 (covering pieces from the calendar year 2001), please enter a complimentary subscription directed to John Wilson, 419 Birch Drive, Wheaton IL 60187.

Many people helped in the preparation of this volume. Thanks first to Steve Hanselman, John Loudon, Gideon Weil, Roger Freet, Terri Leonard, Ann Moru, and the rest of the staff at HarperSanFrancisco, who make publishing a joy. I would also like to thank Elizabeth Wilson, Rick Wilson, Phil Zaleski, and, above all, my wife, Wendy.

John Wilson

It was no dream; I lay broad waking.
— Sir Thomas Wyatt

You hold a striking, engaging, *brilliant* book. I italicize the last to indicate its distinction and the luminescent quality of its chorus of voices, as of flashlight beams striking a forest floor or the transfiguring internal illumination that can send sense racing through not only our thoughts but our most complex and elusive dreams.

The quality is one you might expect in the work of writers enjoined to abide in the light, but too often in the past it has been absent. Sometimes withheld. If all that Christians can offer a needy person, over against the ills of the world, is a theological proposition or a Bible verse or two, then Christians are caught in a rather callous form of *caritas*, unlike the storytelling Shepherd who would search out one lost lamb. I don't mean by this to suggest any insufficiency in the inspired voices that rise from Scripture as one (to my ear), but rather an impercipient use of its contents by respondents to its call, including me, in many earlier incarnations.

I fall, as we all do, into the confines of history, and with the wooziness of the 1960s a damper spread over discerning expression of every kind, including studied clarity in Christian thought. As if to assert a Christian presence in the 1970s, a sort of pugnacious opposition to anything "secular," particularly as it related to the public square, started up. This movement found its fullest expression throughout the 1980s, perhaps, in the organization known as Moral Majority, Inc.

Secular square-keepers hated the heat of religion, and perhaps properly. Free exercise of religion does not mean focusing primarily on political ends or the electoral process, but the freedom to exercise belief. Which means Christians should vote their conscience, but maintain a historical mistrust, epitomized in Jesus, in temporal political power. Christians in the 1980s who were hesitant to cause a polarizing offense—though they saw religious freedoms being legislated away in favor of a secular religion of expanding government—practiced tempered moderation.

But a counterreformation, as it may be seen, appeared, especially at colleges and universities, where intellectual traction is the measure; professors found that when they referred to Christian context or content they ran the risk of being labeled "right-wingers" or worse. Few editors or referees or hiring committees were sympathetic to the Christian tradition, while hostility continued to build to the "logocentricity" of the canon, and the Christian voice retreated to a kind of apologetic peeping.

A few old-liners continued as before, and some table-thumpers emerged, but writing on Christian matters was often tinged with a smiling defensiveness or included such elaborate posturing and justifications that it took a sifting finer than for flour to find grains of Christian salt or light. If writers and apologists could have had access to the remarks of a foremost analyst of the 1970s, Erik H. Erikson, as you will find in his response to Mary Curfman ("Do you consider yourself to be a Christian?" she asked), perhaps their output would have been more even-tempered, more intellectually astute, and sanguine.

My analysis may seem subjective, but I don't believe I was rattling around so exclusively in my pepper-shaker world that I missed most trends. A sensitivity to the exact situation, in fact, along with a response that could be viewed as a call, occurred to quite a number: a series of new publications sprang up. I somewhat anticipate Gilbert Meilaender's "Divine Summons," given substance by passages from the *Aeneid*, and leave it to him to better pursue the point.

A reaction against Christian thinking continues into the present, perhaps as a blessing: that purging clarity the crucible of suffering can provoke. From her present academic post, Elizabeth Fox-Genovese notes, in a nearly scholarly tone that soon turns moving, that "when, in December 1995, I was received into the Catholic Church, my nonbelieving colleagues tactfully refrained from comment, primarily, I suspect, because they literally did not know what to say. More likely than not, many of them assumed that, having lived through some difficult years, I was turning to faith for some form of irrational consolation. . . . From their perspective, I had exiled myself from acceptable conversation of any kind."

Yet she titles her experience "A Conversion Story," and the result is as intellectually gratifying as any "choice" put in prose by, say, Jean-Paul Sartre. That is the difference in this decade, and so this chorus of voices, registering the timbre of forthright expression. It's as if the roadblocks and boulders thrown in the way of Christian expression, besides the detonations of deconstruction, have only served to purify the stream that runs with alternating breadth and depth and clarity since the beauties of *Beowulf*—now in a translation by Seamus Heaney that emphasizes rather than obscures its Christian interweavings.

What brought about the change can be explained only fully perhaps as a work of God, through his Spirit, a whirlwind of it, though the way was paved by the emerging publications I've mentioned, including *Radix, Image, First Things*, and *Books & Culture*. These especially stand out. Their editors adopted a catholic outlook, in the creedal sense, enabling writers and artists and philosophers and pastors and professors and lawyers and politicians to push through the claustrophobic overlay— similar to the atmosphere of a Soviet state—and speak from the breadth of their Christian experience, few holds barred, exposing every articulate reservation or faith-filled moment dear to them.

The providence of alphabetizing opens the book on one of the most controversial religious figures of the past century, Pope Pius XII, in J. Bottum's "Pius XII and the Nazis." Bottum puts the background and personality of Pius into swift, packed paragraphs, examining his strengths and flaws, and then reviews the nearly dozen books that have appeared recently on Pius, from all directions. The picture isn't retouched, but Bottum does draw a line across the falsities and suppressed information and comes to a conclusion that will, perhaps, not satisfy any faction, but has the feel of soundness, considering the evidence.

Dennis Covington confesses how, in a newspaper article on the civil war in El Salvador, he called a bird he had not really identified an "azure-hooded jay." This compels him, in "The Problem of the Azure-Hooded Jay," to meditate on a topic I fear too few Christian writers address, in reportage or fantasy, much less carry to the nth, as they should—the force of truth, of integrity and ethics, or the lack of them, in writing. Covington concludes: "What appears on the surface to be an inconsequential misrepresentation is, in fact, of critical importance, because the force of human will lies behind it."

Which is exactly where Preston Jones heads as a historian when he notes in "History, Discernment, and the Christian Life" how a Christian writer claims Theodore Roosevelt stood on the legacy of biblical orthodoxy. Rather, he says, "Teddy Roosevelt had little use for 'Biblical orthodoxy,' and to spin Roosevelt as an orthodox Christian is to get him wrong." Besides, "American Christians, who are concerned with truth, should want to avoid coming to wrong conclusions about history, even when that means giving up cherished ideas about the stuff of their nation's past."

Joseph T. Lienhard, in "Origen and the Crisis of the Old Testament in the Early Church," addresses theological matters, yet enters the same territory: "The Old Testament comprises about 80 percent of the Christian Bible. This 80 percent never mentions Jesus of Nazareth and is, in fact, the sacred Scripture of another religion, Judaism. Yet the Christian Church claims these Scriptures as it own. This act has been called the biggest corporate takeover in history."

It may follow as the night the day, then, that Stephen L. Carter should suggest in "Religion, Resistance and the Curious History of America's Public Schools" that something akin to Sovietization is happening in the United States, in public education, and that the subversive element exerting a force like a counterweight against it is religion, primarily Christian religion,

which itself may have planted the seeds of (as it were) the
Sovietization! And how pleasant it is to follow Carter's clear-
cut prose as he works this through, each sentence filled to the
brim with the fullness of his thought, moving with lawyerly
calm from margin to margin, yet jittering with a nervy intensity reminiscent of Twain, and then the far reach of a thought
curling in a whipcrack, with an effect like a slap to your dulled
brain. *Wake up!* You're being adjudicated out of existence!
What is your response as a Christian?

The Solzhenitsyn scholar Edward E. Ericson, Jr., turns to
Cabrini Green and the ghettos of Chicago to illustrate one
response, his father's, as he carried the gospel to inner-city
youth ("A Father to the End"). Deborah Smith Douglas places
us within the walk of two women in seventeenth-century York
("Standing Fast on the Pilgrim Way: Margaret Clitherow and
Mary Ward"), Alan Jacobs tracks down the true character of
Jean-Jacques Rousseau ("The Only Honest Man"), David Hansen
dramatizes the power of ministerial listening ("Beneath the
Surface").

The burden of the book, truth over deception, keeps up;
Virginia Stem Owens exposes a staged enactment of reality in
"Death and Texas"—a Didionesque gem of reportorial reserve.
In "Seminary Sanity" Sarah E. Hinlicky provides a comic attack
on sanity, or the tests meant to measure it, and her consterna-
tion at how the results of an MMPI can slam the door on seminary graduation. In the end, humorist that she is, she turns
the tables and makes her comedy moving, by confessing what
she can't help but construe as sin—again an issue of evasion
and deceit. Again by alphabetization the book concludes
on its central theme, as Philip Yancey's "Living with Furious

Opposites" explores the monstrous chasm that can exist between the Christian faith as it is professed and lived, and the tensions this creates for believers as they examine the hypocrisies in their redeemed hearts—so blatant in others! Are we grace-conscious sinners or fallen saints?

The rhythmic dash of Alice McDermott's "Confessions of a Reluctant Catholic," with its seasoning of irony, addresses this: "I must confess (it's a genetic thing, no doubt) that it occurs to me that it doesn't bode well for our church at this millennium to have the likes of me as any kind of standard-bearer." Her buoyant rhythms build—"pro-life, pro-choice, pro-family, pro-child, and those among us who shrilly politicize, sloganize, bumper-stickerize this complex, personal, and heartbreaking moral issue"—until you're sure she'll stamp a foot, but no; she accedes to her discovery that "the questions I most wanted to ask as a novelist were the questions the church had already given language to." Which is what we sense in the breathless rush of assurance in Catherine H. Crouch's lovely detailing in "The Strangely Relational World of Quantum Mechanics."

None of these are in the spirit of Pollyanna, or mere high spirits, as we note in Reynolds Price's "Letter to a Man in the Fire," written to a young man struck down by cancer. We learn how, beginning at the age of six, Price has experienced "moments of sustained calm awareness" assuring him of "the Creator's benign, or patiently watchful interest," an assurance that hasn't left him, no matter what route his own path has taken. It was Price's earlier account of a "transport" to the Sea of Galilee, where he was washed and healed by Jesus of his spinal cancer, that prompted the young man to write to him in desperation and hope.

Only one piece is, to me, more moving: Roger Lundin's confession of one of the lowest phases in his life, after his brother's inexplicable and "unfair" death, when he found himself locked in a frigid prison of unplumbed grief, unreachable, and then picked up *King Lear* ("Living by *Lear*"). "As I read, for example, of Lear staggering under the weight of his daughter Cordelia's body, I recognized his grief and remembered my own resentful amazement on the day my brother had died." We believe, or some of us do, that writing may coax an anonymous reader into faith, having heard from Abraham Kuyper and others about the matter, and here is a testimony of exactly that for our new century.

Let me turn to two writers not represented here and now no longer living, who didn't trumpet their Christian backgrounds. The novelist John Gardner referred to the writer's immersion in metaphor, especially when it took the grip of narrative, as "the vivid and continuous dream." His first attempts to put into practice intimations of that dream came in the form of sermons he composed and delivered to a local flock—his mother's chickens. True humility. William Maxwell was reared in the Presbyterian church and wrote about relatives who were believers and pastors in *Ancestors*. He himself adhered all his life to Christian standards, particularly those of selflessness and charity—which always go hand in hand—as unwaveringly as anyone I've known. He published only one other book of nonfiction, an expansion on Gardner's vision: *The Outermost Dream*, a collection of writings on writing.

The title is a truncated version of "The Outermost Dream of the Reverend Francis Kilvert," used by Maxwell for his dreamlike meditation on one of the books under his scrutiny, *Kilvert's*

Diary. This was a published portion of the diaries kept by a mild Anglican minister (1840–78) who early in his career served as curate to the vicar at Clyro, a rural parish near the Wye, where he led, in his words, "a humble and uneventful life." He recorded the details of that life with such bravura and aching appreciation for the people he pastored and the natural world, however, that Maxwell noted, "so long as English diaries are read, it is unlikely that Kilvert's humble and uneventful life will pass altogether away."

"The Outermost Dream" refers on one level to a dream within a dream that the Rev. Kilvert, a diffident sort with no sign of violence in him, records in his diary: "I dreamt that I dreamt that Mr. and Mrs. Venables [his rector and wife] tried to murder me." The two of them poison Kilvert, which enrages him so much he lies in hiding and lets his rector have it in the manner of Raskolnikov, with a pickax, then kicks in his face, but dreams on:

> I became so wretched and conscience-stricken that I could bear my remorse no longer in secret and I went to give myself up to a policeman, who immediately took me to prison where I was kept in chains. . . .
>
> I knew it was no dream. This at last was a reality from which I should never awake. I had awakened from many evil dreams and horrors and found them unreal, but this was a reality and horror from which I should never awake. It was all true at last. I had committed a murder. . . .
>
> When I woke I was so persuaded of the reality of what I had seen and felt and done in my dreams that I felt for the handcuffs on my wrists and could not believe I was in

bed at home till I heard the old clock on the stairs warn and then strike five.

Nothing now seems to me so real as that dream was, and it seems to me as I might wake up at any moment and find everything shadowy, fleeting and unreal. I feel as if life is a dream from which at any moment I may awake.

His dream is the reality of the Christian, a sinner awake to a God so stunning in perfection he allowed common soldiers to beat and hang up for public ridicule his perfect son, stainless blood spilling over sin, including Kilvert's hidden ones, the least microscopic speck of which He could not bear—to urge humankind onto the path his son walked so perfectly he fashioned of himself a fit sacrifice.

The unreality of that reality is a dream we daily wake from—aware, too, that the Son is God and God is the Son who handed over his Spirit as helper and aid to us in our terrors at the external world and our worse internal ones. On the best of days the outer edges of this dream seem beyond relating (though we believe a supernatural world exists concurrent to this one, when it impinges on us the effect is of treading the air of a dream), and the present clamor of electronic collusion keeps us so busy we barely have time to attend to any still, small voice.

Readers and writers and thinkers are anyway chiefly involved in the innermost dream, probing the interrelated metaphors that widen and bulge through consciousness for as far as we can see, while the outermost dream, the realm we at times see with a shock we inhabit *right now*, expands to reach and touch the hem of the beginnings of perfection found in God. That is what Christian writers attain to and what each here, in his or her own way, at least for a season, has attempted—listening beyond their innermost dreams to the stilled voice of another country.

The Outermost Dream refers on one level to Kilvert's dream, but Maxwell used it for the title of a book, I submit, to suggest something of the method behind his essays and reviews and, indeed, his writing and editing. He was a fiction editor at the *New Yorker* for forty years, through the era of its peak of distinction, from the 1950s into the late 1970s. He retired in 1978 and a slow sea change, like a glacier giving way in the Arctic, began.

His stories and novels are unprotected unveilings (an effort of courage in the diffident Kilvertian Maxwell) of the nerve ends of emotion attuned to disillusionment and loss, including the ultimate disillusioning loss, death. Maxwell's mother died when he was ten. His fiction dealt with that loss to its end, and is distinguished by an intuitive, clairvoyant grasp of some of the seamiest sinful motivations of upstanding people as they relate to one another (or not) within a particular place and time—set in prose so forthright it achieves a pointillist poetic effect as it causes your hair to stand on end.

He entered a piece he was about to edit with the same sympathetic, clairvoyant openness, respecting its integrity, and removed as much extraneous matter as its metaphor and the writer responsible for it could bear. It was the same way he entered books he would review: "Reading is rapture (or if it isn't, I put the book down meaning to go on with it later, and escape out the side door)." He reviewed nonfiction only, feeling that fiction was "too much of a busman's holiday"—his senses alert to the prose before him, no ax-grinding going on, and in this way was able to intuit the outer edges of the metaphor each writer hoped to reach, consciously or not: this was their outermost dream.

We like to imagine we read, or I do, with a comparable unselfish alertness, but it wasn't until recently that I saw the end of Maxwell's introduction to *The Outermost Dream* for what it was. He mentions how diaries, memoirs, published correspondence, autobiography, and biography

> do not spring from prestidigitation or require a long apprenticeship. They tell what happened . . . in detail after often unimaginable detail they refresh our idea of existence and hold oblivion at arm's length. Looked at broadly, what happened always has meaning, pattern, form, and authenticity. One can classify, analyze, arrange in the order of importance, and judge any or all of these things, or one can simply stand back and view the whole with wonder.

That was his way. And if you will pardon, as I hope, my indulgence, I want to say it is to Maxwell that I owe, if not my writing career, my life. His kindness, coming as it did from his authority, was at times the only balm able to heal me. On July 31, 2000, a week shy of his ninety-second birthday, he died— a blow not only to me and his family and friends, but to the standards he fostered in American fiction as editor of John Cheever, Vladimir Nabokov, John O'Hara, Frank O'Connor, Eudora Welty, Mary McCarthy, and dozens of others, including John Updike, who, in Maxwell's obituary in the *New York*

Times, is quoted as saying, "A good editor is one who encourages a writer to write his best, and that was Bill."

In Updike's own tribute for the *New Yorker,* he wrote that Maxwell was "so large-minded, so selflessly in love with the best the world could offer, that he enlarged and relaxed those who knew him. His was a rare, brave spirit, early annealed in terrible loss. He had a gift for affection, and another—or was it the same gift?—for paying attention."

Affection. Paying attention. If we could only always do so, what we'd learn! The hair-raising moment of this collection comes when in "Born Toward Dying" Richard John Neuhaus, possessor of a gravity of reserve and articulate sensibility akin to Chesterton, in a self-pitying moment, punished by cancer, realizes he is about to die and sees—is jerked out of his body to sit up in bed and see—two "presences," who say in a manner he best describes, *"Everything is ready now."*

Last week in a search through my office, a letter from Maxwell I had photocopied for somebody and decided not to send fell from a file. I skipped to its last half, able to appreciate it fully only when I realized Maxwell at the time was eighty-nine, had ridden the train alone to the city from his summer house on Baptist Church Road in rural New York, in hot August, in order to pay tribute, during mundane bodily maintenance, to a lifelong friend, Robert Fitzgerald (translator of the *Iliad* and *Odyssey*), long after Fitzgerald's death, in the manner you shall see—in the breathtaking panache of instantaneous composition:

Last Tuesday I was in the city to have my teeth cleaned and to see an exhibition of paintings by Robert Fitzgerald's son Barnaby. I was surprised when I emerged from the gallery to find there was a heavy rainstorm going on. Which means, of course, no taxis and I had to get to Grand Central. While I was wondering what to do, the light on top of a stationary taxi flashed on, and I rushed out into the rain to get it. The door opened and a young man tried to open his umbrella before stepping out into the rain. He saw me standing there and said, "It's a good thing for you that I'm a friend of Salander O'Reily" (the gallery owner) and as I was saying how indebted to him I was for providing me with a taxi a young woman appeared out of nowhere and insinuating herself between us got into the cab. Whereupon the young man said, "No, you can't do that. It's his taxi" and she got out. Imagine. On the way to Grand Central, at about 59th Street, on Park Avenue, the cloudburst turned into a hailstorm. Shortly after that the motor of the taxi stalled, and wouldn't start through three or four changes of the lights, so I got out, stepped under a marquee, and tried to adjust to the idea of a long walk through rain and hail to Grand Central, when I looked up the street and there was a taxi with his light on. The doorman had a lot of people under the marquee waiting for him to get a cab for them but I was more motivated and shot out into the traffic and nailed it, and made my train with two minutes to spare. With, also, a sense that angels had been taking care of me.

When I was in my twenties Zona Gale [a mentor to Maxwell] said that I was a harmonious being. Pleased with this remark, I repeated it to Fitzgerald, who said, "Be careful when you are crossing the street." But if angels weren't watching over me, one old and decrepit man in the rain, who was?

It is fitting to keep before us elders who serve as examples, and the example I want to emphasize now, as introduction, is the unfeigned faith of Maxwell in the supernatural, and his ease in speaking about it. And then add how happy I am that readers will find reflections and echoes of that example throughout the pages that follow, many of them *brilliant*.

Larry Woiwode

J. BOTTUM

PIUS XII AND THE NAZIS
(From CRISIS)

He was a cosseted Renaissance prince, and he looked like an El Greco painting, as whip-thin and dangerous as a pistol, as ascetic as a razor.

He was a Victorian Italian, born in 1876, and entirely a product of his place and time. But he was also a "big man," in the sense in which a 1920s American industrialist might have used the phrase—one of those people, instantly recognizable to another, who understands exactly how things and organizations work: a getter of things done.

He was hard and competent, perhaps the most sheerly competent man ever to hold his position, though he also showed a tender, almost sentimental streak from time to time, and he trained himself to a habitual charity by force of will. He was more longsighted than most such quick and decisive men, but shortsighted sometimes as well, as they all eventually prove. He lived in a castle and flew in an airplane. He spent three hours a day in prayer. He could never learn to ride a horse. Six months before Hitler's total war of modern tanks and dive-bombers smashed its way across Europe, he assumed control of a vast medieval institution whose international operations

were best suited to solve the question of what to do about
Charlemagne.

Most of all, he was an insider. Inside the Church, inside
the diplomatic corps, inside politics, inside the world. He
knew how a president's office works and what a banker does,
how a scholar functions and what an army colonel thinks. He
came from a powerful and important family, who groomed
him for great things from the beginning. At every point, his
teachers and elders recognized his discretion, his self-posses-
sion, his superiority, and his strength. And they always
responded by taking him further, and further, and further in.

Early in his career, he was the highest example of a type
you sometimes notice at an embassy party or a state reception.
The kind of young politician you can almost sense—like an
ultraviolet color just beyond seeing, a bat-squeak just beyond
hearing—is destined for power. The kind of young diplomat
who has quickly become the ambassador's right-hand man and
is standing near the entrance talking quietly with the other
ambassadors' right-hand men. The kind of young priest who
will run his eye over you as you walk in, weigh you to the last
scruple, file you away for future use in the endless, careful cab-
inets of his mind, and pray for your soul that night on his
knees. He had something finer, harder, sharper than vanity—a
will that had come out on the far side of personal ambition
and turned into an institutional ambition, an ambition for God.

Later in life, he wore round, silver-framed glasses that made
his eyes seem never to blink. He had the kind of physical
courage that allowed him to stare down an armed assassin and
the kind of mental courage that allowed him to keep the secret
of the general's plot against Hitler from even his own closest

advisers. He had enormous rights to expect loyalty and personal freedom, and for six years he was trapped inside a hundred acres in the middle of Rome, walking every day the same path through his garden—spied on by half a dozen major intelligence services, his mail opened, his employees bribed, his telephone lines tapped, his papers copied, his radio signals jammed. He hated extemporaneous speaking. He kept his own counsel.

He was a saint and a failure, a success and a sinner, a man designed by nature to be the finest wielder of the delicate tools of civilized diplomacy the Vatican had ever known— and confronted during his papacy with only blind, monstrous barbarity, like a fencing master forced to duel a panzer tank. He was the most important man in the world and utterly beside the point. From the time he became pope in 1939 until his death in 1958, every thread of world history passed through his hands. But for the most part those threads proved steel cables, and he could never make them bend.

His name was Eugenio Pacelli—reigning as Pope Pius XII— and he was either one of the greatest disasters to sit on the throne of St. Peter, or one of the greatest men to live in the twentieth century.

Slandering a Saint

Perhaps the most curious thing about the man, however, is exactly this bifurcation, for there seems no third option, no middle ground for us to choose. Whenever the topic of his pontificate is raised, Pius XII is either unreservedly lauded as the only significant resister of Hitler to survive on the European continent, or unrelentingly denounced as a cowardly failure who passively or even actively participated in the Nazis' destruction of six million Jews.

So, in the mid-1960s, Broadway gave us Rolf Hochhuth's widely discussed play *The Deputy*, which presented the guilty silence of the Catholic Church during the war as an obvious matter of history, and Hollywood gave us *The Sound of Music*, which presented the Catholic Church as the sole source of shelter for refugees from the Nazis. For the recent British writer John Cornwell, Pius XII is "the most dangerous churchman in modern history," without whom "Hitler might never have come to power or been able to press forward with the Holocaust." But for the Israeli diplomat Pinchas Lapide, in his 1967 volume *Three Popes and the Jews*, "The pontificate of Pius XII was instrumental in saving at least 700,000, but probably as many as 860,000, Jews from certain death at Nazi hands."

These absolute extremes are why Pius XII's papacy is a topic we seem to have forced on us over and over. This spring alone saw the appearance of four books on the question: Cornwell's extremely bitter *Hitler's Pope*, Pierre Blet's careful *Pius XII and the Second World War*, Garry Wills's unhesitating *Papal Sin*, and Margherita Marchione's hagiographical *Pope Pius XII: Architect for Peace*.

And now, for this fall, the latest set of books on the subject has arrived, like the annual falling of leaves: Ronald J. Rychlak's systematic response to Pius's critics in *Hitler, the War and the Pope*, Susan Zuccotti's somewhat belated attempt to join the recent bandwagon of papal detractors with *Under His Very Windows*, Michael Phayer's curious effort to extend the attack to include everything Catholic before the reforms of the Second

Vatican Council in *The Catholic Church and the Holocaust, 1930–1965*, and Ralph McInerny's splenetic defense in *The Defamation of Pius XII.*

On the whole, the current defenders of Pius seem to have the stronger case. Indeed, the best of these new books is Rychlak's *Hitler, the War and the Pope*, and in his epilogue, Rychlak provides a devastating, point-by-point refutation of Cornwell's *Hitler's Pope.*

But "on the whole" is not an option in the argument over Pius. And—to get down to the nub of the matter—it *shouldn't* be an option. The phrase implies a moderated view of the role played by the Church during World War II. And where is there room for moderation?

On the one hand, if from concern for Vatican finances (as Hochhuth claims), lust for power (as Cornwell has it), or hatred of the Communists and latent anti-Semitism (as Zuccotti argues) Pius XII significantly failed to do what could have been done to prevent the war or to save Europe's Jews from the Nazis, then he is guilty and dishonorable, a stumbling block to believers and a scandal to nonbelievers. Indeed, he is, in this case, more blameworthy than anyone except the Nazis themselves, for it was his task—as it was not, in a certain way, the British prime minister's or the American president's—to present a model of moral response.

On the other hand, if Pius XII was a holy and able religious leader who succeeded in saving lives and did the best that could be done when, armed with nothing but a traditional moral authority, he was faced with a set of monsters dedicated to the destruction of traditional morality, then attacks from the likes of Hochhuth and Cornwell are obscene, twisted slanders of a saint.

Behind the Scenes

Between the camps holding these divergent views, the facts are hotly disputed—but the number of facts actually in dispute proves, on examination, to be surprisingly small. Ordained a priest at age twenty-two in 1899, Eugenio Pacelli was one of those talented men that hierarchies exist to find, train, and promote. Pius X made him a monsignor in 1904, Benedict XV consecrated him a bishop in 1917, and Pius XI raised him to cardinal in 1929.

Ever since 1848, the Catholic Church had found itself faced, across Europe, with a swirl of Communists, Socialists, Catholic center parties, and traditional Protestant animus. And the Vatican's solution—even as the Papal States ceased to exist as an independent nation—was to sidestep domestic politics and negotiate as a foreign power with each European state. It was, in its way, a brilliant idea for preventing the seizures of schools and monasteries the Church had suffered in France—and for winning, in a single stroke, protections that would have required years to obtain politically as domestic legislation. But the governments after World War I were not the kind that had existed before. And instead of changing its technique, the Vatican after 1917 *accelerated* its negotiation of concordats with any government that made the least claim to legitimacy—as though dictators, Fascists, Communists, military cabals, and impossibly fragile coalitions could be bound with international law.

Pacelli's relations with Germany began in 1917 when Benedict XV sent him as nuncio to Bavaria. In 1920, he was named apostolic nuncio for all Germany, and he signed concordats with Bavaria in 1924 and Prussia in 1929. That was the same

year the Lateran Accords were completed with Italy, recogniz-
ing the Vatican as a sovereign state. In 1930, Pacelli returned
to Rome to become Pius XI's secretary of state, where he concluded the general concordat with Germany—led then by
Hitler—in 1933.

For all that, Pacelli seems to have understood that the new
governments were not all compatible with Christianity. Before
Hitler's accession, Pacelli gave forty-four major addresses in
Germany, forty of which condemned some aspect of Nazism.
He was deeply involved in the drafting of *Mit brennender Sorge*
("With Burning Anxiety"), Pius XI's 1937 encyclical condemn-
ing German racialism and nationalism. In 1935, at Lourdes,
Pacelli denounced ideologies "possessed by the superstition of
race and blood." At Notre Dame in Paris in 1937, he called
Germany "that noble and powerful nation whom bad shep-
herds would lead astray into an ideology of race."

In March 1939, Pacelli was elected pope, and six months
later the war he dreaded began with the invasion of Poland.
For the next six years, he would speak constantly of peace,
always peace, anything but war—denouncing, for instance,
the Allies' demand for total surrender. He was, at root, a diplomat and believed that clever negotiations, subtle pressures,
and behind-the-scenes manipulations could ameliorate almost
any horror in a time of peace. Many of his best gifts were useless during war.

On March 3, 1940, for example, Pius celebrated his first
papal anniversary by attending a Chopin concert and was
overheard to say, "Poor Poland is being crucified between two
thieves." This was a week before Ribbentrop's official visit to
the Vatican, during which Pius read a list of Germany's racial

crimes and concordat violations in Poland. It was all very strong and powerful—for a world before the Nazis, for a world at peace. A month later, the blitzkrieg swept across France. Italy joined the war.

The Vatican's radio and newspaper, *L'Osservatore Romano*, poured out denunciations of atrocities, and Pius's Christmas message of 1941 deplored "the dishonor to human dignity, liberty, and life." By 1942, the Nazis' systematic plans for the Jews were clear. When the prime minister of Slovakia complained, "I don't understand why you want to stop me from ridding Slovakia of . . . this pack of criminals and gangsters," the nuncio replied, "Your Excellency is no doubt aware of the atrocious fate awaiting these deported Jews. . . . All the world knows of it." In Holland, in July 1942, the Catholic bishops issued an official protest against deportations—and the Germans retaliated by seizing and deporting the Jewish converts who had previously been exempt (among them, Edith Stein). The pope's 1942 Christmas message pleaded for "the hundreds of thousands who, through no fault of their own, only because of their nationality or descent, are condemned to death."

The Nazis, at least, understood clearly what Pius meant. In October 1942, Goebbels's office issued ten million copies of a pamphlet denouncing Pius as a "pro-Jewish pope." His 1943 theological encyclical *Mystici Corporis* was banned in Belgium for containing such lines as, "We must recognize as Brothers in Christ . . . those not yet one with us in the Body of Christ." In an April 30 letter, Pius wrote, "We give to the pastors who are working on the local level the duty of determining if and to what degree the danger of reprisals . . . seem to advise caution." The prudential decision may have been mistaken, but it was a strongly indicated one, and it matched his personal style. "I have repeatedly considered excommunicating Nazism," he told an Italian military chaplain, "in order to castigate before the civilized world the bestiality of Judaeocide. But after many tears and prayers, I have concluded that a protest would not only fail to help the persecuted, it might well worsen the lot of the Jews." Vatican Radio and *L'Osservatore Romano*, under Pius's direction, had repeatedly condemned anti-Semitism and the Nazis' atrocities. But, given the reprisals in Germany— where listening to Vatican Radio was a capital crime—Pius decided that additional public protests would only provoke more deaths.

His personal bravery was never in question. In September 1943, the Germans seized Rome and assigned an officer to "advise" the pope—whose sole response was, "Tell your chiefs that the pope is not afraid of concentration camps." "Papal caution and circumspection," Lapide later wrote, "saved close to 90 percent of Roman Jewry; would papal clamor have saved more—or, conversely, would it have endangered those Jews then in precarious hiding?"

A Question of Judgment

It is not so much these facts that are in dispute between the two camps of Pius interpreters. It is rather mostly "a question of judgment," as the Jewish scholar (and Polish refugee from the Nazis) Joseph Lichten entitled his 1963 essay defending Pius XII. How are we to take statements made on Vatican Radio and in *L'Osservatore Romano*? To whom are we to ascribe the ultimate credit for the good done by some nuncios and

bishops in Greece and France? To whom are we to ascribe the
ultimate blame for the evil done by some clergy in Slovakia
and Croatia? The argument about the Church during World
War II turns primarily on what facts are to be taken as central
and what facts are to be set aside as incidental.

So, for instance, in a private conversation on July 14, 1933,
Hitler boasted that the German concordat Pacelli signed on
behalf of the Vatican "will be especially significant in the
urgent struggle against international Jewry." But then, recorded
in the "table talks," we find Hitler's tirade on July 4, 1942:
"Once the war is over we will put a swift end to the Concordat. . . . Not only the history of the past, but also present times
afford numberless examples of the very hard-boiled diplomats
to be found in the service of the Catholic Church, and of how
extremely cautious one must be in dealing with him." And
which of these are we to take as Hitler's actual view?

In 1939, in the formal letter announcing his election as
pope, Pius wrote to Hitler: "At the outset of Our pontificate,
We wish to assure you that We have an intimate affection for
the German people consigned to your care. . . . As papal nuncio, We labored to organize the relations between the Church
and the State in a reciprocal agreement and effective collabo-
ration, . . . a goal at which We aim particularly now with all
the ardent desire that the responsibility of Our office charges
Us." But Pascalina Lehnert, his longtime secretary, recalls:

> On one occasion I asked the Nuncio if he did not think
> that [Hitler] could . . . perhaps help the German people.
> The Nuncio shook his head and said: "I would be very,
> very much mistaken in thinking that all this could end well.

This man is completely obsessed: all that is not of use to him, he destroys; all that he says and writes carries the mark of his egocentricity; this man is capable of trampling on corpses and eliminating all that obstructs him."

And which of these are we to take as the pope's actual view?

The problem for writers in one of the Pius XII camps is always to explain why writers in the other Pius XII camp cannot see what seems so apparent from the chosen facts. At times, the explanations are almost comic. In a relentless section of *The Defamation of Pius XII*, McInerny, with some accuracy, dismisses—as the psychodrama of lapsed Catholic faith—the papal attacks by the likes of the ex-seminarians Wills and Cornwell and the ex-priest James Carroll (whose 1997 article in the *New Yorker* began the latest round of attacks on the memory of Pius). Zuccotti, more tendentiously, devotes her conclusion in *Under His Very Windows* to disparage—as ill-informed, mistaken, or even devious—the praise Pius received from such Jews as Lapide, Golda Meir, and Albert Einstein.

Reordering the Time Line

But if there is a solution to the puzzle of Pius XII, it must lie most of all in the rejection of anachronism. We make a historian's mistake when we insist that the everyday people and busy leaders of the time should have seen things as sharply as scholars who have devoted their lives to studying the period now can. We stumble when we apply the same moral condemnations to those who instigated the atrocities of World War II

and those who did not foresee or prevent them. Judgment is the
historians' task, but we err most of all when we substitute not
only our judgment but our reactions for that of the observers of
the time—when we say, for instance, that because a document
is not phrased in a way to evoke a strong reaction from us, the
people who reacted strongly to it then must be mistaken.

For someone like Cornwell, anachronism is almost the only
available tool for his anti-Catholic project. In *Hitler's Pope*, he
denounced Pius XII for his failure to speak as forcefully about
the Jews as John Paul II has done. But that same spring in
which *Hitler's Pope* appeared, he wrote an article in the *Times* of
London mocking the "sclerotic pontificate" of John Paul II. For
Cornwell, it amounts to a double bind in which the Church is
dismissed as corrupt because prior popes were not like John
Paul II, and John Paul II is dismissed because he leads a Church
thereby found corrupt.

But even McInerny seems not to escape the trap entirely.
In *The Defamation of Pius XII*, he devotes four sections to Zion-
ism and the confusing, contradictory statements of Jewish
leaders: "If I knew that it would be possible to save all the children in Germany by bringing them over to England, and only
half of them by transporting them to [a new Jewish state in
Palestine]," the Zionist David Ben Gurion once declared, "then
I would opt for the second alternative." McInerny's purpose is
a kind of *reduction:* If you want to play the anachronistic game
of interpreting statements from the 1930s and 1940s by the
standards of today, then there are plenty besides Pius XII open
to ridicule and blame.

This is, however, a dangerous strategy. And it is, in any case,
an unnecessary one. If we dismiss the errors of anachronism and

consider how Pius XII's pontificate was perceived at the time, the defense of the Catholic Church's behavior before and during World War II becomes clear. That behavior was not perfect by any means. It was not always wise even by the standards of the moment, and it was often unwise in retrospect. But it was clear and coherent, and *everyone* knew it—the Nazis knew the Church opposed them, the Nazi sympathizers within the Church knew they had lost the fight to influence the papacy, the Allies knew the Vatican was not under Axis control, and the observers of the time knew Pius XII alone stood against the tide.

So, for example, we must take seriously such things as the October 27, 1939, story in the *New York Times*, which observed, "a powerful attack on totalitarianism . . . was made by Pope Pius XII in his first encyclical. . . . It is Germany that stands condemned above any country or movement in this encyclical—the Germany of Hitler and National Socialism." The March 14, 1940, issue reported Ribbentrop's visit to the Vatican with the subhead "Jews' Rights Defended." "Vichy Seizes Jews; Pope Pius Ignored," ran the *Times* headline on August 27, 1942. "Pope Said to Help in Ransoming Jews," added the headline of October 17, 1943.

A New History

What would make all this clear is a kind of writing about history that we haven't quite had yet (though Rychlak's *Hitler, the War and the Pope* comes close and is, for now, the magisterial volume on the subject). We need a history that selects not only the actions undertaken during Pius XII's pontificate, but also the recorded reaction to them—which refuses to decide how things ought to have been perceived, but limits itself to reporting how they were perceived.

What we will arrive at from such a systematic history is, I believe, an ability to recognize both the sanctity of Pius XII and the failure of all he longed for. An ability to recognize that he did more than anyone else to prevent war, and nonetheless war came. An ability to recognize that the Catholic Church saved more than 700,000 Jews from the Nazis, but nonetheless six million others died. An ability to recognize that no one could have done better than this good, brilliant, powerful man, and nonetheless, it was not enough.

STEPHEN L. CARTER

RELIGION, RESISTANCE, AND THE CURIOUS HISTORY OF AMERICA'S PUBLIC SCHOOLS

(From *The Responsive Community*)

Religion is, at its best, subversive of the society in which it exists. Religion's subversive power flows from its tendency to focus the attention and, ultimately, the values of its adherents on a set of understandings often quite different from the understandings of the dominant forces in the culture. The larger culture will always try to impose a set of meanings on all of its subcultures; of all the subcultures in a society, religion is almost always the one best able to resist. That resistance, in turn, is the source of diversity, of dialogue, and, ultimately, of change.

A simple example is the continued insistence of tens of millions of Americans, most of them evangelical Christians, that the Genesis story of creation is literally true and the theory of evolution, to the extent that it is inconsistent with Genesis, is false. Biologists, paleontologists, and other academics deride the believers who refuse to accept what modern science wants to teach. In the face of much derision, it is religious community, and nothing else, that sustains these believers in their certainty. To answer by saying that we would be better off if they believed something else is imperialism, not argument, for it presupposes a cultural monopoly not only on truth, but on the range of permissible belief about truth. And the same answer could have been offered to the abolitionists, who were also sustained by their faith communities in their certainty that the Biblical injunction to love our neighbors meant slavery was impermissible. Abolitionists, creationists, pacifists, pro-lifers: what religion at its best supplies to the larger society is a veritable cornucopia of difference.

I have always liked the way theologian David Tracy puts the point in his book *Plurality and Ambiguity*: "Despite their own sin and ignorance, the religions, at their best, always bear extraordinary powers of resistance. When not domesticated as sacred canopies for the status quo nor wasted by their own self-contradictory grasps at power, the religions live by resisting." The culture may press the religions to change; but the religions, at their best, press back, often in surprising places. And they press back in a way that no other force does, for the transcendence of religious belief proposes an answer higher than mere human striving. The Western religions in their traditional forms all share the model of transcendence: the answers to the most profound questions are found not in human argument, but in the will of God, which exists in the world in written form and sometimes in an oral heritage as well.

When religion presses back against the dominant culture, both are changed as a result of the encounter. One reason the culture changes may be that we are constructed in a way that causes our souls to resonate to religious language, even when we prefer to avoid it. The spirituality of religion, for most Americans, fills a hole in the human soul that the more material aspects of our world leave agape. Of the theistic religions this is particularly true, but a nontheistic faith, such as the more refined forms of Buddhism, can play the same role. We might, of course, take the totalitarian view that we should allow no forces that press us to be other than we are; but then we would not be either genuinely democratic or religiously free—and, indeed, we would not be America.

Ensuring Space and Autonomy

Resistance is part of religion's power and part of its danger. In either case, resistance is often necessary for religious survival. If a religion is indeed to be free, one of the things it must be free to do is to reinforce itself—that is, to strengthen itself against the inevitable incursions of state power. If we focus our understanding of free exercise on the needs of religion rather than on the needs of the state, especially on the need for religion to create meaning in the lives of the faithful, we can see at once the necessity of carving out a sphere in which religion is immense, not only in its ability to teach or even in its authority, but in its scope, its ability to fill a life—all in an effort to balance the subduing immensity of the state.

In practice—that is, in the practice of constitutional law— the construction of the space of religious freedom remains a rather tricky proposition. In *Corporation of the Presiding Bishop of the Church of Jesus Christ of Latter-Day Saints v. Amos*, upholding the right of religious groups to hire, in most of their activities, only coreligionists, the Supreme Court gave rare and much needed judicial recognition to the notion that this space must be protected. As Justice William Brennan wrote in a concurring opinion:

Determining that certain activities are in furtherance of an organization's religious mission, and that only those committed to that mission should conduct them, is thus a means by which a religious community defines itself. Solicitude for a church's ability to do so reflects the idea that furtherance of the autonomy of religious organizations often furthers individual religious freedom as well.

Maybe it does, maybe it doesn't—I think Brennan is right, although the last point is not perhaps so obvious as to need no argument. Although many Protestants believe that God's call to grace is irresistible (for those few who are called), the constitutional understanding of religious freedom is surely motivated in part by the sense that followers of a faith possess an absolute power to exit. This understanding, in turn, meshes with our cultural attachment to liberty. We mistrust what we sometimes call "cults" precisely because we believe their leaders have somehow overwhelmed the ability of followers to reason, so that the followers lack that freedom to exit. (Some theorists, unfortunately, mistrust the family for the same reason: parents are perceived as possessing too much influence over their children, who possess only limited rights of exit from that influence.)

But Brennan's principal suggestion is not about individual liberty at all. His perfectly sensible concern is with the liberty of the group—including its liberty to exclude. If the religious community cannot define itself, cannot set rules for membership, including rules of behavior, then it is not, in any realistic sense, a religious community. This implies that protection of religious freedom requires a high degree of deference to the definitional process within the community, that a religion must possess a large sphere within which to undertake the activities of worship and following God. Within this sphere, a religion might well teach and preach moral lessons that the larger community would dispute. But the state nevertheless must stay out, for it is only through the process of defining, creating, strengthening, and, sometimes, reinventing itself that the religion gains the power to resist not only the competing meanings proposed by the larger society, but also the inevitable incursions of the state, which will, more often than is probably comfortable, pressure the religion to change. It is in the nature of religion to resist; it is in the nature of the state to battle against that resistance. A just state will therefore allow a broad range of religious freedom in order to tie its own hands.

Schools and Religion: A Not-So-Neutral History

This understanding of religious resistance helps explain why the battles over the education of children are so intense. A religion exists through resisting the meanings pressed on it by the state and projecting its narrative of the people's relationship to God into the future. It will be impossible to do so if the religious community does not have significant control over the upbringing of its children. This is the point the Supreme Court understood in its much maligned decision in *Wisconsin v. Yoder*, which permitted the Old Order Amish to remove their children from school after the eighth grade. The Justices noted, correctly, that "the impact of the compulsory attendance law on respondents' practice of the Amish religion is not only severe, but inescapable"—that is, that the law hurt the religion and there was no way around the law unless the courts carved out an exception.

Critics of the decision have cast it as an abandonment of the "right" of the children to an education different from what their parents prefer; but language of this kind only obscures what is at stake. On the one side is a religious view of the world; on the other, another view—maybe religious, maybe not— held by the state. Both the claim that the children are being harmed and the compulsory attendance law itself simply represent the state's way of looking at the world. To conclude that it is superior to the parents' way of looking at the world is an extension of the state-centered approach to religious freedom. In particular, to lift the individual child from the context of the family, the place where the religion's set of meanings is most closely inculcated, is a coercive act that is very likely to destroy, in the long run, those religions with which the state is unhappy. The state will place few obstacles in the path of domesticated religions that seek to project their narratives into the future but seem supportive of the state itself; it is only religions that are subversive, particularly those that are radically so, that are at risk if, as many scholars believe, *Yoder* is wrong.

The separation of individual child from family is a dangerous staple of the contemporary understanding of education. The state requires all families (with the exception of families with the resources to make a different choice) to send their children for education for six to seven hours a day, 180 days a year, for at least a dozen years of the child's life. Many parents complain that parts of the content of the public-school curriculum interfere with their ability to raise their children in their religion—what we have been calling, more formally, the ability of their religious community to project its meanings into the future. Elsewhere, I have argued for very strong deference to the judgment of parents who object to the curriculum, at least those who want to remove their own children from certain classes, but that is not to the present point. Rather, I wish to show how our assumptions about the role of family and state in raising children not only retain the state-centeredness that is always poison to religion, but largely (although, of course, not entirely) originated in religious, not secular, visions of education.

It is hornbook constitutional law that the religious training of the young is a responsibility of the family and must take place outside the bounds of the public-school day. Where does this understanding come from? It has emerged, at least in part, from the nation's complicated religious history.

First, consider public schooling itself, including the rather extraordinary fact that education is compulsory, which, for roughly half the nation's history, it was not. Why the change? Some might credit the ideology of Progressivism, which held that important tasks should be performed by trained experts. The elevation of schoolteachers into a well-regarded if under-compensated profession is one outcome of Progressive social theory. In the late nineteenth century, moreover, industrial capitalism began to demand a better prepared workforce, and educational theory began to make important strides in understanding the proper building blocks for learning. At the same time, a jingoistic vision of Americanism grew in popularity and seemed to most a perfectly sensible component of a compulsory school curriculum. In short, there are plenty of solid secular explanations for the swift and sudden rise of compul-

sory public schooling in the years between the Civil War and
World War I.

But what we have come to accept as the given form of public schooling also represents the outcome of a fierce battle in
late-nineteenth-century America between nativist Protestants
and Roman Catholic immigrants. The Catholics, arriving on
these shores from a Europe in which there were few common
schools, saw religious instruction as pervasive, something to
which youngsters should be exposed all day, every day. The
Protestants saw religious instruction as something easily confined to that odd invention of America's Protestants, Sunday
school. The idea that children needed any more religion than
they could get at home and in Sunday school was, to the
Protestant mind, simply ridiculous—not least because such
public schools as existed in nineteenth-century America were
designed to further the dominant Protestant ethic of the day.
The Protestants won the battle, which is one reason the
school day is shaped the way it is, without formal religious
instruction. They won by inventing a constitutional principle
against state aid to religious education, which nobody discovered until this battle was joined. And that is why there are so
many Catholic schools.

Indeed, there is some reason to think that common school
was *designed* to make it harder for Catholic parents to raise
their children as Catholics. Certainly the early-nineteenth-
century movement to create, as Horace Mann called it, "universal, free, public education" generated little support until later in
the century, after the great post–Civil War wave of European
immigrants. The movement that might have prevailed in solid
liberal fashion under the banner of equality prevailed instead

under the banner of nationalism: the children of the immigrants had to be "Americanized," supporters of compulsory
schooling argued, meaning that they had to internalize the
norms of American culture—in short, they had to be assimilated. In its historical context, the movement to Americanize
the immigrant children meant to Protestantize their religious
beliefs—particularly their Catholicism.

The same religious battle created our strange American tradition barring state aid to religious schools. When I say that
the tradition is strange, what I mean is that it is difficult to
explain. The tradition is shared by few other countries, not
even those, like France, that zealously separate church and
state. Most countries—and all Western European countries—
consider direct aid to religious schools as part of a portfolio of
pro-family policies, like generous family leave for all workers
and, for those governments that can afford it, a regular stipend
for parents. All these programs together are aimed at supporting families by supporting the choices that families make—
the choice, for example, whether to stay home with a child, or
whether to send that child to a religious school.

In America, we have gone our own way—or rather, we have
lost our way. So parents who stay home with their children are
penalized in the employment market. Parents who send their
children to religious schools are penalized in the pocketbook.
Both American policy failures have the effect of channeling
parental choices in the direction the state presumably wants
them to go: parents should spend less time with children and
more time in the paid workforce, and, instead of educating
their children in the close-knit, nurturing environment of
the religious school, should send them to the bureaucratized,

often impersonal, and aggressively secular public school. Although these may appear to be liberal values, they are, in practice, merely the values of capitalism.

Well, we Americans have always been the wonders of the world, and we are what we are. Still, even in the United States, the tradition against public aid to religious schools is of relatively recent vintage; it is only, perhaps, a century old. During the first century of the nation's history, such "public" schools as existed were for all practical purposes Protestant parochial schools, supported by local communities. (Whether we should think of local communities in the late eighteenth and early nineteenth centuries as "the state" raises tremendous risks of anachronism.) The schools of the day, supported by local assessments, featured both prayer and formal religious instruction. As the common-school movement spread, instruction in Protestant values, along with school prayer, spread with it. Nobody doubted that government funds could be used to pay for these schools. For all the virtues of the movement, the schools it produced often amounted to little more than state-supported efforts to preserve Protestantism and kill the "un-American" religions before they could take their pernicious hold on the immigrant children. Unsurprisingly, Roman Catholic and Jewish immigrants quickly denounced the schools as what they were.

Yet the climate of the times was such that nobody bothered to hide any of these facts. On the contrary. It is hardly an accident of history that the first compulsory education law in the country was adopted in Massachusetts during the period when its legislature and state house were in the hands of the rabidly anti-Catholic Know-Nothing Party. And Governor

William Seward, during his two decades of running New York, fought for state money to pay for separate Catholic and Jewish schools, on the interesting ground that immigrants should not be forced to send their children to schools where they would encounter prejudice. In New York City, the plan was partly adopted, as the municipal government, for a time, paid the salaries of teachers at the Catholic schools.

Supporters of compulsory education laws in the late nineteenth century were quite explicit about their goals. From politicians to schoolteachers (including the head of the fledgling National Education Association), they argued that it was the task of the schools to wean immigrant children from their foreign religions; and, under this banner, compulsory public education triumphed. At the same time, the nativists suddenly discovered—*invented* might be a better word—the principle that prohibits the use of state funds to support religious education, a mischievous idea that killed federal legislation that would have benefited the Catholic schools, while allowing local governments to continue to pay for their Protestant "public" schools.

But look at the result. We inherit from this battle the shape of the school day, which we take as a given, notwithstanding its ridiculous assumption that parents struggling to offer one set of meanings can easily compete with the state, which prefers another. Yet it is not obvious that we have correctly calculated the number of hours children must attend school, and educational theory, although hunting around the margins in search of an hour more or an hour less, also begins with the baseline that we have: six hours of classroom instruction a day, or thirty hours a week, is always the starting point.

I am not against the public schools; I am a product of public schools. I am, however, against the reckless continuation of policies and principles designed to make it difficult for families to teach their children moral principles with which the dominant culture disagrees. The millions of parents who choose religious education for their children, as well as the millions more who say they would make the same choice if they could afford it, evidently feel the same way. If we do not protect the space for the religious teaching of children, we are not really protecting religious freedom at all. Instead, we are preserving a system that began as an effort to domesticate religions that were seen as un-American, and, however more noble our rhetoric than the rhetoric of the nativists, there is every reason to think it plays that role even today.

Forced Liberalism

There are theorists who defend the role. Amy Gutmann, in *Democratic Education*, is quite explicit in urging that the schools be used to limit the ability of parents to raise their children in intolerant religious beliefs. Stephen Macedo calls for a liberalism prepared to do battle, including through its schools, with religions that teach "illiberal" ideas. Suzanna Sherry warns that educational policy must be crafted to limit the effect of the bad choices that religious parents will inevitably make for their children. Quite apart from its totalitarian bent—America is envisioned as the land of the single true meaning, which the elite-controlled state, distinct from the people it governs, alone decides—this literature seems to assume that the purpose of the schools is to minimize the aggregate cost of parental error. The error is defined as raising children who do not approach problems the way the state wants them to. The family, in this vision, becomes a little baby-making factory whose purpose is to create children for the benefit of the state.

This is also the unspoken message of much of the criticism of *Yoder*—including, I would say, Justice Douglas's famous dissent, in which he explains why the parents' liberty to choose a religious education for the child is not unlimited: "Where the child is mature enough to express potentially conflicting desires, it would be an invasion of the child's rights to permit such an imposition without canvassing his views." The image that comes to mind is of a state bureaucracy charged with determining, each time a "mature" child is sent to a religious high school, whether the child objects; the fact that we might call the bureaucrats judges does nothing to alter, from the point of view of the religiously resisting family, the totalitarian implications of the idea itself.

The case that here comes to mind is of course the Sixth Circuit's rather controversial 1987 decision in *Mozert v. Hawkins County Public Schools*. The case involved religious parents who objected on religious grounds to a curriculum aimed at teaching what school officials described as "tolerance." (The official title was "critical reading.") The parents believed that the contents of the critical reading course were actively at odds with the teachings of their faith. The court, siding with the school, responded that learning the tools of tolerance would not be harmful to the children and would not force them to reject the parents' beliefs. As Nomi Maya Stolzenberg has pointed out, however, the judges actually rejected not only the parents' legal claim, but their religious claim. The panel simply did not believe that teaching tolerance could be religiously objectionable.

The *Mozert* decision represents what I hope will be the zenith of judicial endorsement of the idea that we as individuals should lead unsituated lives, or lives that are situated only by a choice informed by the analytical methods of liberalism, with emphasis on self-expression and self-satisfaction—in other words, on the self. In this model, we are, or should be, able to create and re-create ourselves constantly according to the new theories to which we are exposed, so that our convictions, such as they are, are ever open to challenge. Nothing constitutes us but our ability to think and choose. This approach treats humans as consumers in the world of values, encouraging us to live our preferences, whatever they are, simply because we prefer them.

The view more common among traditional religions is that we are, each of us, deeply connected to a community, and that the community and its norms are as constitutive of our selves as anything else. These norms, moreover, are given, not cho-sen, for they are God's norms, not our own. The fact that much of our cultural elite would not want to be bound by norms that are not freely chosen does not justify the imposi-tion of that philosophy on everyone else. The very question of the givenness of norms is one on which religious communities are likely to dissent from the values of the elite; to insist that the children spend most of their young lives attending schools that teach the opposite is simply another way of limiting reli-gion's ability to subvert the dominant culture.

I am not, quite, arguing that vouchers, or other forms of state support for parents who choose private education for their children, is another issue around which the religious should all rally. There are strong reasons for religions not interested in vouchers to support them for other parents, especially poor ones, in order, for example, to maximize the ability of dissenting faiths to survive in a culture often hostile to them. But there is also the common objection: why should my tax money go to assist a religion I not only do not follow, but may actually consider dangerous? This argument is far from unanswerable, and there is plenty of literature answering it, but taking on that burden is not to the present point.

I do believe that the religious should unite behind a very strong norm elevating parental interest above the interest of the state (except in extreme cases, such as physical abuse), so that dissenting religious communities have the chance to survive and thrive rather than drowning in the cultural sea that, if left unchecked, will eventually overwhelm them all.

Trusting the State

I would not want readers to imagine that my argument represents the mainstream view in constitutional law or philosophy. *Mozert* has plenty of academic defenders; I suspect its academic defenders outnumber its academic critics. The strongest form of their argument might be summarized, in formal terms, this way: the family holds the potential to exercise enormous power, and power, in the liberal understanding, must always have a liberal justification. Arming the children with the tools of critical inquiry, then, might be seen as a way of limiting the power the family would otherwise be able to exercise.

But the student of religion as resistance cannot help but be troubled by the degree of trust this approach places in the state.

By positing a right of the children to gain sufficient critical insight to allow them the possibility of rejecting the religious community of the parents, *Mozert's* defenders risk undermining the ability of the community to resist state domination. Once we concede the authority of the state to set up its own schools and compel attendance except for those wealthy enough to make other choices, we already give the state an enormous advantage in deciding which meanings to inculcate in children, and so we reduce the possibility the dissenting religions will successfully project their subversive meanings into the future. We domesticate the religions through the simple device of taking their children.

We can justify this, of course, by following the lead of the icons of the public-school movement, Horace Mann and John Dewey, who argued with some force that the state needs citizens raised to respect certain democratic values if it is to function—in principle, a very good idea. Yet now our state-centeredness becomes simple statism, for the argument assumes—on the basis of what evidence one can only guess—that the state, as an empirical matter, will make better judgments than the parents about what the children need to know. Or, more formally, it assumes that the aggregate costs of the errors the state will make if it is the central source of meanings will be smaller than the aggregate costs of the errors the parents will make if the family is the central source of meanings.

Moreover, the very idea that we can aggregate these costs—or, for that matter, that we have measured them correctly—rests on the assumption that the dominant paradigm will remain undisturbed, that no subsequent shift, perhaps led, as so often, by a radically subversive religious vision, will undo what we have thought settled moral and even scientific knowledge. Once we kill off the ability of the religious to create centers of meaning in serious opposition to the meanings of the state, we are left without the possibility of future prophets calling us to righteousness. Perhaps some would prefer an America without any truly subversive, and truly effective, prophetic voices. But how do we know that the system established today to promote liberal hegemony by wiping out opposing centers of meanings will not be captured tomorrow to promote racist or fascist hegemony? How do we know, in other words, that the good guys will always, or even usually, be on top? (I leave it to readers to decide whether the good guys are on top now.) Nothing in the history of the state as an entity, or of humanity as a species, justifies so extraordinarily optimistic an assumption.

DENNIS COVINGTON

THE PROBLEM OF THE
AZURE-HOODED JAY

(From *Image*)

The first journalism I ever wrote was a series of newspaper articles about the civil war in El Salvador. It was called *Road to the Volcano,* and it ran in my local paper and a couple of others in the Scripps Howard chain. Although I was a fiction writer, I took my role as a novice journalist very seriously. My job was to report only and exactly what I saw and heard. I wrote in the first person, present tense, because I thought I could get away with it. What I knew I couldn't get away with was altering or misrepresenting the facts. But in the very first article, while describing a trip to the top of the volcano San Salvador, I did a terrible thing. I reported that I saw an azure-hooded jay fly into the dormant volcanic crater the Salvadorans call El Boquerón.

I did see a blue bird swoop into the crater, a nice detail to set the scene. I even consulted my guide to the birds of El Salvador in order to identify the exact species of that bird. I couldn't. I mean, hell, it was a blue bird. That's all I knew. But in the article I called it an "azure-hooded jay." Now, there was in my Salvadoran bird guide a photograph of a bird called an azure-hooded jay. And it was blue. But I did not choose to call the bird in my article an azure-hooded jay because I had identified it as such. I just liked the sound of the name, and the way it looked on the page. For all I know, the bird could have been an azure-hooded jay, but I had no reason to think it was, except for the fact that it was blue.

I still suffer for that indiscretion. Okay, maybe not *suffer*. Let's just say that the pain and guilt associated with the memory of that blue bird, whatever its species, is now outweighed by the bird's usefulness as the starting point for an essay about fiction and nonfiction, and about the role of the reliable witness in reporting the truth.

What is the truth? When I went back to El Salvador a few months after the azure-hooded jay incident, I noticed bumper stickers on cars in the upper-class neighborhood of Escalón. "*¡Periodista!*" the stickers read. "*¡Diga la verdad!*" Journalist! Tell the truth! I didn't think these stickers were referring to that blue bird. Nonetheless I took the admonition personally. Foreign journalists were being tortured and killed by right-wing death squads who did not think the journalists were telling the truth. I wanted to report the truth. I am a real people-pleaser when it comes to matters of torture and death.

So I roamed the countryside trying to find the answer to that very question: "What is the truth?" "*¿Que es la verdad?*" I would ask, until a Salvadoran friend told me I was phrasing the question wrong. In Spanish there are two words that mean "what"—*que* and *cual*. The word *que* at the beginning of a question implies a single, definitive answer. For example, "*¿Que es un perro?*" "What is a dog?" "A dog is an omnivorous, mammalian quadruped that chews up your sneakers and pees on the floor."

But the word *cual* at the beginning of a question implies that the listener must choose between a number of possibilities. *"¿Cual es la verdad?"* "Which one of these is the truth?" Or, as my Salvadoran interviewees would often put it back to me, "Which truth do you want?"

In the American legal system, there appears to be no ambiguity. Witnesses swear before juries of their peers to tell "the whole truth and nothing but the truth." But the whole truth is enormous, infinite. You think the courts are slow now? Wait till everyone brought before a judge and jury tells "the whole truth." The whole truth is an impossible ideal unless we think of the word "whole" as meaning not all-encompassing, but having "integrity," that quality of being impermeable. No holes in it, no way for the facts to leak out. Maybe this is just an ideal, too, but it seems to me a more approachable one at least.

"You can be an unethical person, and still be an ethical writer." That's what I told my wife Vicki during the writing of our joint memoir *Cleaving: The Story of a Marriage.* I had no idea until the book came out how painfully that line would be tested and tried.

Last summer, Vicki and I went into marriage counseling. Those of you who have read the book may wonder why we hadn't thought of this before. Anyway, first session, our therapist tells us he hasn't read the book about our marriage and isn't going to. "I don't think it would be relevant," he said. "I suspect that you're going to be talking about things in here that you don't even mention in the book." He was right. Almost none of what we've talked about during counseling is in the book. The book was true. But inevitably it was only one of a number of truths about our marriage.

Cleaving was not the "whole" story, but the story we told in it was "whole."

And uncomfortable to a lot of people. On account of the book, we were urged to resign our positions of leadership within our local Baptist church. A Birmingham radio talk-show host, who had not read the book, suggested our children be taken away from us. Acquaintances avoided eye contact. Friends reported back to us the terrible things other people were saying about us, something writers Pat Conroy and Fannie Flagg had warned us would happen. A few of our closest friends deserted us entirely, or perhaps we deserted them. Family members expressed their shock and disapproval. Others remained uncharacteristically silent, as though the next ice age had precipitously descended only upon the particular neighborhoods in Birmingham where they lived.

The public criticism has eased with time, but one Baptist minister, not somebody we knew, recently wanted to resurrect the issue by bringing a resolution about "the Covington matter" before the Birmingham Baptist Association. When we found out what this minister was planning to do, we called him up. He acknowledged that it was not our past or present behavior that was causing him to take the action. It was not what we had done during the course of our courtship and marriage; it was the fact that we had written about it. It was the fact that, as witnesses to our own lives, we had told the truth. This minister was not satisfied with a confession of our sins to God, or with the public confession that was, in fact, the book itself. He wanted us to remove all copies of the book from the stores and library shelves, and do I don't know what with them—burn them, bury them? But I do know that when the minister brought his resolution before the Birmingham Baptist Association, an old Black preacher stood up before the assembled body and said, "Don't listen to this man. He crazy!"

Writers make mistakes. They "miss the mark." Some of the time, the mistakes we make are unintentional. In the hardcover edition of *Salvation on Sand Mountain*, for instance, I wrote that one of my snake-handling preacher friends and his wife, Carl and Carolyn Porter, lived in a double-wide. That's a kind of house trailer, for those of you not from around here. Carolyn was furious. She didn't mind my descriptions of her speaking in tongues or picking up piles of live rattlesnakes. But she and Carl did not live in a double-wide. And she was right. I was wrong. I had been to their home once, at night. I thought it was a double-wide. It wasn't. It was too late to correct my mistake in the hardcover edition. But I got the correction into the paperback. Carl and Carolyn Porter lived in a house, and spoke in tongues, and handled rattlesnakes. Maybe drank a little strychnine.

Some of our mistakes are like that, mainly innocent, bred of stupidity or inattention. Or a failure to understand consequences. Once the *New York Times* sent me to Missouri to write a piece about the small college where Russian ex-president Gorbachev was scheduled to proclaim the official end of the Cold War. It was the same college where Winston Churchill, in a famous speech after World War II, had coined the phrase "Iron Curtain."

In the course of my article, I quoted the president of the college as he spoke to faculty members gathered at his home. The quote had something to do with competition among similar colleges, and the need, in this age of multiculturalism, for the Missouri college to establish its identity as an upholder of Western civilization and Anglo-American ideals and then, in the president's words, to "sell the hell out of it." I think it was a joke of sorts. The man had had a couple of glasses of wine. But because I reported that quote in the *New York Times*, the college president lost his job, a victim of then-raging political correctness. I still can't believe it. I would never have repeated that line had I anticipated or foreseen the consequences.

It wasn't a factual error. It was an error of professional judgment, probably related to the naïveté and inexperience of the reporter. These things happen. But in fairness to writers, an astonishing number of errors, both factual and interpretive, emerge from the editing process. Before the widespread use of the modem, or let's say a modem that worked half the time, we stringers used to file by telephone into a recording device. The results would be listened to by a transcriber, who would type what he heard into the newspaper's computer system. Need I point out that Southern reporters were at a disadvantage here? Sometimes, for instance, I'd be in the middle of recording some riveting article about a gruesome murder, complete with catfish heads, magnolias, and funeral homes, when the voice of the transcriber would interrupt me with: "Hurry up, buddy, you're running out of tape!" One time I described a small Alabama town in the aftermath of a sensational kidnapping: "The town itself, immaculate in the gold light of the first cool days of fall . . ." The phrase "gold light" appeared next morning in the nation's newspaper of record as "dull light." The transcriber had misheard my accent? I don't know.

Other such editorial changes are more subtle, but less innocent. I once described the onlookers at a snake-handling minister's attempted murder trial as having "unfortunate teeth," which someone on the national desk changed to "bad teeth," the exact judgmental language I had been trying to avoid.

The most egregious example of this institutional meddling in the reporting of facts centered on the issue of gay rights. The Alabama state legislature had voted to cut off funds to a student organization at Auburn University because the organization openly described itself as gay. I went to Montgomery to interview the legislators and was struck by how carefully they phrased their arguments in order for it to appear that the sexual orientation of the group's membership had nothing to do with the legislature's decision to cut the funds.

But then I settled into a comfortable chat with a legislator and his staff over coffee in their offices. When I asked why the student group at Auburn had been singled out—why not a similar group at the University of Alabama's Tuscaloosa campus, for instance?—one of the legislative aides said, "Look, we don't care how many queers Tuscaloosa's got; we just don't want any at Auburn."

I later saw the legislative aide in the hall. He said, "You're not going to use that quote, are you?"

I told him what I tell everyone who asks me a question like that after the fact. I said, "I understand how you feel." For some reason, the aide looked relieved, although I had not, in fact, told him I wouldn't use the quote. But I worried about the ethics of the situation. I asked the editor manning the national desk that day, not my usual editor, what I should do.

This is what the editor told me: "As a general policy, if a person quoted in a story asks that the quote not be used, the *New York Times* respects those wishes, unless, of course, issues of national security are involved. Ultimately, though, it's your call. The guy knew you were a reporter, he said what he said, and when he later asked you not to print it, you made no promises. So it's your decision. But let me make the decision easier for you in this particular case, okay? There is a much more straightforward policy of the *Times* that applies in this instance. We never use the word 'queer' in an article that appears in this newspaper."

The result? Well, that quote did not appear in the article. And one of my cousins, who happens to be gay and lives in the New York borough of Queens, called to congratulate me on the piece, but added that he was somewhat disappointed I'd been so soft on the Alabama state legislators. Surely, there was a strain of homophobia at work in all this. How could I tell him that I had the smoking gun, but that a *Times* policy with which he probably agreed had prevented me from introducing it into the article?

One final *Times* story, related to what John Gardner called "precision of detail." When *Salvation on Sand Mountain* came out, I received a letter from the legal department at the *New York Times*. They were complaining about the book jacket copy, which said I wrote on the South for the *New York Times*. While technically correct, the letter went on, the legal department did not want me to give book readers even the slightest impression that I might be on the *staff* of the *New York Times*. The letter instructed me not to use the phrase "writes for the *New York Times*" in future publicity or biographical sketches. I was, after all, a mere freelance journalist. I suppose I was to leave the impression that I wrote for the *Times* for free, or simply for the honor of having my byline appear there. Considering what the newspaper paid me per article, this was perhaps not an unreasonable assumption.

In short, that letter pissed me off, and I threw the nasty thing into the garbage can. As a writer, I was simultaneously convinced of my own invincibility, and terrified that the legal department of the *Times* had discovered the truth about me—that I was an impostor. Occasionally, though, even for a writer, there is justice in life, and I took unseemly joy in the fact that when *Salvation* was named a finalist for the National Book Award, the *New York Times* proudly announced in its article about the selections that I wrote for their newspaper.

"Precision of detail." What is the truth? Is it relative, like beauty, residing in the eyes of the beholder? What's wrong with fictionalizing certain aspects of a fact-based article, if the result is a different, but better kind of truth? What is the real harm in making up a quote or inventing an incident if the quote and incident are consistent with other, actual words or events? Isn't the truth contained in fiction more profound anyway than that contained in a newspaper or magazine account?

Well, there is only one difference between fiction and nonfiction: the events in a nonfiction piece actually happened; the events in a piece of fiction did not necessarily happen. But that difference paradoxically contains a similarity as well. We all know the reporter's job. It is to provide, as Sergeant Joe Friday, of the '50s television program *Dragnet* used to say: "Just the facts, ma'am." But when John Gardner used the phrase "precision of detail," he was talking about fiction, not nonfiction. In other words, whether the events in a narrative actually occurred or were made up, the relating of the events ought to be "accurate," or "on target." A story, whether fiction or nonfiction, ought to have "integrity," an impermeable membrane through which facts cannot leak out.

Skip forward a few decades from *Dragnet* and enter, with me, the new field of creative nonfiction, a genre the Associated Writing Programs calls "factual and literary writing that has the narrative, dramatic, meditative, and lyrical elements of novels, plays, poetry, and memoir." I carry this definition in my wallet, by the way, because I am often asked what creative nonfiction is and I can't ever remember exactly. Some people prefer the term literary journalism. Others, literary nonfiction. Whatever it is called and however it is defined, its importance here in America at the beginning of a new century can hardly be denied, even if we reject Seymour Krim's pronouncement that creative nonfiction is "The *de facto* literature of our age."

The first thing we notice about this new field of literature is that there's nothing new about it. Defoe and Carlyle practiced the form. So did writers centuries before them. Creative nonfiction so far predates what we think of as literary fiction that C. S. Lewis argues the ancient biblical book of John, by virtue of its form and technique, must be reportage of actual events. Either that, Lewis says, "or some unknown writer in the second century, without known predecessors or successors, suddenly anticipated the whole technique of modern, novelistic, realistic narrative."

Novelist Reynolds Price agrees with Lewis in his book *Three Gospels.* Citing the scene in which Jesus, in His resurrected form, calls His disciples to eat fish and bread around a charcoal fire on the shores of Galilee, Price says: "Nothing in this unprecedented book, nothing in any other gospel, consistently comes so near to convincing me of reliable human witness as this last scene of John. By its *reliability* I mean its tenor of honest report—*I saw this happen, now I tell it to you plainly."*

The burdens for the author of John as a writer of creative nonfiction were great. Either he would help perpetuate the most elaborate hoax of all time, or he would faithfully record details in the life of a man who was God incarnate. Since then, the journalistic stakes have never been that high. But the principle holds for the writer doing a piece about teenage pregnancy in Omaha or the writer infiltrating a heroin-smuggling ring in New York City or the writer covering a foreign war or the writer simply reflecting, in an essay like this, on the times and trials of his own life.

We're all going to make mistakes. The question is, what kind? Will they be mistakes bred of ignorance, inattention, or inexperience, a failure to properly foresee consequences? Or will they be mistakes of intentionality? Unfortunately, I'm afraid, most of our mistakes, both in our professional and personal lives are conscious, intentional, willful. Of course, these are the mistakes most difficult to talk or write about. But these are the very mistakes, if we are conscientious writers, that we have to write about.

It is the problem of the azure-hooded jay, that singular blue bird winging its way into the crater of a dormant volcano in El Salvador. I don't know what kind of bird it is, but I decide to report it as an azure-hooded jay for no better reason than I like the sound of the name. What appears on the surface to be an inconsequential misrepresentation is, in fact, of critical importance, because the force of human will lies behind it.

CATHERINE H. CROUCH

THE STRANGELY RELATIONAL
WORLD OF QUANTUM MECHANICS
(From *re:generation quarterly*)

In the popular imagination, Albert Einstein represents the ultimate physics genius—when people want to personify the stunning role that physics has played in the development of the modern world, they turn to the bushy-haired German Jew whom *Time* named "Man of the Century."

But although Einstein is rightly celebrated for his association with relativity, one of the two major innovations in twentieth-century physics, it's less well known that he vehemently opposed the other theory that rocked the twentieth-century scientific world—quantum mechanics. The brainchild of several of Einstein's contemporaries, quantum mechanics makes mind-bending predictions such as simultaneous causes and effects, particles that seem to be in more than one place at the same time, and an unsettling randomness at the heart of the universe.

Albert Einstein was convinced it couldn't be the whole story, largely for the same kinds of philosophical and aesthetic reasons that caused an earlier world to reject Copernicus's idea that the earth was not the center of the universe. The story of why Einstein, along with other less well known physicists, violently opposed certain aspects of quantum theory—and why they were probably wrong—has many parallels for Christians who want to make judgments about, or draw theological conclusions from, the ever-changing world of basic science.

And, surprisingly, in recent years the theory that reportedly caused Einstein to protest, "God does not play dice [with the universe]," not only has turned out to be right, but may be remarkably congruent with Christian convictions. Call it the quantum leap of faith.

Outside of the physics world, the theory of relativity has much more name recognition than quantum mechanics. Not that either is widely understood, of course; relativity is often assumed to be the scientific justification for the ideological relativism now popular in coffeehouses and dorm rooms everywhere. On the contrary, relativity was actually developed to preserve certain absolutes—namely, to demonstrate that the laws of physics apply regardless of whether the person observing them is moving or at rest, and regardless of the speed of the observer's motion. Under Einstein's brilliant tutelage, physicists realized that the physical universe is governed by underlying laws that are not dependent on human perspective. Certain uncomfortable issues left unexplained by previously known physics became entirely comprehensible with the application of Einstein's theories, leading to an understanding of the universe that was in one sense less random and more coherent than had ever been achieved before.

Quantum mechanics (QM), although not directly contradicting the theory of general relativity, did appear to turn its beautiful rationality on its head. In QM, most physical events are described not in terms of definite outcomes, but in terms of probabilities. Previous physical theories, such as Sir Isaac Newton's tremendously successful theory of universal gravitation, were *deterministic:* if we knew an object's initial properties and a few basic laws, we could predict with mathematical confidence exactly how that object would behave. Their universe was orderly, rational, and predictable—the kind of universe a modern Westerner might happily embrace.

The only problem was that when classical physics, which works so well at describing many phenomena, was applied to certain fundamental questions like the underlying structure of atoms, something was clearly missing. In fact, experimental evidence obtained by Lord Ernest Rutherford at the beginning of the twentieth century, indicating that atoms were made up of a core nucleus surrounded by electrons, simply could not be understood classically. If the classical picture was all there was to it, atoms should immediately collapse in a burst of radiation.

Quantum mechanics was proposed, in a remarkable instance of scientific synchronicity, out of the concerted work of several physicists in the 1920s. The new theory was a terrific success at solving some of the mysteries that had bedeviled classical theorists, at least at the level of providing a mathematical apparatus whose predictions fit the experimental data exceedingly well.

In the QM world, physical objects have not well-defined properties, but *probabilities of having properties.* Take the location of any given particle—QM is stubbornly unwilling to tell you where each electron in your body's roughly billion billion billion (10^{27}) atoms *is* right now. Chances are, they're all pretty much where you think they are, but there is a real (though extraordinarily small) chance that right now, at least one of your electrons "is" outside of your personal space. In fact, QM refuses to commit to where the electron is, preferring instead to say merely that at any given time, that electron has a certain probability of being in a certain place. This idea—that chance, rather than definite predictability, describes the behavior of the universe—prompted Einstein's uneasy comment about God playing dice.

But the trouble with QM goes well beyond randomness. In 1935, Einstein, together with two colleagues (Boris Podolsky and Nathan Rosen), identified a consequence of QM that, at best, seemed paradoxical and, at worst, flew in the face of conventional ideas about cause and effect. In certain situations, a measurement made on one particle (known as an EPR measurement, for Einstein, Podolsky, and Rosen) appears to *instantly* affect the properties of another particle, *no matter how far apart the two particles are.* This seemed to directly violate one of the cherished ideas of relativity, namely, that nothing can travel faster than the speed of light. One consequence of this cosmic speed limit is that interactions between particles, such as the electric attraction between positive and negative charged particles, do not happen instantly if the particles involved are separated by some distance; it takes time for the field that mediates the attraction to travel between the two particles. For Einstein, Podolsky, and Rosen, the apparently instantaneous effect of an event in one place on a particle elsewhere was strong evidence that something was rotten in QM's picture of the universe.

It took many decades for the technology of experimental physics to catch up with the EPR challenge. But in the past decade physicists have performed many experiments to determine whether the EPR paradox in fact is reflected in reality. The outcomes of these experiments indicate that, indeed, nature is as bizarre as QM tells us, confirming Einstein's worst fears. Physicists like Stephen Hawking of Cambridge University (who followed Sir Isaac Newton over three hundred years later in a prominent professorship of mathematical physics) have heralded these results as indicating that God does indeed "play dice" with the universe—if there is a God, this God cannot be purposeful or act deliberately in the world, since the randomness and irrationality of QM demonstrate that no one, even God, can foresee the future, much less exert control over it.

So it's not surprising that when they think about physics at all, many thoughtful Christians are tempted to bury their heads in the postmodern sand. Surely Einstein was right to resist the idea of a God who is little more than a cosmic gambler, wondering where his electrons are today. The situation is not made easier by QM's manifest success at driving scientific and technological progress in physics, chemistry, biology, and computer science (quantum computing, which depends on some of QM's more bizarre features, is coming eventually to a chip near you). Like medieval theologians confronting the uncomfortable evidence that Copernicus's theory just worked better than Ptolemy's, biblically informed people may wonder if cosmos is giving way to chaos.

In truth, though, it's not so simple. First, the world of classical physics was hardly friendly to the biblical picture of a personal God involved with his creation. In a world of billiard balls bouncing off one another with immutable mathematical

precision, the idea that God (or, indeed, free wills of any sort)
could intervene in the process seemed increasingly incredible.
The French scientist Laplace reportedly said, when asked by
Napoleon what role God played in his cosmology, "Sire, I
have had no need of that hypothesis." For orthodox Christianity, those were certainly not the good old days.

But, second, there is a big difference between a physical
theory—the equations and predictions of QM—and its interpretation—the conclusions we draw from the equations about
reality itself. Since the development of QM, physicists and
philosophers of science have argued with one another about
what it actually means. Does the probabilistic nature of QM
imply that randomness is a fundamental quality of our universe?
While the orthodox interpretation (known as the "Copen-
hagen interpretation" for the home of Niels Bohr, one of its
main advocates) insists that the behavior of particles really has
a random quality, others hold that the world only *appears* to be
governed by chance—we simply have not found the laws that
divulge its underlying purposefulness. Such metaphysical questions are not answered by the theory of QM itself.

Since curiosity is a required characteristic for a physicist,
and since most physicists do not observe disciplinary boundaries to their curiosity, a number of theoretical physicists have
ventured to the very edges of their turf to speculate about the
meaning of QM. Out of their speculations, a number of different interpretations have emerged. One deserves particular
attention from those who believe in a Creator. Sometimes
known as the "Ithaca interpretation of quantum mechanics,"
because it was devised by N. David Mermin of Cornell University in Ithaca, New York, this interpretation, surprisingly,

makes contact with some of the most fundamental Christian beliefs about God and creation.

Mermin's central idea is simple: the basic elements of physical reality are not individual objects but *relationships* between what we perceive to be individual objects. (To use Mermin's more technical terminology, correlations between the properties of individual objects, rather than the "correlata," the properties of the individual objects themselves, are the basic constituents of a physical theory.) Individual objects as such most certainly exist. However, if we insist on knowing the properties of *individual objects* rather than the properties of *relationships* between objects, our efforts are doomed to appear paradoxical and incoherent. Physics, it turns out, is not about probing the properties of smaller and smaller billiard balls (electrons, quarks, or neutrinos)—it is about the properties of the relations between those objects, which indeed derive their identity from their relations. The primacy of objects gives way to the primacy of relationships.

It is beyond the scope of this essay to explain the technical argument that can be made after taking this interpretive step. But, essentially, Mermin's approach eliminates QM's apparent violations of cause and effect. If we consider the relationships to be fundamental, rather than individual objects, then the outcomes of EPR measurements are no longer paradoxical, but follow naturally from what is known about the relationships between the objects involved. The universe is rational, Mermin suggests, because it is *relational*.

Christian readers of Mermin suddenly find themselves in familiar territory, for any deeply Christian account of the creation seems bound to have a relational quality. From the enigmatic "us" in Genesis 1:26 to the fully formed descriptions of the Trinity in the creeds, Christian thought posits a relationality in God himself. And the universe exists, Jewish and Christian theologians have long asserted, in continuous, ongoing, dynamic, loving relation to God. (In a suggestion that has particular resonance with QM's emphasis on the role of the observer, the eighteenth-century philosopher Berkeley went so far as to say that the reality of the universe comes from God continually regarding it.) Under Mermin's interpretation, at least, QM turns out to be as much an ally as a foe to the Christian understanding of the world, and some of its most "irrational" elements actually compel a more relational rationality.

Does all of this prove anything? Not really. For one thing, Mermin's interpretation is just that—an interpretation, probably not subject to experimental verification in the way a true scientific hypothesis would be. Even if it is ultimately persuasive because of the elegant way it solves several knotty puzzles, a picture of a fundamentally relational cosmos does not by itself lead us very close to the Christian picture of a God who is Creator, Redeemer, and Sustainer of creation. Many other theological and philosophical options are compatible with Mermin's interpretation, including notably the "panentheism" of Charles Hartshorne and process theologians, which falls well short of the biblical witness to God.

Similarly, the probabilistic nature of QM has been taken by Hawking as proof positive that the universe lacks purpose and design; yet others, such as the British physicist and Anglican priest John Polkinghorne, see an opening for divine and human free will that had been excluded from previous models of the cosmos. Indeed, Polkinghorne points out that in certain kinds of complex physical systems, although the outcomes of microscopic events are governed by probability, the behavior of the system as a whole proceeds within certain boundaries. This could serve as an analogy for how the cosmos as a whole could be working out the purposes of God while permitting freedom of choice to individuals and the possibility of random determination of atomic events. Most, if not all, of the time, several different theologies are consistent with the same evidence.

This is hardly surprising if the Gospel of John is to be trusted in its claim that "no one has ever seen God. It is God the only Son, who is close to the Father's heart, who has made him known" (John 1:18). Or if Genesis is to be believed when it describes God making humanity in his own image. Or if the whole of Scripture does indeed, as it claims, make God's character clear precisely through his interactions (his relations!) with human beings, especially Israel and the Church. Compared to these sources, the creation as a whole is a minor witness. It was made by God and thus reflects some of his qualities, just as a sculpture tells viewers something about the sculptor. But simply seeing an exhibition of sculpture does not give a complete picture of who the sculptor is, whereas reading the sculptor's letters to her family, meeting her children, and especially meeting the sculptor herself tell much more.

So, like every other scientific discovery, QM (which itself is subject to being superseded by a more adequate theory, just as classical physics was) tells us something, but not enough, about God. It is fascinating to speculate, though, on how Einstein might have responded to the dramatic experimental confirmations of QM, that theory he found so unpalatable, near the close of the twentieth century. Would he have given up, with Stephen Hawking, and concluded that God was a cosmic gambler after all? Or would he have begun to suspect that far from playing dice, God was more intimately and personally involved in the world than classical physics ever imagined?

DEBORAH SMITH DOUGLAS

STANDING FAST ON THE PILGRIM WAY: MARGARET CLITHEROW AND MARY WARD

(From *Weavings*)

It is exhilarating to walk atop the city walls of York—especially on an April morning with the sun flashing on the River Ouse and the wind scattering apple blossom before me like confetti. I revel in knowing that I am, through the soles of my shoes, in direct contact with (my guidebook assures me) one of the finest surviving examples of medieval fortification in Europe, looking down on a thriving city that remembers not only the Middle Ages, but the Vikings, the Saxons, and the Romans. The massive wall is itself both rampart and road—protecting the city from its foes and providing a walkway for its citizens to follow. These twin qualities of standing fast and moving forward are also exemplified by two extraordinary seventeenth-century women of York, Mary Ward and Margaret Clitherow. It is because of them that I am here.

From my vantage point atop the encircling wall, at the ancient gate of the Micklegate Bar, I can see just on the far side the decorous brick façade of the Bar Convent. This house was established in 1686 by the followers of Mary Ward (1585–1645), who was in her life both praised as a "great servant of God" and condemned as a "heretic, schismatic, and rebel," and who is honored today as a dauntless visionary, a pioneer of unenclosed religious life for women.

For thirty years this intrepid woman traveled tirelessly across Europe, founding schools for Catholic girls and laboring to establish a rule of life for women based on the Rule and Constitutions of the Society of Jesus. The Jesuits were themselves at that time a new and controversial order of priests, their life being based not on medieval monastic norms of stability and long hours in chapel singing the divine office, but on freedom and mobility; being ready to go in obedience to the ends of the earth at a moment's notice "for the greater glory of God."[1] This was a revolutionary idea for men in vowed religious life; it was unheard of for women. Furthermore, England had seen no convents of any kind for seventy years, since the dissolution of the monasteries by Henry VIII. Young Catholic girls in Tudor England who felt called to cloistered life had to accept lifelong exile in Catholic Flanders or France. Nevertheless, Mary Ward knew from the age of fifteen that she had been called by God to religious life—not to conventional enclosure in a convent, but to a life of action inspired by the love of God and modeled on the example of the Jesuits.

Serenely undeterred by ferocious opposition to her dream, and aware that only papal approval would secure the future of

---

1. For a fascinating glimpse into the amazing adventures of the Jesuits in England, see Philip Caraman, S.J., *A Study in Friendship: St. Robert Southwell and Henry Garnett* (St. Louis: Institute of Jesuit Sources, 1991).

the congregation she envisioned (the Institute of the Blessed Virgin Mary, as it was eventually to be known), she crossed the Alps four times, in winter, on foot, to present her case to the pope in person.[2] She established schools for girls and Institute houses in England, France, Italy, Germany, Hungary, and the Low Countries. Her schools were much admired, but the radical notion of nonenclosure for women drew much opposition. Mary, however, was adamant. "I will not accept as much as two crossed sticks in the way of enclosure," she stoutly declared.[3]

She faced hostility not only from within the Catholic Church, but from the Anglican establishment as well. She was so ardent and effective a Catholic in Elizabethan England, where Catholics were hunted as spies and executed as traitors, that the archbishop of Canterbury declared in frustration that she had "done more harm [to the Protestant cause] than many priests."[4] Imprisoned both by order of the Inquisition and by the Protestant authorities, she lived to see her beloved Institute suppressed and dissolved by order of the pope, her schools closed, her life's work shattered.[5] Yet Mary Ward was steadfast in hope, and peaceful to the end, urging her companions with

2. Mary Ward wished the Institute to be called "Society of Jesus," like the Jesuits, which proved impossible. Her companions were long known as "the English Ladies." From the middle of the eighteenth century, Mary Ward's foundation was known as the "Institute of St. Mary," which was finally granted the Ignatian Constitutions in 1978.
3. Sr. M. Gregory Kirkus, I.B.V.M., "Mary Ward," a lecture given at the Bar Convent, York, 1996, unpublished ms., p. 19.
4. Margaret Mary Littlehales, I.B.V.M., *Mary Ward: A Woman for All Seasons* (London: Catholic Truth Society, 1974), p. 14.
5. *Till God Will: Mary Ward Through Her Writings*, ed. M. Emmanuel Orchard, I.B.V.M. (London: Darton, Longman & Todd, 1985), p. 102.

characteristic "imperturbable gaiety"[6] to "be merry and doubt not our Master."[7] Today the Institute of the Blessed Virgin Mary, which continues as a vibrant teaching order, numbers several thousand members in five continents. The oldest house is the Bar Convent here in York.

From its founding, the Bar Convent provided secret Masses for the Catholic community of York, as well as covert schooling for its daughters. In 1765, when the convent was rebuilt, it still was illegal to build a Catholic church in England.[8] The convent's magnificent chapel is completely hidden at the center of the house, invisible from the outside. A pitched roof conceals the sunken dome, and a hiding place for the priest was included as a matter of course. It was discovered about fifty years ago, when electrical wiring was being installed. The elegant Georgian brick building still presents a courteously bland face to the world, protecting the secret chapel at its heart, bearing architectural witness to a long era of persecution—and of standing fast.

Severe anti-Catholic decrees, born of Henry VIII's and Elizabeth I's insistence on being recognized as the sole heads of the Church in England, made it illegal even to attend Mass. Those Catholics (called "recusants," meaning "refusers") who chose fidelity to Rome over obedience to the Tudors needed great

---

6. Littlehales, *Mary Ward*, p. 30.

7. Letter from prison, 1631, cited by M. Immolata Wetter, I.B.V.M., *Mary Ward* (Regensburg, Germany: Schnell & Steiner, 1996), p. 18.

8. It was not until 1778 that the first Catholic Relief Act was passed by Parliament, and not until 1828 that English Catholics were allowed to vote in elections or hold public office. See David L. Edwards, *A Concise History of English Christianity from Roman Britain to the Present Day* (London: HarperCollins, 1998), pp. 100, 107.

courage. The illicit practice of the Catholic faith, especially the indispensable sacrament of the Mass, required clandestine gatherings with priests. These priests—often Jesuits—had been educated and ordained overseas, smuggled into England, and secretly passed from house to house to celebrate their forbidden Masses. This was an act of treason and was punishable by death not only for the priests, but for the families that sheltered them.[9]

The *élan* of these recusants, determined to remain faithful Catholics whatever the consequences, still is striking today. Young Robert Coulton, challenged by the Protestant authorities, spoke for many when he said, "I hear say that England had been a Catholic Christian country a thousand years afore this queen's reign and her father's. If that were the old highway to heaven, then why should I forsake it?"[10] Those who remained committed to "the old highway" paid dearly for that allegiance. Recusants were stripped of land and title, forced to pay heavy fines, and sometimes spent years in prison for the privilege of nonattendance at Anglican worship.

Others paid for steadfast commitment to "the old highway" with their lives. During Elizabeth's reign, more than a hundred Roman Catholic priests were hunted down, imprisoned, tortured, and hanged as traitors, joined by ninety courageous laywomen and -men. First among them was another valiant Yorkshire woman, St. Margaret Clitherow, who is revered by Catholics around the world today as one of the Forty Martyrs of England and Wales.

---

9. See Robert Ellsberg, *All Saints: Daily Reflections on Saints, Prophets, and Witnesses for Our Time* (New York: Crossroad, 1998), pp. 41–42, 133–34.
10. Edwards, *A Concise History of English Christianity*, p. 54.

Continuing my walk along the city wall, I come to the Lendal Bridge where it spans the broad Ouse. From the bridge, looking east inside the wall's embrace—and looking back in time a generation before Mary Ward—I can see the medieval guildhall, where Margaret Clitherow was sentenced to death for harboring priests and hearing Mass in her home. Just down the river, at the next bridge, is the unmarked site of her execution.

These two remarkable women never met—Margaret died in 1586, at the age of thirty-three, when Mary was just one year old—but their lives connected in deep places, rooted in realities and allegiances that continued to sustain the faithful who came after them. The steadfast love of God and confidence in God's purposes that illumined both their lives shine across the centuries like the rhythmic signal of a lighthouse.

Margaret Clitherow was born in 1553, the year of the Catholic Queen Mary's accession, so in all probability she was brought up as a Catholic until she was eight, when her widowed mother married a Protestant. After that—Queen Elizabeth having ascended the throne—the religious influences in Margaret's growing-up life were all Protestant. At the age of fifteen she was married to local widower John Clitherow, a Protestant butcher old enough to be her father.[11] Within three years of her marriage, however, Margaret had been reconciled to the Catholic Church. By the time she was eighteen, her house was established as the principal Mass

---

11. John Clitherow remained Protestant all his life, but loyally paid the fines for Margaret's recusancy. When she died, he wept aloud, grieving the loss of "the best wife in all England, and the best Catholic." See Philip Caraman, S.J., *Margaret Clitherow* (London: Catholic Truth Society, 1986), p. 14.

center—and thus the heart of the underground Catholic community—in York.[12]

For the rest of her life, Margaret befriended and harbored priests in her home, running a small (and highly illegal) school for the Catholic education of children, and "providing place and all things convenient" for the celebration of the Mass. For most of a decade she was in and out of prison for these crimes, released once only long enough for the birth of one of her children. Margaret's time in prison, in company with other recusant Catholics, seems to have been a profound experience of religious community. She used the time to study, pray, and strengthen her faith. During one of her long captivities, she learned to read and write.

But the deadly risks of recusancy caught up with her at last. A raid on the Clitherow house in March of 1586 revealed the existence of the priest's hiding place in the attic (although the priest had time to escape), as well as the altar and chalice and books and vestments for the Mass. Margaret was arrested, imprisoned, and formally charged. She was allowed no counsel, and conducted her own defense, repeatedly refusing to consent to a trial ("Having made no offense, I need no trial," she calmly told the judge), lest her own and others' children be compelled to give testimony against her.

This compassionate and courageous stand doubtless saved several lives, but cost her her own. Her refusal to enter a plea left the court no alternative, under law, but to pronounce the sentence of death by *peine forte and dure*—being pressed to death

---

12. Ronald Connelly, *Women of the Catholic Resistance: In England 1540–1680* (Durham, England: Pentland Press, 1997), p. 49.

by heavy weights laid upon her prostrate body. This terrible death had been known to take as long as three days, but was swift in Margaret's case. As the weights were laid on her, she prayed, "Jesu, Jesu, have mercy on me." Within a quarter of an hour she was dead.

The story of Margaret Clitherow is one Mary Ward would have heard from her cradle. The whole audacious enterprise of harboring fugitive priests was "very much a woman's affair"— and shaped the heart of every household in which Mary lived as a child.[13] The underground Catholic community in England in those days was essentially a matriarchy. As Father John Mush, one of the priests befriended by Margaret Clitherow, himself put it, "The gentlemen hereabouts have fallen away from the priests but the gentlewomen stood steadfastly to them."[14]

I suspect that Mary Ward was influenced in her vision of the Institute not only by the Jesuits, but by the "women and specifically wives" who sheltered and assisted the priests, educated the children, prepared candidates for baptism, in fact shaped and nurtured the community under persecution and in exile.[15] Mary's experience was blessed by a large number of these women, who made their prisons into schools and retreat houses and their homes into sanctuaries. Ursula Wright, Mary Ward's maternal grandmother, spent fourteen consecutive years in prison. Mary's aunt, Lady Grace Babthorpe, began married life at the age of fifteen with a two-year stint in jail; when she was arrested and asked how many Masses she had

13. Connelly, *Women of the Catholic Resistance*, p. 3.
14. Connelly, *Women of the Catholic Resistance*, p. 2.
15. Bossy, *The English Catholic Community*, cited by Connelly, *Women of the Catholic Resistance*, p. 2.

heard, her spirited response was "so many that I cannot count them."[16]

In seeking this kind of life for vowed women religious, Mary Ward was in some ways seeking a freedom for single women that had long been the prerogative of wives. She wanted both the mobility of the heroic Jesuits who risked their lives to tend the Catholic flock in England, and the devotion of the heroic women who risked their lives to keep the Jesuits.

From her prison cell the night before she died, Margaret made a final bequest: she left her shoes to her eldest daughter, Anne, who was then twelve years old—and who, as a scholar in her mother's illegal school, also had been arrested and imprisoned following the raid. There is strong motherly admonition implicit in the gesture—*follow in my footsteps*, the wordless gift seems to say; *carry on*. Anne seems to have taken the hint: she was to be imprisoned again for "causes ecclesiastical" after her release at the time of her mother's death, and she later escaped an arranged marriage and made the hazardous journey to the Continent, where she became a nun in a Flemish convent. Like her mother before her, and like Mary Ward and her grandmother, Anne Clitherow chose the "old highway to heaven" and walked it faithfully.[17]

Mary Ward's shoes are similarly eloquent of steadfastness. Her worn leather shoes, in which she walked from Brussels to Rome, some fifteen hundred miles, are reverently displayed in the museum of the Institute house she founded in Alt Ötting, Germany.

---

16. Littlehales, *Mary Ward*, p. 4.
17. See Connelly, *Women of the Catholic Resistance*, p. 153–55.

I am intrigued by these two pairs of shoes. I think they have much to teach us as we seek to know what it is to stand fast while moving forward. Our world and our still divided church have changed in many ways in four hundred years, but still are in need of Christians with the wisdom and courage to persevere in what matters most.

These two women remind us that to stand fast is not to stand still. Steadfastness of purpose does not imply a rigid obduracy, a heels-dug-in refusal to move into the future. On the contrary, to stand fast is to be deeply willing to continue on the way. We are called to be a pilgrim people, headed ever deeper into God, on whatever highway we have chosen. Like Mary Ward and Margaret Clitherow, we may need to know when to speak truth to power, when to live with failure, and even when to die in apparently complete ignominious defeat, planting what seeds we may, and entrusting to God and the future a harvest we will never see.

EDWARD E. ERICSON, JR.

A FATHER TO THE END

(From *Perspectives*)

When he was sixteen, he threw his father down the eight steps from the front porch to the sidewalk. The same year, when his father awakened him on a Sunday morning to get ready for church, he stood up and said, "Dad, I'm not going today, and I'm not going ever again. I'm bigger than you now, and you can't make me." And he kept his word for the next sixteen years, not going to church even to get married.

Fast-forward a quarter century and see the now middle-aged white man standing in the midst of a bunch of black kids at a Sunday school he superintends on the worst Skid Row in Chicago. I, the firstborn of five, know his story firsthand from this point. Only gradually did I learn the earlier parts. The bad stories came late—and they came hard, the ones that came at all, confessions of an aging man laying on his children the burdens along with the blessings of their inheritance.

Dad's good stories were often sports stories. He whipped through high school in five years flat, failing English twice but extending his eligibility to play quarterback on the football team and bat third on the baseball team. His academic delinquency drew only a mild rebuke from his stern father, who always dropped his insurance selling to see his boy play. We kids pestered Dad to tell and retell the story of the high-school baseball game between the city champs of New York and Chicago, routinely won by New York but not this time. It is the bottom of the ninth in Wrigley Field, tie score, and Swede (as they called my Norwegian father) gets a single. He and the next batter, best buddy Luke Johnson, flash their own hit-and-run signal brought from the neighborhood prairie. Now there are men on first and third. Next the boys' prairie sign for the double-steal. Game over. Chicago's Carl Schurz High School wins, 4–3. Coach Kohler somehow fails to give the boys a hollering proportionate to the athletic crime.

The University of Kentucky recruited the star athlete for its baseball team, and in his sophomore year he won the Southeastern Conference batting title. Major-league scouts drooled over a catcher who hit for power and for average, who threw to second on a rope, and who ran like an outfielder. Then, in the spring of his junior year, the second most impor-tant event of his college years happened: he threw out his arm. The scouts looked elsewhere. Later, he would muse about what might have been—and thank God for sparing him temp-tations he'd never have been able to handle.

The most important event of his college days was a telegram from home that said, "Father dying. Come home." He arrived too late and, sobbing with grief, grabbed and shook his father's corpse in the coffin. Then the nineteen-year-old who hadn't been in church for three years turned to his godly mother and asked, "Was he saved?" Yes.

University left hardly a mark on the man. He majored in commerce because its classes didn't conflict with baseball practice. Leaving school without a book-reading habit, he brought back three things: a letter sweater that hung in the closet unworn, a diploma that his children never saw, and a fraternity paddle that they saw plenty of.

Stories of the young man's misspent twenties are sparse. From the shards he retrieved for me, I'd guess those stories weren't terribly bad, if comparing evils serves any purpose. But they were very bad for one standing before a holy God with shame for his sinful past. The best story comes toward the end, when the meat worker frequently sees an attractive young woman from a nearby meat-working plant waiting for the bus after work and, with a spiffy new 1934 Ford bolstering natural hormonal drives, finally gets up the courage to offer her a ride home. The belle from the sticks of southern Indiana whose family has come to the big city to find work accepts. They will marry.

It is not likely that the most important event in the life of an independent man who faithfully visited his mother would be one of those visits. But real life is full of improbable turns that fiction could not bear. His mother was listening to her favorite radio preacher, and her grown son heard a Bible verse: "For other foundation can no man lay than that is laid, which is Jesus Christ" (1 Cor. 3:11). If one may say so, other verses seem likelier grabbers, but the man will tell you that the Holy Spirit used this verse to stop him in his tracks and turn him around for the rest of his life. That's what happened at age thirty-two to the man who two years later became my father.

Dad spent too many evenings away from home. His kids thought so, and so did his wife. But he never missed his teenage sons' basketball games. In Chicago, as a crime-fighting move, these games had been switched from evenings to school-day afternoons, and Dad would abandon the office two winter afternoons a week and often be the only parent in the stands, to his sons' delight and their teammates' envy. He coached the church softball team, and his boys got to play for and with him. Which also meant winning a lot. And the old man with a bad back who could scarcely chug to first base always led the team in batting average.

Every adult child of a good dad has his favorite dad story. Mine comes from third grade when we were learning cursive writing. I was left-handed, ballpoint pens were new, and the combination resulted in an outer palm stained dark blue and a sheet of paper comprehensively smudged. I should become a right-hander, the teacher decreed. I refused. Dad was called. There we were, in the principal's office, I with my great big teacher and my great big principal and my great, great big father. The principal explained that, unlike most in our blue-collar neighborhood, I might rise to an office job, and phones in a right-handed world were on the left side of the desk. The long, persuasive speech finally wound down. Dad was always quick to quip, but this time he sat uncharacteristically mute.

"Well, don't you agree, Mr. Ericson?" pressed the principal.

The father, stern: "Son, do you want to write with your left hand or your right hand?"

Boy's soprano, quavering: "My left hand, Daddy."

Then the broad man drew himself up to his full height. "The boy wants to write with his left hand. Let him write with his left hand."

The principal, shrunken: "Yes, sir, Mr. Ericson."

The teacher, squeaking: "Yes, sir. Thank you, sir."

Then there were all those evenings Dad spent away at a church board meeting or a gospel service at one rescue mission or another. Christ came to save sinners, he explained, and there were plenty of those on West Madison and North Clark and South State Streets, just outside the Chicago Loop.

And it came to pass that, shortly after the Chicago Gospel Mission started a Sunday school for the neighborhood children, the superintendent resigned, and the other board members prevailed upon my father to fill in until a replacement could be found. There were eighteen white children, including six Ericsons, on that first Sunday morning. Soon the Ericsons added one more to the group, the neighborhood turned from white to black, and attendance started to climb. It topped out above four hundred.

This did not just happen by itself. The railroad clerk at Chicago's Union Station put to work his untapped entrepreneurial skills. But now he was counting souls, not money. Where to find staff for the growing number of pupils? Moody Bible Institute, nearby, required Christian service of its students. Bring in the teachers. With so many unreached children in the neighborhood, maybe the Moody students could come an hour early and go to the tenements and walk the kids back? Agreed—bring in the learners. Just beyond walking range, by the old Chicago Stadium, were the teeming Henry Horner housing projects. What to do? Sell the family car and buy a Volkswagen microbus—in which a cop who pulled it over for its sardined overload once counted twenty-two toothy grins. If a family microbus, why not a mission bus? Why not a small fleet of buses?

One rainy Sunday, Dad drove two brothers and a sister home, stopping for a moment to discuss their spotty attendance with their mother. When he returned to the car, parked on the wrong side of the street, a policeman was there, his book of tickets in hand. Out shot J.W., age eleven, and his brother Punkin, age ten. "You can't give that man a ticket! He's the Sunday school man! He tells us about Jesus! You go away and leave him alone! You're just an old copper!" The copper allowed as how Dad had too many friends around there for him, so no ticket, but don't disobey the law again.

Of all Dad's firm convictions, the firmest was that Scripture had been written for us to memorize. So he started keeping the mission kids after Sunday school for a few minutes of drill. They took to it. After x number of Bible verses perfectly memorized, with reference said before and after each, he reinforced positive behavior with the gift of a softball. After y number, roller skates. After z number, a basketball. The numbers of kids hiding verses in their hearts grew, as did the prizes, until eventually (you need suburban donors for this one) the big winners went to a week of summer camp in Michigan.

Dad's own children were now mostly grown, but he had a large stock of father love still to give and hundreds of new kids to give it to. Once this man started being a father, he stayed being a father to the end.

On the principle that lights should not be hidden under a bushel, Dad formed a traveling group. He named them the "Scripture Kids." Sunday night remaining open on his schedule, he called around to churches to see if they'd like a special program of kids reciting Bible verses. He got some takers. Word spread, and he soon had more invitations than he could accept.

The minimum age to be in Scripture Kids was seven. The minimum entrance requirement was three hundred verses stone-cold perfect. The first sixty-six verses were one apiece from the sixty-six books of the Bible, so that the young would know the books in order and where to find the verses to come. Many kids who hit three hundred didn't stop there, and more than a few reached seven hundred, eight hundred. We're talking about kids from the worst schools in the inner city, often kids with no discipline at school and sometimes little at home, kids some might predict would be hard-core unteachables and later unemployables.

See now a line of black kids with approximately matching clothes standing on a church platform, eyes glued to an aging white man with his back to the congregation, marching through the Bible a verse per book. Sit and hear Deuteronomy 32:4, Joshua 1:9, 1 Samuel 3:9 in King James English. Luxuriate in several Psalms in a row. After Proverbs 22:6, "Train up a child in the way he should go: and when he is old, he will not depart from it," the leader might turn to the congregation and express his hope for these kids' future. The program (never call it a show) grows a bit stylized.

"What about Amos 3:3?"

"Can two walk together, except they be agreed?"

"Well, can they?"

"NO!"

Soon it's off to a heavy dollop of the New Testament. Reciting is completed by understanding; if you're going to have to pronounce *propitiation*, you might as well know what it means. Soon the stylizing includes theological mini-lessons attached to verses and chanted back and forth between leader and group. Twenty or more youngsters, ages seven to seventeen, letter perfect for an hour.

Food is another leitmotif in the story of the Scripture Kids. The best was what they ate at the home of Mr. Ericson. Of course, they received a good feeding after night church, too, in the church basement. Dad did once admit to feeling sheepish when some kids said they preferred white churches because of the food. You can't stop kids from thinking, but you can sternly instruct them not to say everything they think.

Friends who knew that Dad spent many evenings in the projects were afraid for him. He did have experiences that for others would have been hair-raising, but he was never harmed. Though sure that God protected him, he did carry his Bible prominently as "armor," in case some bruiser asked why he was where he wasn't supposed to be.

One night, when the elevators were not functioning, he started trudging up fourteen flights of steps to his destination. Opening the metal doors to one landing, he came upon young toughs playing craps. A surly voice asked where he thought he was going. Before he could answer, a voice from the corner said, "Hi, Mr. Ericson." Focusing hard, he replied, "Is that you, Jo-Jo?"

"Yeah, it's me, Joe."

Asked surly voice, "You know this man?"

"Yeah, he's the Sunday school man. He's all right."

Who wouldn't leave it at that—glad to escape? Dad wouldn't. "Joe, you haven't been to Sunday school for a long time. You're never too big for Sunday school." And then he witnessed Jesus' love even for craps players.

In the late 1960s, the cities were burning. Headlines screamed "Race Riots!" Once, Mrs. Turner called and told Dad he shouldn't

come that night; men who had just been rioting were gathered
in front of the project. Dad replied, "I'll be there at the regular
time. The Lord'll protect me." Dad saw the gathered mob and
heard the banging bongos. He walked right into the middle,
picked out a possible leader, greeted him, showed off his Bible,
explained he was there to teach kids Bible verses. Then he said,
"You guys need Jesus, too, you know. You're never too old for
Jesus to love you. Say, will you give me five minutes to tell you
about Jesus? Here, hold my watch and tell me when my five
minutes are up. Okay?" The scowling men kept scowling, but
no one said no. Drumbeats resumed after Dad walked into the
building a little while later, as did the riots on the following
evenings. But no one menaced him when he came back out
later. This is the only time I know of that Dad admitted he
was a little scared.

Young people who learn Bible verses still have other things
going on in their lives. Dad entered into these other concerns,
willy-nilly. The kids would open up to him about trouble at
school and trouble at home, about dreams of going to college,
about boys (if they were girls) or girls (if they were boys). For
sex education in his household, someone silently placed on a
son's bed a copy of *A Christian Boy's Problems.* With this next
generation of children, though, Dad turned more frank, and
he gave them the only ennobling counsel about sex many of
them ever heard.

Sometimes it was the parents who needed an old-fashioned
lesson in self-esteem. One unemployed father needed reminding, Dad thought, of his responsibility to provide for his family.
Shortly after, the man landed a job at the glue factory, where
(one might say) he stuck. This man's son became a minister.

It was hard to hold teenagers with just Sunday school. What to do? Dad's prayer was for a youth center, and a warehouse for sale two blocks from the mission was the answer to that prayer. The building was remodeled, a full-time director was hired, and the Sunday school moved into spacious quarters.

Well into his seventies Dad kept his dates with the Scripture Kids. But the stairs inside and the snow outside finally came to be too much. So, catching him at a moment of weakness, we kids moved the Chicago-loving man and his wife down to Texas to be near their elder daughter.

Except that the end was not quite yet. The Scripture Kids, against all expectation, carried on. Without the old guy around as father figure, they changed "Kids" to "Crusaders." One of the group's alumni, Ben Curtis, who had gone on to Moody Bible Institute, became the leader. And as Dad's eighty-second birthday approached, his Chicago kids decided they should pay him one last visit. They washed cars and sold cookies to raise money; they rented vans; they booked hotel rooms. For the big dinner these young-adult kids took us, at Dad's request, to a cheap steak house. The suburban restaurant had only white customers that evening except for the fifteen or so black ones arrayed along two tables. One of the kids stood up and prayed before our food came, and all the restaurant hushed. The air conditioning was too much for Dad, so one skinny fellow took off his two-tone royal blue, tuxedo-cut jacket, tied the sleeves around Dad's neck, and arranged the jacket to cover as much of the burly back and shoulders as it pitifully could. Dad expressed himself warm enough now. He looked so ludicrous we couldn't stop laughing. Someone said we should sing "Happy Birthday." After the first few notes, the whole restaurant joined in and capped off the singing with sturdy applause and some strangers dabbing their eyes. ("Who is that man, anyway?") That evening is my favorite restaurant memory. That visit is the last time his Chicago kids saw their "father."

Alive, that is. Some saw him dead. Dad died at eighty-three in his own bed, with a daughter on either side, each holding a hand of his and singing. He had long told us to put him in the ground in a plain pine box wherever he died. The Lord would know where to find him. Vans set out from Chicago for Texas again. On the early March day of the funeral, a mean snowstorm hit. Not your usual Texas weather, but we figured God wanted this Chicago man to have a Chicago funeral. The director of the funeral home had other ideas and called to cancel. No one could get there, he said. We said Texans might not make it, but we had gathered from around the country and we'd be there.

A caravan of vehicles struggled from my sister's house through unplowed streets to the funeral home. Ben Curtis and a childhood friend of mine co-officiated. At Mom's request, her marimba-playing daughter shook off her rust and played "Amazing Grace." I read a eulogy. Ben quoted lots of verses in his sermon. Then we trundled the casket across the street and lowered it into the Chicago-cold ground.

What ever happened to all of Dad's "other kids"? Stories still reach us. Recently, a friend who was seeking board members for his nonprofit foundation came upon one Gary Jones, a Christian African-American entrepreneur in his thirties who owns a company that refurbishes buildings. In the interview for the board position Gary was asked how he became a Christian.

"Through the Chicago Gospel Youth Center. Through a man named Mr. Ericson."

Dad has been dead ten years now, but sixty or seventy members of his "second family" still get together every year to reminisce and support one another spiritually. Among them are pastors, teachers, businessmen, and other professionals. Ben Curtis and the Scripture Crusaders are still performing.

ERIKSON ON HIS OWN IDENTITY
(From *DoubleTake*)

During the 1960s, when she was a social worker at a school for autistic children in Denver, Colorado, Hope Curfman became interested in the writings of child psychoanalyst and biographer Erik H. Erikson. In 1976, she helped to lead a church workshop on Erikson and was often asked about his religious faith. She posed the question to Erikson directly in a letter that began a short but fruitful correspondence. Erikson's reply, published here for the first time, is a candid discussion of his own spiritual concerns. Shown this letter, Yale University professor Kai Erikson remarked that his father "often used occasions like this to audition ideas he thought he might one day want to share with a larger audience—letting the sentences season in the back of his mind, as it were, without having to commit them (yet) to print." Two dozen years later, Erikson's words still retain their trenchant power. As Mrs. Curfman recently told us, "His writings and personality continue to influence me now, in my eighties."

Tiburon, California
December 30, 1976

Dear Mrs. Curfman:

The Season seems to be a good time to respond to a letter which, when it came, was put aside as too important to answer lightly. Early this year you wrote to me to tell me of your church group which was studying my ideas. You wrote, "Frequently, the question is asked: 'Is Erikson a Christian?'" And you added, "Of course, answering such a question . . . depends on one's definition and timing. Today I consider myself a Christian; tomorrow I may not; and yesterday I struggled with it. Each has his own definition, so I shall restate the question. Do you consider yourself to be a Christian?"

It is because of your thoughtful statement as to what such a question would mean to yourself (a frankness altogether rare in questioners and critics) that I would like to try to answer it.

I also like your formulation that I seem to "put emphasis on health as wholeness," and I agree with your diagnosis that such wholeness to me does not seem possible without some pervasive faith—although I would not, as you suggest, call it "therapeutic." Anxiety may call for therapy; dread demands faith.

That a statement of faith, then, cannot be simple, you have anticipated in your question. My ruminations will, in fact, respond to some doubts and questions raised by others. I address them to you precisely because of your awareness of the power of "yesterday," "today," and "tomorrow" in our sense of supreme value and of belongingness. But nothing except a lengthy auto-historical account could convey the cataclysmic transvaluations with which this century underscored the life crises of persons my age. To be an approximate age mate of the century means a childhood in a period before the world wars and the revolutions; it means a young adulthood when Nazism was, as yet, inconceivable; it means professional education, marriage, and immigration to this country before Hitler's total threat or World War II seemed imaginable. Then, too, the discovery of relativity and of the unconscious gave new dimensions to our experience. But all the more important is the simple question as to what—after all—touched us and touches us most immediately in this ocean of uncertainties.

All right, then: some passages in the Gospels—the Word made Flesh and the Child and the Kingdom—have always touched me and continue to convey a creedal immediacy which to me is the simplest and deepest resource of a universal faith formulated in the Western world. To me, the shining newness, above all, of Jesus' parables attests to the genuine presence of a singular man. His teachings are, of course, unthinkable without the elemental steps of Judaism, even as they derive their revolutionary strength from the way in which they point for point overturn (nonviolently) the ritualistic logic that seems to have then pervaded the Judaic establishment—as it will always pervade establishments.

Yes, the Gospels present an indispensable step in the development of human conscience and consciousness—a step that, historically seen, seems to have been basic (if often by way of a radical counterpoint) to the great traditions of the Western world.

And then, the core of the Gospels has one totally singular aspect. I mean the utter simplicity in which those sayings were perceived and preserved by small communities of the Mediterranean world of the first century. For such elemental renewal I would accept no doctrinaire explanation from declared believers or nonbelievers: such an immediate message (*and* its falsifications) must be newly understood in each era with new resources of insight. Today and to me this means also psychoanalytic-historical insight.

But before I come to that, let me ask you: you refer to my "mixed Jewish and Christian origins." Does your question imply another one, namely, whether or not I consider myself a Jew?

Yes, I went along to synagogue as a child, and I underwent Bar Mitzvah, the Jewish confirmation, at the proper age. But although I was touched by the rituals performed at home (such as Passover), the synagogue services, at the time, impressed me as rather ritualistic performances, and this probably because of their "reformed" style. All this was part of a quiet alienation from my whole childhood setting, German *and* Jewish. My alienation was (lovingly) ascribed by my family to my artistic temperament, and I remember as an adolescent writing a long letter of disengagement to our rabbi. Then, there was the gradual awareness (this was the family secret) that while my mother was a Danish Jewess, my father had been a Danish Gentile. Also, my mother was a faithful reader of Kierkegaard, and I early received from her a quiet and uncombative conviction that to be raised a Jew did not preclude a reverence for the core values of Christianity. Later, personal fate removed me from my background, and world events destroyed it altogether. My mother and my stepfather died in Israel.

Now to the point: I know that nobody who has grown up in a Jewish environment can ever be not-a-Jew, whether the

Jewishness he experienced was defined by his family's sense of history, by its religious observances, or, indeed, by the environment's attitudes toward Jews. For that very reason, however (as I told Coles [see pp. 180–81]),* to profess one's Jewishness can, in our day, imply a diversity of "confessions": from a proud affirmation of a unique racial history to the confirmation of the Judaic faith or to the mere undeniability of a fact; and from the eager claim to the potential right to become an Israeli (on the basis of having had a Jewish mother) to the survivor's admission that he (on the same statistical grounds) would have been eligible for the holocaust. None of these aspects can ever be stricken from the Jewish part of one's historical identity, which, in fact, is made up of their unique combination. The question is only how one will eventually combine them with the developing worldview dictated by one's overall identity.

As you saw, my first response was a statement of faith concerning the original Christian vision—rather than its institutional fate. I know, of course, that churches and associations, ritualizations and rituals, are necessary for the survival of ideas and of ideals. And I do feel on occasion the need to participate, with my wife, in a church service in order to affirm and to receive affirmation from the ritual formulations of a devotional community. My wife's church is ministered to by a clergyman

---

Erik H. Erikson: The Growth of His Work, by Robert Coles (1970). The bracketed interpolation is Erikson's. He told Coles: "You rightly ask about the Jewish part of my background as an identity issue: my mother's family was Jewish, but in Denmark baptism and intermarriage are old customs, so one of my ancestors (so she told me) was chief rabbi of Stockholm and another a church historian and pastor in Hans Christian Andersen's hometown. I have kept my stepfather's name as my middle name out of gratitude (there is a pediatrician in me, too) but also to avoid the semblance of evasion."

singularly able to convey the basic terms of original Christian- ity; and he is hospitable toward my kind. Also, he does seem to understand and to be willing to take for granted the basic his- torical fact that Jesus was a Jew and had his being among Jews who were ready for his message. For, indeed, even such a new universal being is always co-defined by his cultural place and his historical time and must ground his message in their imagery. Yet, while being a product of previous history and while causing unpredictable future events, a truly significant moment gains its momentum from its presence in a present—which is as close as a human being comes to a sense of the immortal—or the holy—within the timebound reign of mortality.

Such perception, then, is the basis for my sense of identifi- cation with Christians. This, however, does not exclude, it intensifies a deep anger over the ritualistic forms the world reli- gions have assumed, not to speak of the cruel indulgence in the hate of otherness of which they periodically have been guilty throughout history. Organized Christianity, through the ages, has made colossal deals with political and economic establish- ments, thus conspiring even for a collusion of world empires— and the Kingdom. Jews of the Diaspora could, at least, avoid the linking of churches with empires. I would even submit that after two millennia there are, ever again, individual Jews who seem to be dedicated to the messianic tenets of a more univer- sal love and who seek for radical ways of realizing it through new political, economic—and psychological methods.

This, finally (and "naturally"), brings me to the fact that I am a psychoanalyst—if, again, one of a particular kind. It is true that in my field matters of faith are, more often than not, delegated to the sphere of irrationality, if not of pathology or dishonesty. This is related to Freud's early scientistic devotion which, up to a point, rightfully gave exclusive validity to a newly verified and, oh, so elusive lawfulness. That this must not escape us again and that all human phenomena must be sifted through to detect the pollution by wayward instinctuality and by individual and mass anxiety—that is a commitment worthy of devotion. But it also commits us to seeing the difference between (more or less repressed) anxiety and man's (more or less dissimulated) existential dread.

Nor is it enough to explain man's a-rational need for faith solely on the basis of its precursors in early childhood—and in prehistory. The study of the life cycle makes it very clear that adult generativity needs the guidance of all-inclusive world-images (ideologies, if you will). And here the previous mile-stones of human consciousness must be re-avowed as an intrinsic element of our devotional experience, studied with our means of verifying relevance, and made contemporary in our engagement with social reality.

In conclusion, I want to quote to you a phrase my wife used when I asked what she (who happens to be an Episcopal minister's daughter) would say in response to your question. She said, "I would tell her that I am a Christian apprentice." I like this, because (as your own remarks indicate) it seems so much more important to recognize the frontier on which one is struggling for insight and communality than to let oneself be totally committed to categories that—important as they are for the factual definition of one's daily duties—foreclose one's infinite search.

Dear Mrs. Curfman, a trusting question deserves a precise answer. Instead, as I warned you I would, I am sending you a small essay. All these words—do they tell whether I "consider myself a Christian"? I would say "yes" in the sense that in order to perceive and to study the living implications of Christ's message I am not only willing but determined to live on the shadowy borderline of the denominational ambiguities (whether national or religious, political or professional) into which I seem to have been born. I know that this border area also can invite a certain shadiness of expression, and certainly arouses much shady comment. But knowing this, it seems all the more necessary to live in it as one studies it, if for no other purpose than that of helping us overcome the (potentially fatal) human need for what I have called pseudospeciation—that is, the unthinking equation of one's own kind with humankind itself and the bolstering of one's identity by the categorical exclusion and rejection of otherness.

Well, you have read what I wrote about that, so let me stop here.

Thanking you for your inquiry, and with the Season's Greetings for you and your study group,

Yours sincerely,
Erik H. Erikson

A CONVERSION STORY

(From *First Things*)

An adult conversion to Catholicism—or indeed to any form of orthodox Christianity—is not an everyday occurrence in the American academy. Most secular academics seem to receive any profession of Christian faith with a vague sense of embarrassment. Adherence to Judaism or Islam is another matter, although why is not immediately self-evident, since both impose stringent demands upon their faithful. Perhaps they meet with greater tolerance because they are less familiar, perhaps because, whatever the reality, they do not carry Christianity's taint of having long figured as the religion of a male European elite that allegedly used its faith to cow others into submission. Nor does it change anything to remind skeptics that, in the United States, Catholics long suffered a discrimination that was, in its way, almost as implacable as that suffered by black Americans. A vague, nondenominational Christianity— or, better yet, Unitarianism—may be acceptable, but Catholicism lies beyond the pale. Catholicism is not something that people "like us" embrace.

Thus when, in December 1995, I was received into the Catholic Church, my nonbelieving colleagues tactfully refrained

from comment, primarily, I suspect, because they literally did
not know what to say. More likely than not, many of them
assumed that, having lived through some difficult years, I was
turning to faith for some form of irrational consolation. Conse-
quently, from their perspective, to acknowledge my conversion
would, implicitly, have been to acknowledge my vulnerability.
Others, who were less sympathetic, doubtless assumed that my
turn to Rome reflected what they viewed as my reactionary politics, notably with respect to abortion. From their perspective, I
had exiled myself from acceptable conversation of any kind.

I have no intention of berating my colleagues or other secular academics, but rather to call attention to aspects of the
prevailing secular mind-set that make the idea of conversion
virtually incomprehensible. For secular academics, the language
and practice of faith belong to an alien world. Not understanding faith, they are ill prepared to understand conversion
to it. Having long participated in the reigning discourse of
secular intellectuals, I understand all too well where they are
coming from, and I readily acknowledge that indeed "there
but for the grace of God go I." More important, however, my
long apprenticeship in their world allows me to reflect upon
their unreflective assumptions, for those assumptions cut a
broad swath through our culture as a whole, challenging faith
at every turn. So firm is their hold upon our culture that they
are imperceptibly permeating the fabric of faith itself, constantly challenging the faithful to justify and rejustify their
beliefs.

Believers, in sharp contrast to nonbelievers, welcome
conversion stories as heartening evidence of God's grace and
the workings of the Holy Spirit. The conversion of a secular

intellectual in particular seems to snatch a soul from the very jaws of feminism, communism, nihilism, atheism, or some other fashionable secular ideology. Given the broad gap between belief and nonbelief that both sides perceive, it is not surprising that both hostile and sympathetic observers expect conversion stories to be dramatic. Like St. Paul on the road to Damascus, the convert is generally expected to have experienced a moment of blinding illumination followed by a radical change of life. This expectation testifies to a widespread sense that the tenets of faith and those of the world, of Jerusalem and of Athens, are in conflict. Though emphatically not disputing the significance of the deep differences between the views and attitudes of believers and those of nonbelievers, I did not myself experience conversion as a radical rupture with my past. This is not to say that I did not experience the journey to belief as what my students call "life-changing": in essential ways, I did. Nonetheless, in other ways I did not. In many respects, my conversion fit neatly—almost seamlessly—into the continuum of my life, and, from this perspective, it was a natural stage in the journey rather than a new departure.

For practical purposes, I grew up a nonbelieving Christian. Wait a minute, you may fairly protest, is that not an oxymoron? How can a nonbeliever describe herself as Christian if faith constitutes the essence of Christianity? Time and again throughout the Gospels, Jesus evokes belief in himself and the Father who sent him as the only test or standard. Think of Martha at the time of Lazarus's death: "Yes, Lord, I believe that you are the Christ, the Son of God, he who is coming into the world" (John 10:27). And Martha is not alone. Time and again

petitioners receive what they seek because Jesus fulfills their
belief. As he tells Martha, "I am the resurrection and the life;
he who believes in me, though he die, yet shall he live, and
whoever lives and believes in me shall never die" (John
10:25–26). A Christian, by definition, is one who accepts Jesus
Christ as his or her personal savior and, no less important, as
Lord. Everything depends upon belief.

The story of modernity has arguably been one of the mar-
ginalization and discrediting of belief or, perhaps more accurately, its relegation to the realm of radical subjectivity.
Modernity, in other words, has systematically divorced faith
from moral and intellectual authority. Until well into the twentieth century, however, the mounting assaults on faith did not
entirely erase the living legacy of Christianity from Western
culture. If nothing else, the moral teachings of the Decalogue
and the Sermon on the Mount continued to receive a measure
of respect—in exhortation if not uniformly in observance. My
early years conformed precisely to this pattern, especially with
respect to the Decalogue, which my parents took with utmost
seriousness. In retrospect, it seems to me that my father especially never doubted the truth of Dostoevsky's troubling question: "If God is dead, is not everything permitted?" Yet neither
he nor my mother was a believer, and neither taught us to
believe. Like many other honorable and upright modernists,
they apparently grounded their strong sense of morality in the
integrity of the individual.

Throughout my non-churchgoing, nonbelieving adult years,
I had always considered myself a Christian in the amorphous
cultural sense of the world. Having been reared on the Bible
and Protestant hymns, I was conversant with the language and

basic tenets of Christianity. I had, moreover, been reared with a deep respect for the great Hebrew prophets, assorted Protestant leaders and Catholic saints, and even the unique value of Jesus Christ as the preeminent exemplar of loving self-sacrifice. Never, I am grateful to say, did I, like too many secular intellectuals, denigrate or disdain believing Christians, whom I had always been inclined to regard with respect. But for long years, I did not give much thought to joining their number. By the time I had completed college and then graduate school, I had so thoroughly imbibed materialist philosophy that it did not occur to me to look beyond it. My quests, such as they were, focused upon the claims and contours of moral worthiness in a world that took it as a matter of faith that "God is dead."

Over the years, my concerns about morality deepened, and my reflections invariably pointed to the apparently irrefutable conclusion that morality was, by its very nature, authoritarian. Morality, in other words, drew the dividing line between good and bad. During the years of my reflection, however, the secular world was rapidly promoting the belief that moral conviction, like any other idea, expressed the standpoint of the person who enunciated it. And it was becoming a widely shared belief that there were as many moralities as there were people and that it was inappropriate to impose one's own morality on another whose situation one could not fully understand. Although as predisposed as any to respect the claims of difference, whether of sex, class, or culture, I increasingly found this moral relativism troubling. It seemed difficult to imagine a world in which each followed his or her personal moral compass, if only because the morality of some was bound, sooner or later, to clash with the morality of others. And without some semblance of a common standard, those clashes were more than likely to end in one or another form of violence.

My more wrenching concerns, however, lay elsewhere. Thinking and writing about abortion had led me to an ever greater appreciation for the claims of life, which were so often buried beneath impassioned defenses of a woman's right to self-determination, especially her right to sexual freedom. When I began to think seriously about the issue, my commitment to women's right to develop their talents predisposed me to sup- port the legality of abortion, at least up to a certain point. Even then, I found it impossible not to take seriously the life of the fetus that was being so casually cast aside. The emerg- ing discussions of assisted suicide only intensified my discom- fort, as I found myself worrying about one human being deciding whether another's life is worth living. "How do we know?" I kept asking myself. "How ever can we know?"

Today, it is easy to see that I was instinctively revolting against a utilitarian or instrumentalist understanding of the value of human life. I did understand that as soon as we admit as a serious consideration whether our obligations to others are inconvenient, the value of any life becomes negotiable. At this point, as you will note, my internal struggles still unfolded within a secular framework, although I fully appreciated that devout Christians and Jews viewed reverence for life in its most vulnerable forms as a divine commandment. Indeed, I was slowly coming to envy the certainty that religious faith afforded, and I began to think seriously about joining a church. At the same time, I knew that no matter how noble and well-intentioned, worldly preoccupations were not an adequate reason for doing so.

As if barring my path to church membership stood the figure of Jesus Christ. The churches I most respected all required that prospective members affirm their personal faith in Christ as Lord and Savior. I did not question the legitimacy of the requirement, but nothing in my previous life seemed to have prepared me to meet it. To the best of my knowledge, I had no personal experience of religious faith and no real grasp of its nature. When I was twenty, André Amar, a brilliant professor of philosophy and a devout Jew, had spoken to me of religion as a realm unto itself, irreducible to any other, and his words had lodged in my mind, but I did not fully understand them. To this day, I cannot point to a single moment of conversion, no blinding light that opened my eyes, no arrow that pierced my heart. Almost imperceptibly, the balance between doubt and faith shifted, and, on one ordinary day, it came to me that I had decided to enter the Catholic Church.

It would be easy to think that my decision, however lacking in drama, represented the end of my journey to faith. Instead it marked only the beginning of what is proving to be an adventure I could not previously have imagined. The Sunday after reaching that decision, quietly and alone, I went to Mass at the Cathedral of Christ the King in Atlanta. Both my Catholic-born but at the time unbelieving husband and my devoutly Catholic friend and graduate student Sheila O'Connor would happily have accompanied me, but I did not tell them where I was going.

I had not attended a Mass since my youth, during visits to France, and then only rarely. I had no clear idea of what to expect, although I knew enough to know that I could not receive communion. Yet an almost visceral instinct told me that this first direct encounter with the faith I was planning to embrace was something I could not foresee and must undertake alone. By now, most of my specific memories of that morning have merged with the countless times I have attended Mass at the cathedral since. All that stands out is my response to that first hour, as a Catholic-to-be, of confronting the figure of the crucified Christ that dominates the cathedral. There, directly in front of me, was the Lord I had pledged myself to serve—a Lord whom as yet I barely knew and who nonetheless seemed to hold me fast.

Shortly thereafter, thanks to the help of Sheila's mother, I began to receive instruction from Father Richard Lopez, the remarkable priest who remains the confessor and spiritual director for my husband and me. Fr. Lopez rapidly determined that I was much more familiar with Catholic theology than he had reason to have expected, and thereafter his instruction focused primarily upon the practice, rituals, and traditions of Catholicism. Between our meetings, I read the *Catechism* and other books on the elements of Catholicism, attended Mass, and learned and said prayers. During the meetings, Fr. Lopez guided me through the practical meaning of words and rituals. We discussed the significance of the colors priests wear during the different seasons of the liturgical calendar, the role of the Virgin Mary and the saints as intercessors, the structure of the Mass, and more. In retrospect, what astonishes me is how much I learned and how little I truly understood. For the words we exchanged, valuable as they were, remained mere words. Learning them felt like a privileged initiation, but I used them rather in the way in which one learns to say the beads of the Rosary before one begins to grasp the immediacy of the events they signify.

In deciding to enter the Church, I had decided that I believed in Christ Jesus and accepted him as my Lord and Savior, but even as my love for and commitment to the Church deepened, I remained unsure of precisely what my faith meant or from whence it derived. Fr. Lopez reassured me that faith and faithfulness were, above all, matters of the will rather than the emotions, which, he insisted, remain inherently suspect. His words conformed to what I had learned from my own reading in Catholic theology and eased my occasional misgivings about the elusiveness of my own feelings. On the day of my reception, which included the sacraments of baptism, confirmation, penance, marriage, and communion, a transformative joy consecrated a decision that now seemed to derive as much from the heart as the mind.

That joy, although varying in manifestation and intensity, has persisted since. But my understanding of its meaning has not ceased to change and grow. Today I see more clearly than I could at the time that much of my initial hesitation and diffidence derived from my unconscious persistence in materialist habits of thought. Like any good rationalist, I kept looking for unambiguous explanations for my turn to faith, and, although the possible candidates abounded, none clearly stood out as *the* reason. It took two or three years for me to begin to understand that the decisive action had not been mine, but God's. In principle, we all know that faith is a gift or grace, not a personal accomplishment. But if my case is as common as I suspect it is, we find that knowledge surprisingly difficult to believe and make fully ours. Thus, with the best of intentions, we try to earn that which lies beyond the reach of even our most heroic efforts and which exceeds any merit we can conceive.

An important part of what opened me to Catholicism—and to the peerless gift of faith in Christ Jesus—was my growing horror at the pride of too many in the secular academy. The sin is all the more pernicious because it is so rarely experienced as sin. Educated and enjoined to rely upon our reason and cultivate our autonomy, countless perfectly decent and honorable professors devote their best efforts to making sense of thorny intellectual problems, which everything in their environment encourages them to believe they can solve. Postmodernism has challenged the philosophical presuppositions of the modernists' intellectual hubris, but, with the same stroke, it has pretended to discredit what it calls "logocentrism," namely, the centrality of the Word. In the postmodernist universe, all claims of universal certainty must be exposed as delusions, leaving the individual as authoritative arbiter of the meaning that pertains to his or her situation. Thus, what originated as a struggle to discredit pretensions to intellectual authority has ended, at least in the American academy, in a validation of personal prejudice and desire.

Sad as it may seem, my experience with radical, upscale feminism only reinforced my growing mistrust of individual pride. The defense of abortion especially troubled me because of my inability to agree that any one of us should decide who has the right to live. But my engagement with faith drew me into more general reflection about the importance of charity and service in the life of the Christian. Initially, I had shied away from the idea of the imitation of Christ and even from the entreaty in the Universal Prayer to "make me holy." Such aspirations struck me as the ultimate presumption: who was I to pretend to holiness, much less the imitation of our Savior? Gradually, those fears began to dissipate, and I found myself meditating upon the Gospels' teaching on service, above all, that "the Son of Man did not come to be served, but to serve and to offer his life as a ransom for all." Having been received in the Church on the day after the feast of the Immaculate Conception, I also pondered the Holy Mother's response to the Annunciation: "Let it be done unto me according to Thy Word."

The injunctions to charity and service unmistakably applied to all Christians, but it was difficult to deny that, since the moment of the Virgin Mary's response to the angel Gabriel, they applied in a special way to women. Her example, as Hans Urs von Balthasar has reminded us, offers the exemplary embodiment of faith. "Faith is the surrender of the entire person: because Mary from the start surrendered everything, her memory was the unsullied tablet on which the Father, through the Spirit, could write His entire Word." It is incontestable that, throughout most of history, women have suffered injustices and abuse that cry out for redress. It is no less incontestable that the path to justice and dignity for women—the recognition of their equal standing with men as human persons—cannot lead through the repudiation of the most basic tenets of our faith. No amount of past oppression can justify women's oppression of the most vulnerable among us—or even our repudiation of our own specific vocation as women.

Pope John Paul II has written extensively on the special dignity and mission of women, frequently provoking the shrill opposition of feminists, especially Catholic feminists. Above all, feminists deplore his insistence upon the abiding differences between women and men and upon women's exclusion from the priesthood. I would be astonished if, at one point or another, every woman has not tasted some of that anger, the outraged sense of "Why me? Why should I always be the one to give?" And it does not help if men interpret women's yielding as proof of men's superiority. Not expecting heaven on earth in the near future, I see little prospect that either of these responses will simply evaporate. Yet both miss the key to the Holy Father's theology of the person, namely, that the essence of our humanity lies in our capacity for "self-gift." This understanding links our relations with one another to our relation to God, reminding us of the danger of treating another person as an object. It also suggests that, whether in relation with others or in communion with God, our highest realization of self results from the gift—or loss—of self.

In our time, it is countercultural indeed to see the loss or effacement of self as an admirable goal. Our culture's obsession with identity and the rights of the individual seems to suggest precisely the reverse. You will nonetheless recall the First Beatitude: "Blessed are the poor in spirit, for theirs is the kingdom of Heaven" (Matt. 5:3). For years the passage, when I thought of it, puzzled me. In what way was poverty of spirit to be seen as desirable, especially in a Christian? And what, precisely, did poverty of spirit mean? I had left the question, together with others that I hoped some day to understand, in the back of my mind until I happened upon Erasmo Leiva-Merikakis's eye-opening explanation in his *Fire of Mercy, Heart*

of the Word: Meditations on the Gospel According to St. Matthew
(1996). Pointing out that this is not merely the first of the Beat-
itudes, but the only one in the present tense, Leiva-Merikakis
explains that the poor in spirit are those who literally "beg for
their life's very breath"—those who depend upon God the
way we all depend upon air to breathe. Poverty of spirit is the
grace of those who have emptied themselves of everything
but the desire for God's presence, "who offer God a continual
sacrifice from the altar of their spirit, and the sacrifice in question is the very substance of their being." And those who
achieve poverty of spirit have their reward in the present as
well as the future, for to live in poverty of spirit is indeed to
live with God.

A decisive moment in my journey in faith came when, one
day, seemingly out of nowhere, the thought pierced me that
Jesus had died for my sins. And, immediately on its heels,
came the devastating recognition that I am not worth his sacrifice. Only gradually have I come truly to understand that the
determination of worth belongs not to me, but to him. God's
love for us forever exceeds our control and challenges our
understanding. Like faith, it is his gift, and our task is to do
our best to receive it. The knowledge, even when partial and
imperfect, that he loves us also opens us to new responsibilities and obligations. For if he loves us all, he also loves each of
us. And recognition of that love imposes on us the obligation
to love one another, asking no other reason than God's injunction to do so. As fallen human creatures, we are nonetheless
likely to continue to search for human reasons that justify our
loving service to those in whom we find little or no obvious
redeeming value. And the best human reason may be found in

the faith that God has freely given us: our nonjudgmental love of the other remains the condition of God's love for us. For, knowing how little we merit his love, our best opening to the faith that he does, lies not in the hope of being better than others, but in the security that his love encompasses even the least deserving among us.

BENEATH THE SURFACE

(From *Leadership*)

"Let's make a bow. Here, I'll put my finger right there to hold the ribbon, and you tie the bow."

"Okay," she answered cautiously.

Slowly she reached for the slant-cut ends of red ribbon. Holding one between her right thumb and forefinger, the other end between her left thumb and forefinger, she stopped.

She appeared unsure of the next step. Latent muscle memory suggested to her that some time ago she could tie ribbons into bows. But she could not remember ever, actually, tying a bow. She looked at a finished product. She could not reverse-engineer the process of tying a bow (most of us could not do this either).

She watched a happy patient succeed. Her short-term memory deteriorated, she could not watch a step and reproduce it.

"We're not in a hurry," I said to her.

"Thank you," she said.

Continuing to grasp the ends of the ribbon, she slowly waved her hands circularly over the spot where my finger held the ribbon in place. Perhaps she hoped the movement might trigger a recollection. It did not help. She squinted. I suggested an alternative.

"How about if you hold the ribbon, and I'll tie the bow?"

"That would be nice," she responded.

She smiled because she could help. We tied a bow together and smiled together. I wondered if I was supposed to let her try again. I looked over to the program coordinator. She smiled and nodded. The point was to enjoy being together, not relearn kindergarten.

So we worked away quite happily, and with seven other Alzheimer's patients we assembled forty little bags of candy for a party. Each red and gold cellophane pouch, bound by a ribbon, held a caramel, some candy corn, and a chocolate kiss or two. We felt pride in the heap of packages in the middle of the table.

The stash would have been larger if we had not consumed our supplies. That was part of the plan, however. Our discomfiture in bow tying—she could not tie and I could not teach—dissolved as the candy melted in our mouths.

The group moved to a different table. My job was to lead a "service." I'd forgotten my Bible in my car and I cannot recite the Twenty-third Psalm without the text in front of me, so I asked the program coordinator if they had one. She dug through some drawers and hauled out a Bible as big as a sofa. I was glad for the King James. Modern idioms and unfamiliar cadences are not good news for old people with widely spaced brain cells.

Slowly and rhythmically I read a bit of Psalm 23. "The Lord is my shepherd; I shall not . . ." I stopped precipitously before the last word.

"Want," said a few, timidly.

"Good job," I said. They sat a little straighter.

"He maketh me to lie down in green . . ."

"Pastures!" they replied triumphantly. Even my bow gal clicked into the game.

"He maketh me to lie down in green pastures; he leadeth me beside the . . ."

"Still waters!" This time they remembered two words. I still need the text before my eyes. We continued in a great triumphal procession.

"And I shall dwell . . ."

"In the house of the Lord, forever!" The old voices rang like bells.

I leafed through the Bible looking for other passages that might ring a bell. Some fell flat. But it surprised me how many verses they could recite with simple cues.

Slowly, softly, and tenderly I sang a few hymns, some sang along, some hummed, no one looked bored. Tears formed.

The woman who could tie bows said, "I can play the piano!"

She could not tell you her address, the year or the day she was born, but she could play old hymns by memory. What a joy that was! The more she played the more we sang. By the end we felt warmed and loved and accomplished. And we felt the Spirit of God.

What did I see in this picture? People short of brain cells whose souls work just fine. Their brains incarcerate their souls.

The holistic/monistic school of theological anthropology tells us that body and soul are an indissoluble, indistinguishable thing. The view cuts across liberal and conservative theological boundaries. It makes sense to healthy, happy people who, in the normal course of their lives, don't experience a dichotomy between their physical and spiritual selves.

Indeed, it is ideal to feel no separation. Healthy people do not feel separation in their bodies. They don't feel their kidneys, or their blood, or their intestines as they work. Healthy people don't even feel their bones as they go about their day. They feel themselves as whole beings. That's the way it is supposed to be. When they sing a song they love, it moves their being; they feel it from head to toe, in their mind and in their heart.

In worship—trendy or traditional—we don't stop and think, *Here's my soul worshiping; here're my toes worshiping; here's my mind worshiping.* We worship as whole persons.

But how about disadvantaged persons? What if they can't stand to sing? What if they can't read the words? What if they can't hear? Do their souls flunk because their bodies fail?

If the soul and the body are the same thing, then a sick body should make for sick spirituality and a healthy body should make for healthy spirituality. Likewise, spiritually healthy people should all have healthy bodies and spiritually sick people should all have sick bodies. But as life clearly teaches, physical health and spiritual health are two very different things. Very often the healthiest bodies are spiritually self-centered and the healthiest spirits are enveloped in deteriorating bodies.

Many healthy people think that someone with Alzheimer's is boring, or scary, or as good as dead—unless that person happens to be their grandfather. In which case, if you ask them if their grandfather has a soul, most people will instinctively answer yes.

The soul is an engine. It is the spiritual center from which the self emerges as the will to live. Almighty God is "I Am That I Am," and made in his image we are little "i am's." We use the verb *to be* in the first person singular constantly in our simple, normal speech patterns.

We say, "I am hungry." The phrase sounds self-centered, or it sounds like the desire to eat and survive. We say, "I am able." We may be bragging, taking responsibility, or asserting ability. "I am not able" may be frank self-appraisal, the refusal to work, or one more confession that our dust devolves toward the grave.

To say, "I am not able, but Christ is able, and in Him I am able," expresses the mystery of the gospel, the power of ministry, the hope we share, and an ultimate fear of life's penultimate end. "Therefore we do not lose heart. Though outwardly we are wasting away, yet inwardly we are being renewed day by day" (2 Cor. 4:16).

Max's Camouflaged Soul

Max, an old Dutch dairyman, made few concessions in life to the demands of ease. Nevertheless, he hunted and fished and after he retired he played a mean game of golf. As his pastor, to be asked to an all-family dinner with children and grandchildren was an honor and joy. There was sure to be much laughter and horseplay.

Unfortunately, in his late sixties Max suffered a series of strokes and bleeds in his brain, which left him bedridden, blind, and mentally incompetent. One of the most pragmatic men I ever knew became delusional. He told everyone he was a colonel in the army—though he had never been in the military. And though he'd been as conservative as a fossil bed—he was now taking helicopter rides to the Great Wall of China with Ted Turner and Jane Fonda.

At first he loved the Communion we served him in the convalescent hospital. But after more bleeds he didn't seem to know what it was.

At one point his family told me that they had heard him say something like "God the Father Almighty" over and over. The family warned me because they thought he might be swearing. In Max's state it wouldn't be unusual. Still I wondered what his expletive meant.

The next time I visited Max he growled out agnostically, "God the Father Almighty."

So I said, "I believe in . . . "

"God the Father Almighty," he said calmly.

"Maker," I countered.

"Of heaven and earth," he responded.

Thus, we recited the Apostles' Creed together. By the end he was weeping and my eyes weren't all that dry either.

For a few minutes we conversed in a normal way. He remembered who he was, who I was, and where we were. He seemed to enjoy the encounter, but I think it also made him feel sad. The touch with reality reminded him of his present condition and, naturally, he didn't like that.

In subsequent visits, sometimes we connected and sometimes we did not. He continued to have slight strokes and bleeds. He slept more.

After twenty years of visitation with infirm people, I am quite sure that people we normally call "out of it" have emotional ups and downs like we do. Sometimes we want a pastoral visit. Sometimes we want to be left alone. In places like nursing homes with little privacy and much loneliness, sometimes visits soothe and sometimes they invade.

Unconscious and delusional patients can't tell us to go away. That's why I always ask infirm people if they want me to read Scripture and pray. I look for the slightest clues for "Yes" or "No." If I sense hesitancy from them, I politely refrain. If I cannot tell anything, I read and pray, but briefly. It is not their responsibility to desire my ministry. It is my responsibility to find out if they want me there.

Sometimes Max desired my presence and other times he didn't.

Connecting on a Deeper Level

We can't see the soul. But we can see the soul at work. We can see the ground of our being in the field of our life. In some ways, it's easier to distinguish the soul when the body and mind are damaged.

To minister to normal, healthy people, we need to differentiate what really matters to them amid the fluff and stuff of their lives. We need to distinguish the negligible from the nonnegotiable. It's a field-ground issue. How can you see the particular camouflaged in the general?

In the river valleys of Montana, just about Mother's Day, morel mushrooms pop up through dead cottonwood leaves in moist, shady places. Deer love them! These delectable and exotic mushrooms are easy to distinguish from their deadly relatives. They look far different from the ones that grow in your lawn. But they are devilishly difficult to distinguish from the decaying forest fall in which they spawn.

A friend of mine can spot a morel at a hundred yards in a total eclipse. He's been picking them for years. When we go out together, I pick a few, he shares with me, and then he goes out later to fill his freezer. However, if a light spring snow blesses the season and we arrive after the snow melts off the conical delicacies but before it leaves the ground, even I can fill a five-gallon bucket with the precious fungi. When the color and texture of the ground are suppressed, the mushrooms are easy to see.

Seeing the soul is a similar field-ground issue. To see the soul, we must distinguish it from the physical and mental life surrounding it. With the physical and mental life suppressed, the soul is easier to see.

That's at least one reason why many pastors find calling on the sick to be simpler than calling on the healthy. When the outer life is wasting away, the existence and the necessity of the inner life are far more obvious to both pastor and parishioner.

What does it mean for the mental life to be suppressed so that the soul becomes more obvious? Aren't the mental life and the soul the same? Consistent with our approach to the question of seeing the soul, we ask: Can mentally ill people have healthy souls? Does a schizophrenic person have a real, human soul? Does a person who suffers from chronic depression have a fully human soul?

Of course they have fully human souls. Their mental life is suppressed or altered, not their soul.

Consider what happens when parishioners experience anxiety (a temporary mental disturbance) due to the onset of a dread disease in themselves or a loved one, or a major financial crisis, or a dramatic change in life. We see the pain, the fear, perhaps the depression. But we also see the opportunity.

Every pastor knows that happy, healthy, wealthy, and wise individuals may be nearly impervious to discussing the things of God. Their mental and physical life is thriving and full. But catch the same persons in a time of crisis, and they may be more open than ever to things of the spirit.

What is not readily apparent is that the soul concerns of a high-flying CEO are the same as those of the Alzheimer's patient. The failure to close a big deal is no different from the failure to tie a bow, because tying a bow is a big deal to an Alzheimer's patient.

We have confused age, gender, racial, socioeconomic, personality, and professional distinctions with the essence of being human. Yet our real essence is seen in the soul, not in the soul's wardrobe.

We may process the circumstances of our world differently, but to see this process at work is to see the soul—at its best and at its worst—in service to God and in rebellion against God. We glimpse the joy of honest accomplishment and the fear of the loss of competency, the peace of love and the angst of strife, the humble acceptance of the righteousness of God and proud assertion of selfish control. That's where the soul becomes visible.

Healthy Soul-Searching

What this means, in the most practical terms, is that you may not have to wait for the focused CEO and the rip-roarin' cowboy to hit life's bottom to minister Christ to the depths of their souls.

The best training for ministering to happy, healthy, thriving humans of all generations, all racial and ethnic groups, is to minister to unhappy, sick, depressed people.

To learn how to minister to people who can think only of themselves, learn to minister to people who can't remember their own name. To understand the stroke victim is to understand the football star; the only difference is the field.

How can this be? Old Max is living the football star's greatest fear. To know the football player's greatest fear, get to know the man living the football player's worst nightmare. And if you can see God's grace and salvation in that fearful place—then you can point to God in the hopes and fears of healthy men and women.

Of course, visiting old Max stretches us to the limit, too, because in facing him, we face our own fears and we know our own soul. Ultimately, we don't have to make great distinctions between the life of a football star and the life of a hallucinating, catheterized old man. It comes down to knowing that we both share similar joys and fears: "All go to one place; all are from the dust, and all turn to dust again" (Eccl. 3:20, NRSV).

The soul we see in the old woman unable to tie a bow is also the soul of a young girl tying bows in her hair before her first dance. The soul of a diapered, deranged man growling fragments of the Apostles' Creed is also the soul of the boy learning it first in Dutch. And the soul of a man hanging on a cross crying out, "My God, my God, why have you forsaken me?" is also the soul of the boy stumping the elders in the Temple.

The deepest soul hopes and soul fears of our everyday, healthy parishioners do not stray far from these poles. These touchstones for the gospel exist in every one of us.

Of course, in and of ourselves we can no more create a soul connection between a person and Christ than a hallucinating old man can recite the Apostles' Creed or a woman *sans* brain cells can tie a bow. But with Christ cuing us, we can speak the Word of true witness and place our finger on the ribbon, while he ties the bow.

SARAH E. HINLICKY

SEMINARY SANITY

(From *First Things*)

When you start out at seminary with an eye toward entering the ministry, the first thing they want to know about you is not whether you believe in God, or pray, or go to church. The first thing they want to know is whether you are a loony-toon. And so, in a move that may or may not make sense, they bustle you off to a psychological evaluation to find out.

This is mildly irritating to someone like me who believes in God, prays, goes to church, and wonders how much sanity has to do with any of it. For the record—and for those who place great import on childhood baggage—I (a) get plenty of positive attention from my dad, (b) approve of my mom's taste in clothes, and (c) adore my one brother, whose only flaw is having learned to play on me all the tricks I played on him when he was smaller than me. But my well-adjusted smile was not enough to convince the People In Charge that I was too healthy to spend an hour in a shrink's office. Instead, I got a whole day there. Before that, though, I had to take a whole battery of tests.

If I wasn't tending toward loony-toonity beforehand, the Minnesota Multiphasic Personality Inventory was nearly enough to trigger it. There is something ethically fishy about that test. The MMPI is approximately 567 true-or-false statements that, in their effort to detect whether one suffers from paranoia or hysteria, effectively induce those very conditions. Here are some sample statements (drawn from memory, since the MMPI is kept safely out of the hands of civilians like me):

> I vomit a lot.
> I have a terrible fear of rats.
> Sometimes I think someone's out to get me.
> I am possessed by evil spirits.
> I enjoy being hurt by those I love.

I am pleased to report that I quickly answered "false" to all of these. (Besides, if I really were possessed by evil spirits, do you suppose they'd tell me so?) But the one that really got me was: I am fascinated by fire. It all revolved around the interpretation of the word "fascinated." Sure, in one sense, I'm fascinated by fire—isn't everybody?—but if I answered "true," they'd probably think I was a pyro. The candidacy committee would have visions of the headline news announcer saying, "Last night a local pastor allegedly charged through the town center wielding a lit paschal candle like a lance and crying, 'Fiery death to the infidels!'" and that would be the end of my vocational prospects. It took me a solid ten minutes to talk myself into lying (a very unministerial thing to do, alas), reasoning that I'd rather commit a venial sin than lose my chances over a stupid psych exam.

The other tests were a walk in the park by comparison. Everybody loves the Myers-Briggs because it reports no negative information on the test taker, just preferences toward one style of operation over another. I personally hated the Thinking/Feeling questions, which make you choose between "head" and "heart," because I think it's a false dichotomy and the source of all Western philosophical ills; however, that probably proves I'm a Thinker beyond any shadow of a doubt. The Campbell interest survey ranks your skills and interests to help you figure out a suitable career. (The fact that I was taking this test while in direct pursuit of a chosen career is, apparently, a matter of indifference to the People In Charge.) You just tick off your level of interest in various occupations like tax consultant, Mary Kay vendor, botanist, or fireman. Later they tell you what you told them. It gets high marks for accuracy.

More creative are the "sentence completions." They give you an opening phrase, and you take it wherever you want to. So you get about forty totally open-ended possibilities like these:

I like it when . . .
Sometimes I wonder . . .
I wish that . . .
Sea anemonae remind me . . . (Just kidding. Nothing
    that suggestive here.)
My favorite memory . . .
I often think . . .
Fire-swallowers at the circus make me feel . . .
I used to . . .

The potential for sarcasm here is truly awesome. I mostly restrained myself, again for fear of headline news fantasies, but after so much soulful introspection I just couldn't take it anymore: When I stop . . . breathing, I turn blue. ("This just in! A local pastor has been hospitalized after a series of self-induced fainting spells.") There was a vocabulary/deductive reasoning test too, but as that was basically objective, there's not much in it worthy of comment.

All that, of course, was just preliminary. The real excitement came on Evaluation Day itself. The plan was to spend the morning with the master's-level counselor and the afternoon with the Ph.D.-level counselor, all for the bargain price of six hundred dollars. I must admit, though, that there are worse things in this world than spending an entire day talking about myself to utterly rapt strangers. It was fun to diagnose and dissect myself as if I weren't even there in the room, saying with absolute authority, "Oh yes, this is just like me," or "Oh no, I would never act like that." Parts of it were fairly enlightening. Other parts were not.

Take, for instance, the chat about my Myers-Briggs profile (ENTP, for the record). The very kind and likable lady who counseled me explained that, like most ministerial sorts, I was a strong N (intuitive/abstract thinking), whereas most laypeople are S's (sensory/practical thinking). "So you mean," I said slowly, trying to take it all in, "that I, as the pastor, will be more interested in theology than the church council, whose main goals will be meeting the monthly expenses, arranging to have the boiler repaired, and organizing a potluck now and then?" Well, gosh. The lady went on to express her concern that I had low self-esteem. I opined that there must be an error in the tests, but she showed me on the little chart that I consistently rated my interest in my favorite areas (religion, teaching, philosophy, etc.) higher than my skills. Therefore I must

be underrating myself. It's hard to argue with that kind of reasoning, so I didn't.

Don't get me wrong—the morning was by no means
wasted. I discovered, to my great relief, that even in this day
and age a little theology goes a long way, even where psych
evaluators are concerned. Luckily for me, the nice lady was
also a "diaconal minister," the phrase my church uses because
for some reason it can't bring itself to say "deacon," so she was
excited by any evidence of orthodoxy. My first indication of
this was after her speech about how my inner sense of call
was sacrosanct, and her intention was not to threaten or question it in any way; she just needed to determine whether I'd
make a good match with the kind of people the synod was
looking for.

After a moment of respectful silence, I said, "Actually, I
don't think there's anything sacrosanct about my sense of call.
I could be wrong. The church is supposed to discern whether
the Holy Spirit is calling me to ordination, so I'm happy to
leave the decision in their hands."

She looked at me in genuine astonishment. "Oh, how wonderful!" she exclaimed. "You just can't guess how many people
walk in here and demand that we give them full rein in the
church as if they were the only ones who counted in the
process." I thought I probably could guess if I tried.

The next time theology saved the day, it was a narrower
escape. We had been reviewing my interest survey. The nice
lady and her assistant confronted me, in a very sweet and loving manner, with the fact that I had not rated counseling very
highly on my interest list. (I began to squirm.) In fact, according to the test, I seemed to have almost no desire to help peo-

ple at all. Did I realize, she whispered, that according to the statistics most pastors rate higher in interest in the helping professions? Did I really have no interest in being a therapist, psychiatrist, health-care professional? Isn't that why people go into the ministry?

At last I bit the bullet and said, "I don't believe that I can help people." Audible gasp. "I believe that Jesus Christ can help people, and my job is to lead them to him and his healing."

Contented sighs. The lady was beaming again, and she thanked me. At that point even I couldn't help but like her, despite my firm resolve to be suspicious of her ilk. By the end of the morning, our common appreciation of solid doctrine made me feel like we'd spent an evening chatting in front of a cozy fire instead of under the glare of the fluorescent lights.

Unfortunately, the treatment wasn't over yet. I still had to see the doctor. My McDonalds lunch was sitting none too well in my insides as I pondered what sort of horrible secrets he would try to get me to blurt out. When I finally sat down in his office and introduced myself, I felt myself blushing fiercely— and immediately panicked at how he would interpret it. Maybe he'd think I was hiding something. Worse yet, maybe he'd think I had a crush on him.

"Hi," he said. "How was your morning?"

"Fine! It was fine," I replied quickly. Why did he ask? Was he going to tell the nice lady what I said about her?

"Good," he said blandly as he started rustling papers around. "All we have to do is look over the results of your MMPI."

The MMPI! My old nemesis was back. I tried to focus while he explained in a monotone about the threshold line on the charts, which means, in lay terms, that as long as you're below it, you're not a psycho.

"But I'm over the line on that one," I said, pointing to the column labeled Bizarre Mentation. "What does that mean?"

"Oh, that," said the doctor dully, waving it away like a fly with his hand. "Don't worry about it. All religious people score high on that one." He went on to explain that if you mark "true" for statements like "I believe there is an afterlife" or "I think angels exist," the test chalks it up to potential mental illness. I didn't know whether to be insulted or strangely comforted; either way, the doctor didn't care and proceeded with the results.

After droning on for a while, lulling me into a false sense of security, he asked me, "So, did you have a happy childhood?"

It was too quick and sudden, the sneaky jerk. I wasn't prepared for the question and he knew it. I almost just said yes. But I caught myself in time, looked him square in the eye, and said, "I had such a happy childhood that I've never even been to a psychologist. I don't expect you to believe me, though. I'm sure if I said so you'd think I was hiding nasty secrets or something."

"I'll believe whatever you tell me," he said calmly.

"I had a happy childhood," I said defiantly.

"Great," he said, and started to pack things up. "We're all through here. Do you have any questions or comments before we quit?"

I thought a moment. I looked at him. Then I blurted out, "I lied on the fire question!"

ALAN JACOBS

THE ONLY HONEST MAN

(From *Books & Culture*)

> Most of us know, now, that Rousseau was wrong: that
> man, when you knock his chains off, sets up the death
> camps. Soon we shall know everything the eighteenth
> century didn't know, and nothing it did, and it will be
> hard to live with us.
>
> —Randall Jarrell

When the great poet, satirist, and philosopher Voltaire died in 1778, at the age of eighty-four, he was buried on the grounds of the Abbey of Sellières, near Romilly-sur-Seine, France. But this would not be his final resting place. In the fervent early years of the French Revolution, before the Reign of Terror, the leading revolutionaries agreed that their "glorious Revolution has been the fruit of his works" and decided to bring his body to Paris, where he could receive the honor so rarely granted him in his lifetime. Some such decision had to be made, for the abbey (along with much other property of the Church) had been confiscated by a cash-strapped government and was to be auctioned off, and some of the new national leaders quailed at the prospect of the great philosopher's remains

131

becoming private property. The site they chose for the hero's reinterment was the newly designated Panthéon—what had been the unfinished church of St. Geneviève, now finally completed not as a house of God, but as a monument to those designated by the revolutionaries as *"les Grands Hommes."*

Only two dignitaries had thus far assumed their places in the Panthéon: its original inhabitant, the seventeenth-century philosopher René Descartes, the patron saint of reason as conceived by the Enlightenment, followed in April 1791 by the revolutionary leader Mirabeau, whose unexpected death had bestowed upon him an immediate sanctification. Now, on July 11 of the same year, Voltaire would make the third in this company: his remains were carried on what Simon Schama calls "a monumental chariot, as high as a two-story house," leading an enormous imitation Roman triumphal procession through the streets of Paris. Notable among the many participants in this cortège were "a troupe of men dressed in Roman costume [carrying] as trophies of glory editions of all Voltaire's works."

Strange to say, this bizarre ritual would be repeated three years later, in October 1794—when *la grande Terreur* had run its course, its instigator and sustainer, Robespierre, having been at the end of July one of the guillotine's last victims—but now the exhumed hero was Jean-Jacques Rousseau. Again a procession was organized, this time commencing at Ermeonville, thirty miles from Paris, where Rousseau had died and been buried. (Though eighteen years younger than Voltaire, he had outlived him by only a month.) Again emblems of the great man's life and work were displayed for public approval: musicians played Rousseau's compositions, and at the end of this cortège members of the national legislature held aloft copies of the gospel *du jour*, Rousseau's famous political treatise, *The Social Contract*.

In one sense, nothing could be more comprehensible than this co-elevation of two of the eighteenth century's most versatile and influential writers. Each man had written in a remarkable variety of genres. Voltaire produced tragedies, an epic, a witty philosophical satire that is his most-read work today (*Candide*), many comic tales, and innumerable pamphlets on his time's most controversial subjects. Similarly, in one astonishing nine-year period Rousseau produced a romantic epistolary novel about love and duty (*Julie, or The New Héloïse*), a didactic philosophical tale about the ideal means of educating young men (*Émile*), an extended polemic on the uses and dangers of theaters in various societies (*Letter to d'Alembert*), and a compressed yet ambitious treatise on political philosophy (*The Social Contract*). Such activity left him no time to compose the music that had earlier brought him to the attention of the French. Both Voltaire and Rousseau contributed to the dominant intellectual project of their time, the great ongoing *Encyclopedia* edited by Denis Diderot and Jean d'Alembert. Both were theoretically hopeful about the human race, but by temperament bitterly pessimistic. Above all, both men understood themselves to be celebrants and defenders of freedom, and therefore enemies of the hierarchies and institutions of France's *ancien régime*. Surely a revolution which itself promised freedom from royal absolutism and aristocratic privilege was right to enthrone these two great men?

Perhaps. But it must also be said that Voltaire and Rousseau had loathed each other, indeed, believed themselves to speak for irreconcilable philosophies. Their relationship—which was conducted wholly in letters, since they only met once—began cordially enough, as the aspiring artist-intellectual Rousseau sent flattering letters to the man already recognized as France's leading writer (though Voltaire's polemical nature had generated enough highly placed enmity to drive him from his native country and to the suburbs of Rousseau's home city, Geneva). But in 1754, when Rousseau sent a copy of his second significant work, the *Discourse on the Origins of Inequality*, to Voltaire, things began to change. This *Discourse* was Rousseau's first work to articulate fully a position which would later be almost identified with him: that human beings had once lived in a blissfully anarchic "state of nature," the innocence of which we have since lost through the corruptions of organized society. Nothing could be further from Voltaire's view that the disciplined practice of Reason was, or at least could be, gradually emancipating us from the chains of ancient passions and superstitions, and he replied with predictable irony: "I have received, Monsieur, your new book against the human race, and I thank you. No one has employed so much intelligence to turn us men into beasts. One starts wanting to walk on all fours after reading your book. However, in more than sixty years I have lost the habit."

From this point on the relationship deteriorated. Rousseau became more and more convinced that Voltaire was his greatest enemy, a consuming suspicion that boiled over in 1760 in a wrathful letter, equally paranoid and megalomaniacal, which insured that they would never be reconciled:

I do not like you, Monsieur; you have done me injuries of the most harmful kind; done them to me, your disciple and your enthusiastic admirer. You have ruined Geneva, in return for the asylum you have been given there. You have turned my fellow citizens against me as a reward for the praise which I have secured for you. It is you who have made living in my own city impossible for me; it is you who force me to perish on foreign soil, deprived of all the consolations of the dying, cast unceremoniously like a dog on the wayside, who you, alive or dead, enjoy in my homeland all the honours to which a man could aspire. I despise you.

In fact, far from being a dying, impoverished, and rejected man—and far from striving to return to Geneva—Rousseau at the time was living comfortably on the bounty of his friend and patron, the fantastically wealthy and powerful Maréchal de Luxembourg.

Voltaire never responded to this letter, which perhaps only intensified Rousseau's paranoia and determination to oppose the older man in all things. If Voltaire would praise philosophy, Rousseau—who as an aspiring writer had self-consciously given up music for philosophy—would repudiate it. If Voltaire would elevate Reason, Rousseau would condemn it in favor of the more sure way of the heart: "I have abandoned reason and consulted nature," he wrote to a Genevan friend when his alienation from Voltaire, his old friend Denis Diderot, and the whole world of the *philosophes* had become evident to everyone involved, "that is, the inner feeling."

And they quarreled about God. Voltaire always maintained a belief in the existence of some kind of deity—the argument from design appealed to him—but he wasn't sure exactly what kind, since it was obvious to him that this beautifully made world was also filled with incomprehensible evil. When a great earthquake destroyed much of Lisbon, Portugal, in November of 1755, Voltaire wrote a bitter poem that mocked the very idea that such a disaster could be attributed to the sovereignty of a benevolent Providence, and asked whether a good deity could even be thought to rule over this world at all. Rousseau responded—this was before their decisive break— with a long letter pointing out, reasonably enough, that many of the people died not from the earthquake as such, but because their cheaply constructed and grotesquely crowded houses caved in on them: the disaster was more due to the systemic evils of life in unjust human society than to the acts of God. Rousseau warmly affirmed his belief in Providence and in the immortality of the human soul. (For this affirmation, Diderot came to believe, Rousseau had earned the admiration of "the devout party"—that is, the Christians—and would therefore remain popular with and accepted by them. In this he was wrong.)

Voltaire in turn replied only with an apology for not having time to answer substantively, though he proclaimed affection for Rousseau. And so the conversation appeared to end. But when *Candide* appeared two years later—with a repudiation of the idea of Providence, and those who believe in it, still more fierce than that of the poem—Rousseau understood it to be Voltaire's belated reply to his passionate letter. "I wanted to philosophize with Voltaire; in return he made fun of me." If such was the attitude of the age's greatest apostle of philosophy and reason, then who needed philosophy and reason? And indeed mockery would be from this point on

Voltaire's characteristic response to Rousseau: for instance, he amused himself by spreading the rumor that Rousseau had at one time been valet to France's ambassador in Venice. (In fact, Rousseau had been the ambassador's secretary and therefore an important member of the diplomatic corps himself; but since at one time he had indeed been a footman in the household of a rich man, the false report had a particular sting.) And to his fellow *philosophes* he spoke of "that fool Rousseau, that bastard of Diogenes' dog."

Were Voltaire and Rousseau right in thinking that they, and their intellectual positions, were irreconcilable? Or had the Revolutionaries correctly discerned some hidden complicity of the two antagonists, some common vision that lay beneath the surface and that Voltaire and Rousseau themselves could therefore never see? Or could both views be true? There is another way to put these questions: was Romanticism an alternative to the Enlightenment, or its natural heir? It is Jean-Jacques Rousseau who stands at the confluence of these two great movements in Western intellectual history; his life and work, more than those of any other single figure, show us how the two were related to each other. And if Rousseau's life is full of confusions and contradictions, that is largely because he represented within himself movements that were now harmonious, now dissonant, now moving on parallel tracks, now on a collision course. Rousseau is the modern world.

Maurice Cranston's three-volume biography of the extraordinary Jean-Jacques is as full and scholarly and vivid a portrait as we are likely to have; but alas, it is not all that one might hope for. Chiefly this is because Cranston, a longtime professor of political science at the London School of Economics, died before he could complete the third volume. Sanford Lakoff, who was entrusted with the task of putting the manuscript in order, writes that Cranston had finished seven of that volume's eight chapters when he died, but one can only assume that Cranston was hurrying his work, since these chapters cover momentous events in Rousseau's life at a much quicker pace than the first two installments had maintained. There can be few readers of those sweeping yet detailed volumes who will not be disappointed at the thinness of the third.

Such disappointment testifies both to Cranston's skill as a biographer and the extraordinary richness of Rousseau's eventful life. Even the briefest sketch of Rousseau's experiences is enough to illustrate the need for a multivolume biography. At the outset of his second volume, Cranston summarizes Rousseau's first forty years:

Rousseau's early life was that of a wanderer, an adventurer, the life of a hero of a picaresque novel. Orphaned by the early death of his mother and the defection of his father, he had run away from his native Geneva at the age of sixteen to escape the life of a plebeian engraver's apprentice, and found refuge as a Catholic convert in Savoy. Making his own way in the world as a footman in Turin, a student at a choir school in Annecy, the steward and the lover of a Swiss baroness in Chambéry, the interpreter to a Levantine mountebank, an itinerant musician, a private tutor in the family of Condillac and Mably in Lyons, secretary to the French Ambassador in Venice and research assistant to the Dupins at Chenonceaux, he set out with his great friend and contemporary Denis Diderot to conquer Paris as a writer, and, much to his own surprise, did so almost overnight at the age of thirty-eight with the publication of his *Discourse on the Sciences and Arts*.

After this came the prodigious decade already mentioned, in which almost all the works that would make Rousseau famous were written. But these increasingly controversial works alienated the more conservative elements in French society—especially Roman Catholics—and in 1762 two of them (*Émile* and *The Social Contract*) were formally condemned. Rousseau fled France under threat of arrest, and it is with this departure that Cranston ends his second volume. For most of the rest of his life Rousseau lived in Switzerland, though his reputation as an infidel made him unpopular, and he had to move from town to town. For a while he lived in England under the protection of the philosopher David Hume, but Rousseau's increasing paranoia ruined that friendship, as it had ruined many others, and he returned to the Continent. Eventually, in 1767, he was received back in France, and in the years leading up to his death in 1778 was once again celebrated in the salons of Paris, where in lengthy readings of his work-in-progress, the *Confessions*, he praised himself and cursed his enemies to the applause of society.

Again, until the Swiss exile, Cranston is a masterful relater of this history. But it is not just the rushed narrative of Rousseau's later years that creates problems for this biography's readers: also problematic is Cranston's desire to rescue Rousseau from at least some of the bad repute that disfigures his memory. Cranston is consistently sympathetic to Rousseau and tries whenever possible to reconcile Rousseau's versions of events—especially as those versions appear in Rousseau's pathbreaking and self-exculpating *Confessions*—with the available evidence. Sometimes he has to give up the attempt with an almost audible sigh, but for the most part he manages to make Rousseau's view of the controversies that always surrounded him seem comprehensible and even plausible.

Cranston achieves this, at least in some cases, by a kind of withholding of evidence. Rousseau's letters are full of passages that show him in a very bad light indeed, and often Cranston simply doesn't quote such passages; or if he does quote them and cannot explain them away, he leaves them without comment. To some degree he is reacting against earlier biographers and critics who have calumniated Rousseau, but given a work of such scope it is difficult to condone a reluctance to confront the whole truth about the subject.

One may approach this problem, and simultaneously approach what is of crucial importance about Rousseau, by returning to the quarrel with Voltaire. In 1759 Rousseau wrote a letter to an old Genevan friend whom he was coming to distrust because he knew the man to be one of Voltaire's regular visitors. He is particularly concerned to respond to a semirhetorical question his friend had asked him: "How is it that the friend of humanity is hardly any longer the friend of men?" The question had angered Rousseau, and in defending himself he insists, "I am the friend of the human race." When Voltaire saw this comment he seized upon it: "Extreme insolence is extreme stupidity, and nothing is more stupid than a Jean-Jacques talking about 'the human race and I.'" (All of this Cranston relates.)

One might think that Voltaire was unfairly mocking a passing figure of speech, but Rousseau's distinction was by this time in his life fundamental to his character—fundamental in a way that Cranston is reluctant to acknowledge. Three years after the exchange I have just described, Rousseau wrote, "Oh why did Providence have me born among men, and make me of a different species?" And one does not have to read far in Rousseau's letters, or indeed his published works, to figure out what species he thought he belonged to: he was the world's only *honnête homme*, that is, the only truthful and wholly honorable man.

Almost from the beginning of his time in Paris, Rousseau took pains to emphasize his difference from others. He early on learned to make capital of his peculiarities—he had more than a few—and to convince people that what would be rudeness or thoughtlessness in others was virtue in him. He called himself a "bear" and liked it when others did the same; he commented frequently on his inability to make polite conversation or to dissemble his feelings in any way. When friends suggested that he owed some gratitude to Madame d'Épinay, who had befriended him, he replied bluntly: "As for kindnesses, I do not like them, I do not want them, and I do not feel grateful to those who force me to accept them." (He does not explain how exactly she "forced" him to take her gifts, which included a house in which he lived; later he would complain similarly of being "forced" to receive presents from an admiring Prince de Conti.) When the Maréchal de Luxembourg installed Rousseau in his *"petit chateau,"* Rousseau wrote a letter to Madame de Luxembourg insisting, "I shall not praise you. I shall not thank you. But I inhabit your house. Everyone has his own language, and I have said all in mine." This had the exquisitely subtle effect of flattering his aristocratic patrons while simultaneously maintaining the manner of a "bear" who simply cannot behave as other men do.

Rousseau found every possible means of insisting upon his difference from other men. Thus his habit once he was established in Paris of referring to himself, and having others refer to him, as *"citoyen de Geneve,"* when in fact he had repudiated his Genevan citizenship as a young Catholic convert: he found it useful to represent himself as the outlander, the plain-spoken burgher from the wild Alpine lakes. In his Swiss exile he even wore a flamboyant Armenian costume on his daily walks (and then wrote letters complaining that the locals mocked him). His virtues could only be made evident by contrast with the vices of everyone else. In a reproachful letter to a woman who had failed to return his affection, he roundly declared that "there cannot be any peace between J.-J. Rousseau and the wicked"—and who wasn't wicked? "What distinguishes me from all the other men I know, is that with all my faults, I have always reproached myself for them, and that my faults have never made me despise my duty or trample on virtue; and, moreover, that I have struggled for virtue and conquered at times when everyone else has forgotten it." It is this conviction above all that underlies the most definitive statement of his uniqueness, on the first page of his *Confessions*: "I am made unlike anyone I have ever met; I will even venture to say that I am like no one in the whole world."

Rousseau consistently maintained belief in his uniqueness, and almost as consistently, belief in his superiority to other human beings—but at times the latter stance grew difficult. Especially when word got out that his mistress had borne him five children and he had promptly sent each of them to Paris's foundling hospital, he had some explaining to do, and knew it. He writes to several friends, at various times in his life, about that decision, and wavers between staunchly defending himself—on the grounds that he had lacked the resources to raise his children properly and that in the orphanage they would have been educated into an honest trade, which was more than he would have been able to do for them—and expressing remorse. But his general tone of each letter is more or less the same: that he had shown his nobility of character in performing the "rational" act of abandoning his children, and that he continues to show the nobility of his character by experiencing deep remorse even over such a fully justifiable decision. Whether in acting or in lamenting his actions, then, he lived up to his self-description as *l'honnête homme.*

In this case and in many others, Rousseau presents himself as a man whose behavior would be vicious if practiced by others, but on his part is sheer virtue. In a lengthy and extraordinary letter to Madame d'Épinay (one to which Cranston does not refer), Rousseau refuses her attempts to reconcile him to his former friend, the *philosophe* Diderot. He describes for her at some length his expectations in friendship—expectations unmet by Diderot—and concludes the description by saying: "I require from a friend even a great deal more than all I have just told you; even more than he must require from me, and than I should require from him, if he were in my place, and I were in his."

But what does Rousseau mean when he speaks of his "place"? This is important, since the distinction between his place and that of Diderot seems to justify the grossest inequalities in friendship. He immediately goes on to explain, "As a recluse, I

am more sensitive than another man"—and it is Rousseau's status as a "recluse" to which he almost obsessively returns in his
letters and memoirs. In Rousseau's philosophy, only the recluse
can be virtuous, because only the recluse evades the corrupting influences of society and thereby retains a pure natural
honesty. Rousseau the recluse, then, becomes the living
embodiment of his own "noble savage," and Cranston is right
to title his second volume with that phrase.

In his *Confessions*, therefore, Rousseau writes that he "first
began to live" on April 9, 1756, for on that day he retired from
society into a "hermitage," utterly isolating himself from his
Parisian acquaintance. Well, perhaps not "utterly." No self-
respecting hermit could have found Rousseau's residence satis-
factory, since it was a former hunting lodge on Madame
d'Épinay's estate, and he could visit with her whenever he
chose. Moreover, in Cranston's words, this was no "Gothic
cottage but a dignified and symmetrical house, with good-
sized rooms, an elegant door and windows, with both orna-
mental and kitchen gardens and an orchard, surrounded by
fields and the forest." And to top it off, this supposedly remote
and isolated habitation was less than a dozen miles from Paris;
Rousseau would sometimes chastise his friends for not walking
out to visit him.

Later, when living still more elegantly in the Maréchal de
Luxembourg's *"petit chateau,"* he would often visit the Duke's
house in Paris. This was awkward for Rousseau, not only
because of his status as "recluse"—when first invited there he
replied, "Why do you disturb the peace of a hermit who has
renounced the pleasures of life in order to be spared its
fatigues?"—but also because he had vowed never to set foot

on the streets of Paris again. But then he realized that the Duke's carriage would take him directly into the garden of the great townhouse: thus "I could say with the most exact truth that I never set foot on the streets of Paris."

Nevertheless, these various "cottages" and "hermitages" were sufficiently removed from the day-to-day distractions that bedeviled Rousseau in his Parisian years that during the nine years he lived in them he wrote almost every word that would later make him famous. For all his posturing, Rousseau was never reluctant to work, and he was intellectually ambitious as well as prolific—even though he made almost no money from his books and tried to support himself by copying music.

But if one looks at those works from the great decade in isolation from what we know about Rousseau, they are not often impressive. Jules Lemaitre may have exaggerated when he said that the enormous popularity of Rousseau's first book, the *Discourse on the Sciences and Arts*, constituted "one of the strongest proofs ever provided of human stupidity;" in that book, and in each of Rousseau's books, there are certainly striking and provocative ideas. But the works lack coherence of development, and indeed some of them are wildly self-contradictory, as Rousseau himself saw: in the case of his novel *Julie*, he noted some of the contradictions when the book was being prepared for press, but decided not to remedy them. (Perhaps he didn't know how; or perhaps his attitude anticipated that of Walt Whitman a hundred years later: "I contradict myself? Very well, I contradict myself. I am large; I contain multitudes.") Even the book by which Rousseau is best known today, *The Social Contract*, was not widely read in his lifetime—in part because it was frequently censored—and first became influential when the Revolution initiated its cult of Rousseau.

What is particularly important about this first celebration of Rousseau is that, like those that would come afterwards, it was dictated by Rousseau's self-presentation in the *Confessions*. Indeed, the *Confessions* was Rousseau's only book to have precisely the effect he intended it to have: the others were thoroughly misread or not read at all, but this one hit the mark. In the depths of a profound paranoia, convinced that his former friends were conspiring at least to destroy his reputation and perhaps to have him murdered, Rousseau wrote this book to convince the world that he was in fact a new kind of saint: the saint as reclusive hermit, as noble savage, as *honnête homme*.

"I publicly and fearlessly declare," he says at the end of the *Confessions*, "that anyone, even if he has not read my writings, who will examine my nature, my character, my morals, my likings, my pleasures, and my habits with his own eyes and can still believe me a dishonorable man, is a man who deserves to be stifled." It was largely because this rhetorical strategy convinced his revolutionary readers that he was installed in the Panthéon—not because of the influence of *The Social Contract*, which few among the revolutionaries had read, and which was appealed to not because of its argument but because of a couple of striking phrases. There was the famous first sentence of the book—"Man is born free, but everywhere he is in chains"—a resonant utterance in the mouths of self-proclaimed liberators; and then there was the notion of the "general will" of the people, the collective desire or purpose of a culture, a will for which the rebels were quick to claim that they spoke, though they cared little what Rousseau meant by that phrase.

No, it was the Jean-Jacques of the *Confessions* who was the real popular hero, because he stood against the complexities and hierarchies and dissimulations of the *ancien régime* by standing for an unaffected "natural" sincerity. On the first page of that book, he stakes out his territory in memorable terms as he imagines going before the judgment seat of God, not bowing or kneeling, not weeping penitent tears, not in awe or fear, but boldly, with a copy of the *Confessions* in his hand. Indeed, Rousseau imagines the whole company of heaven suspending their customary adoration of the Lord to listen, as raptly as the attendants of a fashionable Parisian salon, to the honest man reading his story:

> I have displayed myself as I was, as vile and despicable when my behavior was such, as good, generous, and noble when I was so. I have bared my secret soul as Thou thyself has seen it, Eternal Being! So let the numberless legion of my fellow men gather round me, and hear my confessions. Let them groan at my depravities, and blush for my misdeeds. But let each one of them reveal his heart at the foot of Thy throne with equal sincerity, and may any man who dares, say "I was a better man than he."

This astonishing declaration needs to be read in conjunction with Rousseau's desire to "stifle" anyone who does not hear his tale with full approval. In other words, the honesty with which he proclaims his every action transmutes those actions, however base they may seem, into the pure gold of virtue. Rousseau claims justification neither by faith nor by works, but by sincerity: sincerity alone enables him not only to transcend his fellow human beings, but also to throw his *Confessions* in the face of God, daring even him to judge Jean-Jacques.

What is so noteworthy, here and elsewhere in Rousseau's writings, is the fierceness with which he demands the recognition and approval of others, even while simultaneously claiming to despise their company and to owe them nothing (not even gratitude for *un petit chateau*). So even when he descends to the public's level and provides just the sort of sensationalistic writing they want to read, he sophistically contends that they are merely getting what they deserve and are able to comprehend. He blames the age rather than himself for the bad taste of his *Julie, or The New Héloïse,* as he explains in the preface to his novel (referring obliquely to his own condemnations of theaters and novels in his *Letter to d'Alembert*): "There must be theatres in large cities and novels for corrupt peoples. I have observed the morals of my time, and I have published these letters. Would that I had lived in a century when my duty would have been to throw them in the fire!" In other words, just as his aristocratic patrons were "forcing" him against his will to accept their lavish gifts, so French culture as a whole was "forcing" him to write corrupt, and corrupting, novels.

This kind of argument had for Rousseau a twofold beneficial effect. On the one hand, it relieved him from the responsibility for any of his actions that might be considered shameful. On the other hand, by condemning so bluntly the very people to whom he addressed his works, he maintained in their eyes his reputation for being bearish, blunt, unaccommodating—in short, honest. One cannot but admire the rhetorical panache with which Rousseau carries this off: to become famous and celebrated by relentlessly praising oneself and belittling everyone else is no easy feat and must be managed with great care.

Here again the contrast with Voltaire is instructive. Voltaire was happy to participate in what he liked to call the "Republic of Letters" and its "reign of critique," and enjoyed not only the honors showered upon him by his fellow intellectuals (such as membership in the Académie Française) but also, when they came, those bestowed by the monarchy. Rousseau by contrast looked upon, or tried very hard to look upon, or pretended that he looked upon all honors as invitations to corruption: for instance, he claimed to have refused membership in the Académie. Likewise, his insistence on earning his bread by copying music—while all the time his patrons were slipping money to his mistress—served to increase the esteem of those already inclined to admire him.

As Paul Cohen shows in his admirable book *Freedom's Moment*, the key to understanding this phenomenon is provided by the sociologist Pierre Bourdieu, who coined the term "consecrated heretic" to describe a recurrent character in French society—a character, Cohen says, created virtually from whole cloth by Rousseau. Again and again since Rousseau, famous French intellectuals have made, or enhanced, their public reputations by the ostentatious refusal of public honors. (Thus the anthropologist Claude Lévi-Strauss, in his own narrative of encounters with "noble savages," *Tristes Tropiques*, speaks for the entire French intelligentsia when he celebrates Rousseau as "our master and our brother. . . . Every page of this book could have been dedicated to him, had it not been unworthy of his great memory.") In repudiating every form of recognition by the society at large—and even by the countercultural intellectual elite—these thinkers demonstrate their intellectual autonomy and integrity. As Cohen points out, the greatest of all such masters of refusal was Jean-Paul Sartre, who in the aftermath of World War II publicly and vocally declined election to the French Legion of Honor, then, encouraged by the admiration this decision elicited, went on to refuse (like Rousseau) the Académie Française, then the Collège de France, and finally, in the grandest gesture of all, the Nobel Prize for literature.

The point of such repudiations, especially in the context of the 1960s, is clear: Sartre was determined to avoid being "co-opted" by the Establishment, that is, lulled into complacency and acceptance of the status quo by the soporific drug "honor." But this determination only made him more heroic in the eyes of the intelligentsia: thus for his very heresy he was conse-crated. At times, Sartre seems to have suspected that his inabil-ity to get himself persecuted by his society compromised his claim to heretical status. After all, would a truly subversive thinker be so lionized? It must have been particularly galling for Sartre when, in 1960, President de Gaulle shrewdly declined to have Sartre imprisoned for subversive activities, saying "one does not arrest Voltaire"—a neat twist of the knife, given Voltaire's enthusiastic acceptance of public recognition!

In this respect Sartre could only have envied Rousseau. As long as he was celebrated and coddled by Madame d'Épinay and the Maréchal de Luxembourg, Rousseau's pride remained more or less in check: his complaints about being forced to accept gifts and his insistence that he was a reclusive hermit betray doubt about the moral validity of his position. But when he came under genuine persecution, his books were banned, and he was driven into real solitude and exile, his self-regard escalated into megalomania: every new misfortune, every word of criticism confirmed his superiority to the human beings among whom he was doomed to live. Rousseau became the ultimate heretic, consecrated not by society—whose praise would have been gall and wormwood to him—but by the only authority whose right to consecrate he could accept: his own heart.

Scholars in many disciplines have identified Rousseau as a decisive figure in the development of modernity. Political theorists have discerned in *The Social Contract*, especially its notion of the "general will," adumbrations of later totalitarian regimes; historians of education have pointed to *Émile* as the originating document of the "liberating" tradition of pedagogy that Americans associate primarily with John Dewey; his "primitivism" and his love of wild mountain scenery (scenery "sublime" rather than merely beautiful) have been acknowledged as sources of the Romantic movement in literature, painting, and music. One could go on. But Rousseau's true gift was for self-creation, and it is this art that he has bequeathed to the whole modern world. He could well have said what Oscar Wilde would later say, that only his talent went into his work: it was his life that exhibited genius.

Peter Gay has defined Rousseau's life as "that melodramatic vagabondage punctuated by angry letters." A brilliant and incisive phrase, but not fully adequate. Those letters—including *The Confessions*, which may fairly be called the longest and most

rhetorically crafted among them—are not always angry: often
they rail, to be sure, but equally often they plead, and, as
occasion warrants, lament, sneer, enthuse, celebrate, and
scold. But each of these moods or tones is put in the service of
one comprehensive and never-forgotten goal: to justify the
ways of Jean-Jacques to the world. The image Rousseau offers
us on the first page of the *Confessions*, of his striding up to the
throne of God with his book in his hand, is the only one we
really need if we wish to understand this remarkable man.

Remarkable, but not—oh, how Jean-Jacques would protest
here—not unique. In many ways his audacious confrontation
of all the host of heaven is but the logical culmination of the
key doctrine he shares with Voltaire and all the *philosophes*: the
doctrine of innate human innocence. Voltaire and Rousseau,
for all their differences, alike inherited what may well be the
decisive event in the last thousand years of intellectual history:
the widespread rejection of the Christian doctrine of Original
sin. Voltaire, Rousseau, and all the *philosophes* never waver in
their conviction that innocence is our birthright, just waiting
for us to claim it.

But why, then, has Rousseau's vision of humanity become
so much more potent and lasting than the *philosophes'* picture?
Why are we the heirs of Jean-Jacques rather than Diderot or
Condillac or even Voltaire? It is an easy question to answer.
Note what each party says:

Philosophe: (1) People behave badly. (2) They do so
because they follow the dictates of passion and superstition rather than those of reason. (3) Therefore an education that systematically disciplines the passions and places

them under the sovereignty of reason will remedy most human ills.

Rousseau: (1) People behave badly. (2) They do so because they live in societies that have miseducated them, led them astray, and made them deaf to the call of their own pure hearts. (3) Therefore an education that isolates them from the corrupting influences of society and liberates them to hear and heed the innocent and natural promptings of their inmost being will remedy most human ills.

Which of these would *you* be more likely to receive as good news?

The *philosophe* tells you that your sins and crimes result from a combination of acts (for instance, indulging your passions) and failures to act (for instance, not training those same passions), for both of which—the acts and the failures—you are responsible. The good news that you are naturally virtuous is scarcely sufficient to compensate for this tough lesson in accountability and the need for hard moral work.

Rousseau, on the other hand, gives you not only the good news of innate virtue, but also the still better news that your habitual failure to realize such innate virtue is always someone else's fault. So omnipotent is this belief in our time that I once quoted, in a classroom full of young Christians, Sartre's famous dictum—the summation of Rousseau's thought, in four words—that "Hell is other people," only to have several students nod approvingly and one mutter, "That's so true." So pernicious is this belief that, despite Rousseau's defense of the goodness of God and whatever approval from "the devout party" he received therefrom, a retreat from Rousseau's principles to those of the *philosophes* would be a salutary move for our society. It is true, of course, that anyone attempting to follow the *philosophes'* program for moral improvement would be hindered and ultimately defeated by the recalcitrance of the fallen human will. But this defeat could be instructive and even redemptive. Rousseau's brand of self-regard, by contrast, eliminates *a priori* the learning of such lessons.

Which leads us back to the French Revolution. As that movement progressed, it came increasingly to be dominated by its more radical parties, until the most radical of all rose to power: the Jacobins. And foremost among the Jacobins came to be Maximilien Robespierre. As Paul Cohen explains, Robespierre's "idol" was none other than Rousseau: from Rousseau he derived his whole rhetorical-ethical apparatus, especially its relentless division of the sheep from the goats. "There are only two parties in France," he declared, "the people and its enemies," the party of "corrupt men and that of virtuous men." But as Robespierre's Reign of Terror progressed, it began to frighten even those who had been enthusiastic at its inception; and as he saw his colleagues deviate from the true path— "There are not two ways of being free," he insisted—the party of the goats grew ever larger, while that of the sheep inexorably shrank. More and more Jacobins found themselves peremptorily arrested, tried, and guillotined, in a terror that claimed to be the instrument of virtue: for, as Robespierre famously said, it may be that without virtue "terror is harmful," but without terror "virtue is impotent."

But how did Robespierre know that his way was the way of virtue? He knew because, like his idol and model Rousseau, he had attended to the testimony of his heart—indeed, this was how he discerned the few good citizens among the many bad: "I believe patriotism not to be a matter of party, but of the heart." One can see where this, inevitably, is headed: toward the paranoia of Rousseau, who came in the end to trust no one but himself, no heart but his own. Thus a caricature that appeared in 1795 showing a formally dressed man releasing the guillotine's blade onto the neck of a solitary victim, with this caption beneath: "Robespierre guillotining the executioner, having guillotined all of France."

It is the tragic culmination of Rousseau's logic: since other people impede my achievement of virtue, in the very name of virtue they must be destroyed. In July 1794 the Jacobins who remained had little choice but to turn on Robespierre and execute him; he would have gotten each of them eventually. And Rousseau had said it all before him: "I publicly and fearlessly declare that anyone, even if he has not read my writings, who will examine my nature, my character, my morals, my likings, my pleasures, and my habits with his own eyes and can still believe me a dishonorable man, is a man who deserves to be stifled." The child of pride is Terror.

PRESTON JONES

HISTORY, DISCERNMENT, AND THE CHRISTIAN LIFE

About twenty-three hundred years ago the author of Ecclesiastes wrote that "of the making of books there is no end." Nowadays Solomon's observation might be modified to say that of the making of books about, say, the American Civil War, women in American history, or a myriad other topics there is no end. Consider the number of works concerned with the study and nature of history itself. Even a cursory glance at some of the older though still available titles—e.g. *What Is History?* (E. H. Carr), *The Idea of History* (R. G. Collingwood), *Truth in History* (Oscar Handlin), *Reason in History* (G. W. F. Hegel), *The Origins of History* (Herbert Butterfield), *Philosophical Analysis and History* (William H. Dray), *Early Christian Interpretations of History* (R. L. P. Milburn)—suggests the extent to which the study of historiography and of various philosophies of history can be a full-time job.

If there are hundreds of available books on the nature of written history, there are probably as many opinions about history as there are people. "History is a nightmare," says Stephen in James Joyce's *Ulysses;* and in Oscar Wilde's opinion, "Anybody can make history," but only "a great man can write it."

H. G. Wells wrote that "history [is] more and more a race between education and catastrophe," Thomas Carlyle that the "history of the world is but the biography of great men." (Carlyle also wrote that history was a "distillation of rumor.") History is an "excitable and lying old lady" (Guy de Maupassant). History is a "great dust heap" (Augustine Birrell). History is "the belief in falsehood" (F. Nietzsche). "History is more or less bunk" (Henry Ford). "History is a pattern of timeless moments" (T. S. Eliot). "History is *magister vitae*"—the teacher of life (Benedetto Croce). The "whole of history is incomprehensible without [Jesus]" (Ernest Renan).

Obviously, a new claim about the nature of history isn't needed, and I am not interested in formulating a Christian philosophy of history. For while I recognize that one's own views, dispositions, personal experience, and temperament will inevitably influence how one sees and thinks about the past, I am opposed to history consciously written or taught from any particular "perspective." The dangers inherent in writing or teaching history from a "feminist" or "Marxist" or "conservative" or "liberal" point of view are also, it seems to me, inherent in studying the past from a "Christian" perspective.

Eager to uncover the depths of America's Christian roots, some Christian writers have embraced the founding fathers' references to God without acknowledging that the God of Thomas Jefferson, James Madison, and John Adams is one most orthodox Christians of whatever tradition wouldn't recognize. Similarly, Christian writers of history have sometimes failed to distinguish between civil religion and cultural Christianity, on the one hand, and, on the other, a consciously biblical Christianity (however flawed in practice). Thus some of the same people who resist casual Christianity and civil religion in contemporary America endorse it in historic America.

"Theodore Roosevelt stood foursquare on the legacy of Biblical orthodoxy," says a Christian writer and "historian," who fails to distinguish between an approach to the Bible that takes it seriously as the Word of God and a very different approach to the Scriptures taken among late nineteenth- and early twentieth-century American nationalists who ransacked the Bible for verses that could be used to justify various political causes. The claim is false; Teddy Roosevelt had little use for "Biblical orthodoxy," and to spin Roosevelt as an orthodox Christian is to get him wrong. And I think that American Christians who are concerned with truth should want to avoid coming to wrong conclusions about history, even when that means giving up cherished ideas about the stuff of their nation's past.

It is inevitable that historians or history teachers will bring their personal commitments with them to the archives and into the classroom. But it is fundamentally corrupting—and as a Christian I think that it is sinful—to turn to the past with the primary object of vindicating preconceived judgments. To keep to the example of Teddy Roosevelt, if a Christian wants to applaud Roosevelt's manly patriotism, that is a matter of fair choice; but I think that Christian readers, writers, and teachers of history would do well to beware spinning Roosevelt's nationalism in strictly favorable—or Christian—terms. The expansionist movement Roosevelt promoted did some good in the world: illiterate people in America's colonies learned to read; people without medicine gained the advantage of Western technology; and Christianity did "uplift" many of the colonized, just as President William McKinley said he hoped it would. But Roosevelt's brand of nationalism also made him a late-nineteenth-century warmonger, which led to a vicious conflict in the Philippines—a conflict protested by, among others, the devoutly Christian William Jennings Bryan. One long-term consequence of America's military presence in the Philippines is the massive and still growing trade in Southeast Asian girls and young women—a skin trade with which the U.S. military is still involved and which in many cases amounts to modern slavery.

The Christian writer I quoted above has claimed that Teddy Roosevelt "led the world into a remarkable epoch of peace," but to say that is to do an injustice not only to the plain historical record, but also to Roosevelt himself. Roosevelt approved of war. He reveled in battle. For him, conflict weeded out weak people who stood in the way of progress. It's true that Roosevelt won the Nobel peace prize in 1906, but it's hard to see how even that time could be called an "epoch of peace," since all the animosities and suspicions that would explode into world war in August 1914 were then brewing.

It isn't that Roosevelt should be painted mainly in a bad light. He was an extraordinary and, in many ways, wonderful man; he was larger than life and is one of the most significant personalities in American history. But, like everyone who has read about him (including, obviously, myself), Roosevelt was a sinner, and his actions helped to set off a series of events that, for good and bad, affect us still.

I want to suggest that Christian writers, such as the one I've quoted, who spin history in simplistic terms so as to boost their favored political, cultural, or theological causes are doing nothing better than politically motivated writers who do the

same. The antidote to secularist historical revisionism isn't
Christian revisionism, but the attempt simply to get things
right, insofar as that is possible. Scholarly incompetence with
a Christian face on it is still incompetence, and one who fabri-
cates myths in the name of saving Christian kids from secular-
ism isn't doing anyone a service.

If I am correct, and if it is wrong for Christians consciously
to put their own spin on history, then what is there for the
Christian student of history to do? For one thing, Christian
writers, teachers, and students of history can strive to cultivate
within themselves a capacity for discernment. Of course, all
students of history should do this, but it seems to me that
Christians in particular should pursue discernment: for to discern is to test something to see whether it is what it claims to
be; it's to be perceptive, keen, and intellectually sharp; it's to
be prudent, even-handed, and cautious in coming to judgment; it's to be judicious in how one speaks of the dead; and,
even as one acknowledges that there is much that cannot be
known, it's to be determined to get things right.

The Bible clearly has a lot to say in praise of qualities such
as these, and, just as obviously, the present sound-bite culture
can hardly stand them. As far as the present culture is concerned, it sometimes seems that it is enough to say that Thomas
Jefferson, author of the Declaration of Independence and slaver
holder, was a bald-faced hypocrite, period; that Christopher
Columbus was a wanton purveyor of destruction and geno-
cide, end of story. An inattentive population can hardly stand
conclusions more complex, and more accurate, than these.
(The same was true a century ago when Jefferson and Columbus
were sometimes described in almost godlike terms.) But time

and again the Scriptures admonish believers to be wise in their approach both to spiritual and worldly matters, to be cautious in judgment, prudent in how they conduct relationships, and keen of mind. The writer of the book of Hebrews says that the "word of God is quick, and powerful, and sharper than any two-edged sword, piercing even to the dividing asunder of soul and spirit, and of the joints and marrow, and is a discerner of the thoughts and intents of the heart." The description is of the Word of God, but I think it also can stand as an ideal to be pursued by every Christian who reads, writes, teaches, and thinks about history. "Be wise as serpents and harmless as doves," the Scriptures say. "Be quick to hear and slow to speak." "With what judgment you judge, you shall be judged."

In the preface to his very fine biography of Abraham Lincoln, David Donald writes that he asked "at every stage of [Lincoln's] career what he knew when he had to take critical actions, how he evaluated the evidence before him, and why he reached his decisions. [This book] is then," Donald continues, "a biography written from Lincoln's point of view, using the information and ideas that were available to him."

What Donald aspired to do is both simple and difficult. It's simple in that he strove to do what all responsible students of history should—that is, attempt to understand historical figures in their own terms, to place them within their own context, and to avoid imposing upon them ideas and beliefs that weren't available to them in their own day. What Donald set out to do is also complex. Just as those who view the American Civil War mainly as a war of aggression against the South would find it hard to give Lincoln a fair and, so far as is possible, objective shake, so must Donald have begun his book on Lincoln with beliefs about the man and his significance in American history. Yet he tried not to impose himself on Lincoln, but to be imposed upon by Lincoln. This is a commendable act of humility, and I don't know the precise extent to which Donald succeeded, but I find his endeavor encouraging, for it illustrates an attitude toward history that is, I think, fundamentally Christian.

In a time when European travelers were exploring the New World, when inventors were in the process of making life easier and more interesting, and when knowledge of the universe was expanding rapidly, a priest in the Church of England named George Herbert wrote a wonderful poem titled "The Agony" (1633). In the poem Herbert doffs his cap with admiration at the scientific and geographic discoveries being made in western Europe and the New World and he compliments humankind's capacity for uncovering knowledge. Yet despite these great advances, Herbert wrote, there remained "two vast, spacious things" the depths of which had never been truly sounded, namely, "Sin and Love."

Since the first time I read Herbert's poem—I was a new graduate student in history at the time—I have thought that in it he suggests, however curtly, an attitude toward history that I, as a Christian, could take. I saw that I should keep ever before me the truth that all have sinned, and that because I am part of the human community of sinners I can't presume myself to be superior to others—either those now living or those who have gone before. I also saw that, my own combative temperament notwithstanding, I am obliged to practice charity toward all men and women, the living and the dead.

With Herbert, Christians know that sin pervades everything—even history teachers. I think that one would be hard
pressed to find a passage of Scripture more obviously true than
St. Paul's declaration that "all have sinned," that is, that all
have failed to lead impeccable, blameless lives. Of course, Paul
knew whereof he spoke. In Acts 15 we find him and Barnabas
in such contention over the trustworthiness of a young Christian named John Mark that, being unable to agree, they res-
olutely "departed asunder one from another."

There's some comfort to be found in this passage of Scripture, for here the same man who in his Letters challenges all
Christians to be of one mind and to live in peace with one
another huffs off, separating himself from a fellow believer.
Now, given Paul's personal record as a persecutor of Christians, his behavior here seems minor, perhaps even encouraging: from murder to occasional anger—that's grace! This passage
also reminds us that even the best among us are tinged by the
Fall. In Paul, whose dispute with Barnabas really was over a
significant matter, Christians can perhaps see themselves
miffed by insignificant slights and inconveniences. We see
Paul's apparent failure and recognize that were we in Paul's
shoes on that day, we probably would have done the same
thing. Similarly—and here we come back to our discussion of
a Christian attitude toward history—if we were among the
brutish conquistadors who won New Spain in the fifteenth
century, we would probably have acted as they did. If we were
Plains Indians in the late nineteenth century, we may have
taken the lives of the children of American settlers too. And if
we were the friends of a family whose child was lost to Indians,
we probably would have been glad to read in the newspaper

that somewhere in the Midwest, a few days before, a group of Indian men, women, and children had been gunned down in their tents.

The point is that Christians know that sin pervades everything, and it shouldn't surprise us when it rears its ubiquitous head in history. Thomas Jefferson, writer of the Declaration of Independence and slave holder. Henry Ford, great businessman and anti-Semite. Aimee Semple McPherson, committed evangelist and distributor of goods to the needy, who's often remembered chiefly for a life tainted by scandal. There's nothing to be surprised about. And what's all the high talk one hears so often these days—talk that suggests that if I or my favored group had been at such and such place at such and such time things would have turned out differently?

The world is warped, sin blemishes every human thing, and even one's best effort to be and do the best one can is itself tainted by the Fall. And because the Christian reader, writer, or teacher of history knows that sin infects everything human, he or she is in a position to exercise charity—compassion, understanding, consideration—toward historical figures, many of whom appear in retrospect to have made vast errors.

Jesus said that his disciples should do unto others as they would want others to do to them, and fifty or a hundred years from now (if there is such a thing), what would we want historians to do with us? Certainly we would want them to try to understand us on our own terms. Yes, we expect that they will be critical of us the way we are critical of people in history. After all, a person who looks at something in retrospect, and who has more information available to him or her than those who lived in the past, may see more clearly than they were able to. But we hope that when we are put to the test our own judges will be careful, prudent, judicious, and kind. We don't want them to make myths of us, to pretend that we were faultless, but we hope that they won't focus solely on our shortcomings. We hope that they won't force us into their mold, but that they will try to shape themselves into ours. We hope that they will not put into our mouths political and cultural agendas with which, for a variety of reasons, we are not concerned. We would want them to treat us fairly. In short, we would want them to be charitable toward us and to keep in mind, even as they must judge us, that they themselves will be judged farther down the road. And, of course, we hope that they will keep in mind, as Christians must always remember, that all men and women will finally be judged by One who himself has no judge. The ultimate archives are kept in heaven, and there are no forgeries there.

Thus we come to the last part of this essay's title—the Christian life—for at bottom, the Christian approach to writing, teaching, thinking about, and judging history is not really much different from the life Christians are called to strive for every day. In his Letter to the Galatians, St. Paul writes that the fruit of the Holy Spirit's work in a person's life is love, joy, peace, patience, kindness, goodness, faithfulness, gentleness, and self-control. The list itself makes me aware of my own failure—my failure to dwell on good things and deeds both in this life and in the past. Like the daily news, written history focuses on misdeeds, war, dissension, and body count; but the great mass of human action that makes up American history comprises acts of kindness, common civility, and quiet service to friends and strangers. Written labor history stresses tension in the workplace, but I think that most American labor history comprises daily acts of trust, duty, and honest work adequately compensated. The Scriptures remind Christian students of history to keep good things such as these things in mind.

Paul's words also remind me to practice self-control in my daily affairs and in my judgments of things past. They challenge me to love—to exercise charity toward—the person nearby and also to those long dead, among whom are included some in the vast "cloud of witnesses" who surround us in heavenly places and, the Scriptures suggest, are cheering us on.

The Scriptures maintain that I ought to be cautious, thorough, and wise in my treatment of people in the here and now, and I think this principle applies to those who have gone before as well. The Scriptures remind me of the fact that my own daily actions are, for good and bad, helping to shape a future that I do not know and cannot control.

Life is a serious business. Whether we are aware of it or not (and however clichéd the statement seems), we are making history every day of our lives, and future generations will estimate for themselves the quality of the history we made. The Christian knows that every decision, every gesture, every word, every purchase, every prayer, and every road taken—and not taken—matters. And not only to us.*

* I would like to thank Father Dwight Duncan, St. Matthias' Episcopal Church, Dallas, Texas, for his comments concerning style on an earlier draft of this paper.

JOSEPH T. LIENHARD, S.J.

ORIGEN AND THE CRISIS OF THE OLD TESTAMENT IN THE EARLY CHURCH

(From *Pro Ecclesia*)

The Christian Bible is the last place most people would look for a crisis.[1] There it is: Old and New Testaments, God's unchanging Word—bound in black leather, edged in gold, covered with a layer of fine dust. But the very phrase "Old Testament" raises a great question. The Old Testament comprises about 80 percent of the Christian Bible. This 80 percent never mentions Jesus of Nazareth and is, in fact, the sacred Scripture of another religion, Judaism. Yet the Christian church claims these Scriptures as its own. This act has been called the biggest corporate takeover in history.

The process by which the Jewish Scriptures became the Christian Old Testament lasted about two hundred years and was marked by uncertainty, disagreement, and strife. I would like to describe this process and, at the end, suggest that it may still not be finished.

---

1. This lecture was delivered in November, 1999, as part of the Joseph Gregory McCarthy Visiting Professorship in Theology at Boston College.

The "Old Testament" as the Church's Bible

From the first day of its existence, from that first Easter morning when "Mary Magdalene went and said to the disciples, 'I have seen the Lord'" (John 20:18), the Christian church had a Bible—namely, the Jewish Scriptures. St. Paul could write to the Christians in Corinth, "Christ died for our sins in accordance with the Scriptures and he was buried and he was raised on the third day in accordance with the Scriptures" (1 Cor. 15:3–4). But there was an all-important proviso: the Jewish Scriptures were to be interpreted in light of the Christians' experience of Jesus the Christ, for the first Christians—who were, of course, Jews—found their Scriptures fulfilled in Christ.

But the Christians had to establish their stance toward these Scriptures. The earliest Christians took one of three basic approaches to the Jewish Scriptures: they were law, they were prophecy, or they were irrelevant.

The first Christian to raise the question of Christ and the Scriptures was Paul.[2] For him, the Scriptures were preeminently law. Paul could not, and did not, reject the truth of the Scriptures. But he came to a new understanding of the law. "Now," Paul writes, "the righteousness of God has been manifested apart from law, although the law and the prophets bear witness to it" (Rom. 3:21). In this one sentence, Paul has taken two crucially important steps. The commands of the Mosaic law, as such, belong to the past. Yet the Scripture as a whole speaks of the same faith and the same salvation that Christ

---

2. See Hans von Campenhausen, *The Formation of the Christian Bible*, trans. J. A. Baker (Philadelphia, 1972), 24–37 for this paragraph.

finally brought to all people. For Paul the law was valid, but temporary. The Epistle to the Hebrews takes the same approach, but applies it to the liturgy.

Other Christians saw the Old Testament principally as prophecy. This understanding appears as early as the Gospels of St. Matthew and St. John, which find single events in Jesus' life foretold by the Scriptures. Matthew writes, for example: "All this took place to fulfill what the Lord had spoken by the prophet: 'Behold, a virgin shall conceive and bear a son'" (Matt. 1:22–23), or "In Bethlehem of Judea; for so it is written by the prophet" (Matt. 2:5–6). John writes: "This was to fulfill the scripture, 'They parted my garments among them'" (John 19:24), or "These things took place that the Scripture might be fulfilled, 'Not a bone of him shall be broken'" (John 19:36). The heart of Justin Martyr's *First Apology* is a long proof from prophecy.

But another tendency, too, appears as early as some books of the New Testament: the tendency to dispense with the Jewish Scriptures altogether, to have no need for them. Several Pauline Letters omit all mention of the law, and of Scripture in general—for example, Philippians, Colossians, 1 and 2 Timothy, and Philemon. The three Epistles of John and the Apocalypse of John never explicitly quote the Scriptures. The same tendency appears a little later in the letters of Ignatius of Antioch, the letter of Polycarp, and the *Shepherd of Hermas*.

The Crisis of the Old Testament in the Early Church

As the Christian church became a church of Gentiles, the relation between Christ and the Scriptures changed. Jewish converts had first known the Scriptures and then confessed their faith in Christ. Gentile converts first accepted faith in Christ and then encountered the Scriptures. What was the Gentile church to do with this book—this collection of historical narratives from creation to the Maccabees; this mass of moral, civil, and liturgical law; this collection of prophecies stretching over eight centuries; this accumulation of wisdom literature, some of which appeared to have no place for God; this series of short narratives, some charming, like Ruth, others less so, like Esther; this collection of hymn texts from the Second Temple? It was not law for the Christians. Was it enough to quote a few dozen verses as prophecies and to ignore the rest? Or, could the Christian church make this book its own?

The crisis of the Old Testament in the early church peaked around the middle of the second century. At that time, two positions emerged that embodied the most extreme attitudes toward the Old Testament possible in the church. They are represented, on one end, by a man, Marcion of Sinope, and on the other end by a document, the *Epistle of Barnabas*. In brief: Marcion interpreted the Old Testament literally, and only literally, and threw it out of the church. The author of the *Epistle of Barnabas* interpreted the Old Testament figuratively, and only figuratively, and took it away from the synagogue.

Marcion of Sinope is one of the more intriguing, if peculiar, figures of the second century. He was a native of Asia Minor, where his father may have been a bishop. He made a fortune in the shipping business and then got serious about religion. Around 140 he moved to Rome and contributed a great sum of money to the church there. A few years later, around 144, the church at Rome expelled him for his wrong teachings and—interestingly—gave him his money back.

Marcion read the Old Testament very carefully, and what he read appalled him. He read, for example, that the god of the Old Testament created Adam and was thus responsible for the entry of evil into the world. This god was ignorant; when he walked in the Garden he had to ask Adam, "Where are you?" This god was fickle, too; he first forbade Moses to make graven images but later commanded him to make an image of a saraph serpent. This god could be vicious; he ordered the most awful slaughters of women and children. Jesus would contradict this god, for this god commanded "eye for eye, tooth for tooth," whereas Jesus bade us love our enemies.

Marcion also read Christian writings, especially St. Paul's Letters, and found there a wholly new religion. He concluded that there are two gods: the inferior god of justice of the Old Testament and the higher God of love of the New Testament. Marcion, in other words, was convinced that every single word of the Old Testament was literally true, and only literally true. And as such, the Old Testament was unworthy of the God of love and of the Christian church and hence had to be rejected.

The other extreme is represented by the *Epistle of Barnabas*. This curious document is classed among the writings known as the apostolic fathers, those eight or nine Christian writings that survive from the first half of the second century. Like Marcion, the author of this strange document also read the Old Testament intensely, but proposed a diametrically opposed theory: the whole Old Testament, he held, is a great allegory, and concealed within it are the truths of the Christian faith. In the process, "Barnabas" put forward some of the most bizarre interpretations of the Old Testament ever proposed by Christians.

On God's covenant with his people, Barnabas set up a simple dichotomy: is the covenant for us or for them? (13:1). His answer is clear: the covenant was meant for Christians only. More precisely, Moses received the tablets on Sinai, but because of the people's sin in worshiping the golden calf, he hurled the tablets to the ground and the covenant was invalidated (14:4). A wicked angel then caused the Jews to take the Scriptures literally (5:6). In a spectacular section, Barnabas contrasts the erroneous, literal interpretation of Scripture with its true, spiritual sense. A few examples will make his method clear.

He deals at length with dietary laws (10:1–9). The Jews had erred by taking the texts literally, as if they really were about food. Barnabas knew better. The prohibition against eating pork, he writes, really forbids us to associate with those who think of the Lord only when they are in need, for swine bellow when they are hungry but otherwise ignore their keepers. The prohibition against eating eagle, hawk, kite, and crow really forbids us to associate with those who refuse to work for a living, since these birds feed on what others have killed. The prohibition against eating eel or octopus really forbids us to associate with the impious, since these creatures are bottom feeders. To avoid eating rabbits, hyenas, and weasels really means avoiding deviant sexual sins. And so it goes on.

But Barnabas's real triumph—one of which he was immensely proud—was his interpretation of Genesis 17:23, which says that Abraham circumcised 318 men in his household. Abraham himself, Barnabas writes, foresaw Jesus in the spirit and received the precious teaching on this number. When the number 318 is written in Greek (which used letters for numbers), 10 and 8 are *I* and *E*, the first letters of the name of Jesus, and 300 is *T*, the cross. This is the higher knowledge, and Barnabas exults, "No one has learned from me a more trustworthy lesson!" (9:7–9). The fact that Genesis was written in Hebrew, not Greek, did not slow him down for a moment. This, of course, is the stuff of madness.

In summary: what was the situation around the year 150? In the technical sense, the church did not have an Old Testament, because it did not yet have a New Testament. As so often, the church first defined its doctrine negatively, by rejecting what it perceived as wrong, and tried thereby to steer a middle way between Marcion and Barnabas. The norm by which the church judged was soon to be called the "rule of faith," that sense of the essence and heart of Christian belief and doctrine. When the church rejected Marcion, it affirmed its belief in one God, and one God only. Further, it affirmed that this one God had revealed himself in the Old Testament to Abraham, Moses, and the prophets, just as he revealed himself definitively in Jesus the Christ. The church also affirmed that the Jewish Scriptures it inherited were indeed the Word of God and would never cease to be that, a conviction later enshrined in the Third Article of the Nicene Creed, which states that the Holy Spirit "spoke through the prophets." And finally and most significantly, the church affirmed that there was no dichotomy between creation and redemption. Matter was not the work of one god and grace the work of another; redemption was not an escape from the corporeal world; and the work of the one God, Creator and Redeemer, was manifested in all of history.

The teaching of the *Epistle of Barnabas* was never explicitly rejected or condemned; it was simply ignored, and Barnabas never found a disciple among later Christians. The church thereby affirmed that the Old Testament did indeed have a literal sense, and that the literal sense was revelatory. The Jews had indeed seen the face of God, and the church, the new Israel, had to be understood in continuity with the old Israel.

Origen of Alexandria and the Solution of the Crisis

The church did not follow either Marcion or Barnabas. But a question remained: what was the church to do with this Old Testament? How was it to make this collection of books its own? The question was answered on two levels, one theoretical, the other practical.

The theoretical solution first appeared in the theology of Irenaeus of Lyons. Irenaeus was born in the Greek-speaking East, but spent his later years in Lyons, in what is now France, and died around the year 200. He set out to refute the teachings of the Gnostics and, in the process, developed the first Christian theology. He integrated the Old Covenant and the New into one great sweeping historical vision, from creation to consummation. He envisioned an ellipse whose two foci are Adam and Christ. There was no disjunction between creation and redemption, but rather a great continuity: what God had begun in Adam he restored and elevated in Christ. In the past few decades Irenaeus's theology has attracted great interest, and the documents of Vatican II cite Irenaeus at least a dozen times. The theory was established, but it still needed to be put into practice.

Before the third century, few Christians had attempted to write commentaries on books of the Old Testament. Jerome reports that he saw a commentary on Proverbs attributed to Theophilus, the bishop of Antioch (died ca. 182/83), but doubted that it was authentic. Clement of Alexandria (died ca. 215) wrote a work entitled *Hypotyposes*, which is said to have dealt with the Old and New Testaments, but the few bits of it that remain treat only the New Testament. The one Christian writer before Origen—and he was only slightly before Origen—who wrote commentaries on parts of the Old Testament was Hippolytus, a cleric at Rome in the early third century. From Hippolytus we have the first surviving Christian commentary on any book of the Old Testament, on the book of Daniel. The occasion may have been the Montanist movement: some Christians thought that Montanism signaled the imminent end of the world, and Hippolytus studied Daniel for its teaching on the end time. Part of Hippolytus's commentary on the Song of Songs also survives. Ancient authors report that Hippolytus also wrote commentaries on the Psalms, the six days of Creation, Genesis, the blessings of Jacob and of Moses, Exodus, Ecclesiastes, the beginning of Isaiah, and selected passages from Ezekiel and Zechariah. But these works are all lost. One reason may be that they were not very good.

It was Origen of Alexandria who fixed the place of the Old Testament in the church. Origen, nicknamed the "Man of Steel," was one of the greatest and most prolific writers of the early church. One trustworthy scholar estimates that Origen wrote more than any other ancient Greek, pagan, or Christian.

Origen was born in Alexandria in Egypt, around 185. When he was seventeen his father, Leonides, who was probably a catechist in the Christian church, was arrested, condemned, and executed. An ancient legend has it that Origen was eager to rush out and be martyred along with his father, and his mother prevented it only by hiding all his clothes. In any case, after his father's death, Origen supported his mother and his six younger brothers and sisters by teaching grammar. Five or six years later, through the generosity of a man named Ambrosius, he was able to devote himself entirely to the study of the Scriptures and theology.

In Origen's day, boys were given their general education through the painstaking explication of a classic text, generally Homer, word by word.[3] Origen, trained in the literary methods of his day, would apply the same method to the Bible. He eventually had the Greek Bible more or less memorized.

Around the year 230, Origen had a serious falling out with the bishop of Alexandria, Demetrius. He packed up his library and moved to Caesarea in Palestine, where he spent the rest of his days. He died in 254, his death perhaps hastened by torture he suffered in the persecution of the emperor Decius.

Origen's writings on the Bible will be the topic of the last part of this paper. But before I go on to his writings, I'd like to say something about the fate of Origen after his death. In his own lifetime and in the century and a half that followed, Origen enjoyed a great reputation. Basil of Caesarea and Gregory Nazianzus prepared an anthology of his

---

3. See Joseph T. Lienhard, "Reading the Bible and Learning to Read: The Influence of Education on St. Augustine's Exegesis," *Augustinian Studies* 27 (1996): 7–25.

works, called the *Philocalia*. Rufinus of Aquileia translated book after book of his into Latin. Jerome and Ambrose, two very different men, based their biblical commentaries on Origen's writings, to the extent that they are sometimes little more than translations. The study that traces the full extent of Origen's influence on the church's exegetical tradition is still to be written.

At the end of the fourth century, however, a controversy arose about Origen. Some Christians called him a heretic, and his reputation never recovered. In the sixth century, the situation grew more serious, and the fifth ecumenical council, the Second Council of Constantinople, condemned Origenists—but not Origen—as heretics.

Glossing over many exceptions and nuances, Origen was generally considered a heretic well into the twentieth century, perhaps more in the Eastern church than in the Western. Constantinople II had condemned some teachings—or rather speculations—of the Origenists, mostly about the beginning and the end of things: that created souls existed eternally, that a second Fall and a second Incarnation are possible, that the Devil would in the end be saved, and—most shocking of all—that the resurrected body would be spherical. Most of these doctrines derived from one work of Origen's, entitled *On First Principles*. This book, many thought, represented the real Origen: the Origen of the biblical commentaries was a pious deceiver.

A turn came in the mid-twentieth century, with the great Jesuit theologian Henri de Lubac. If we can point to a single moment that changed the study of Origen in this century, it is a sentence that de Lubac wrote in 1950: "Observe Origen at work."[4] De Lubac encouraged the scholarly world to look at Origen's writings on the Bible, his commentaries and his homilies, and they did. They found an Origen concerned primarily not with the beginning and the end of things, but with the significance of Jesus Christ and his church, and with the soul's progress in the Christian life.

My thesis is this: Origen assured the Old Testament a permanent place in the Christian church not by an abstract theory, but by working his way through the entire Old Testament, book by book, sentence by sentence, and word by word. Origen provided the church with the first Christian commentary on virtually the entire Old Testament. Seldom, if ever again, would there be any doubt that this book had its proper and rightful place in the Christian church. Someone might say that Lewis and Clark should have followed a better way across this continent; but the fact remains that they were the first to chart *a* way; and so it is with Origen.

Origen was the first great textual critic of the Old Testament. He prepared the enormous Hexapla, a set of books in which six versions of the Old Testament were written out in parallel columns. Among Origen's goals was to know how the Hebrew and Greek texts differed and thus to facilitate conversations with the Jews.

In his study of the Old Testament, Origen wrote three sorts of works: *scholia*, commentaries, and homilies. *Scholia* are learned footnotes. Commentaries are running explanations of a biblical book. Homilies originate in the liturgy: a passage

---

4. Henri de Lubac, *L'histoire et l'esprit* (Paris, 1950), 34.

from the Bible is read aloud, and the preacher explains its meaning and applies it to the lives of the hearers.

A catalogue of Origen's works on the Old Testament will convey some sense of his accomplishment. He wrote *scholia,* or exegetical notes, on Exodus, Leviticus, Isaiah, Psalms 1–25, and Ecclesiastes. He wrote books of commentary (in which "book" means about what a long chapter means today) on the following: 13 books of commentary on Genesis, 36 on Isaiah, 25 on Ezekiel, 25 on the twelve Minor Prophets, 35 on the Psalms, 3 on Proverbs, 10 on the Song of Songs, and 5 on Lamentations—152 books of commentary in all. We also know of the following homilies: 16 on Genesis, 13 on Exodus, 16 on Leviticus, 28 on Numbers, 13 on Deuteronomy, 26 on Joshua, 9 on Judges, 4 on 1 Kings, 32 on Isaiah, 45 on Jeremiah, 14 on Ezekiel, 120 on the Psalms, 22 on Job, 7 on Proverbs, 8 on Ecclesiastes, and 2 on the Song of Songs—375 homilies in all.

What Old Testament books did Origen not write about? With the exception of a few homilies, the double books of Samuel, Kings, Chronicles, and Ezra-Nehemiah, along with Esther and Daniel. Pierre Nautin thinks that Origen was hired as the catechetical preacher at Caesarea for a three-year term (perhaps 239–242), to preach a course of sermons on the whole Bible, but got sacked before his contract was up, and this is the reason why he never completed his homilies on the later historical books.[5]

Was Origen's work any good? There is no doubt that some of Origen's exegesis can be ridiculed. But ridicule avoids a

---

5. Pierre Nautin, *Origène: Sa vie et son œuvre* (Paris, 1977), 434.

question; it doesn't answer it. A Lutheran scholar summed up the believer's approach to the Bible in three short sentences: the Holy Ghost is one, the Holy Ghost is no fool, and the Holy Ghost speaks to me. The Holy Spirit is one; hence the Bible, which he inspired, contains one truth. The Holy Spirit is no fool; hence the Bible contains nothing that is useless. And the Holy Spirit speaks to me; hence the Bible will always profit me. The condition is that the Bible is read in faith and rightly understood. Origen would have agreed with that man.

The accusation most often brought against Origen is that he allegorized the whole Bible and thus made it mean whatever he wanted it to. But to say this is to distort Origen's intention. One who observes Origen at work notices two things: he pays painfully careful attention to the literal sense, but he always strives to read the Old Testament as a Christian. Both statements are worth examining further.

Origen begins with the literal sense. But he does not mean by that what modern scholars mean. In Henri Crouzel's perceptive phrase, the literal sense for Origen is "the brute materiality of the words,"[6] before any figure of speech is invoked. He traveled across Palestine to find out if there was indeed a "Bethany beyond the Jordan" as John's Gospel has it. He wonders why there is a "Sidon the Great" when he cannot find a "Sidon the Little." He tries to work out the practical details of Noah's disposition of the ark, down to speculating that the fifth and lowest deck may have been used to store manure. Origen drew on the best learning of his day, in history, geography, philosophy, medicine, grammar, even zoology, to explain

---

6. Henri Crouzel, *Origène* (Paris and Namur, 1985), 93.

the Scriptures.[7] He learned Hebrew and asked rabbis about Jewish interpretation and traditions. In other words, he refused to treat the Bible, or any part of it, like a Platonic myth. One of Origen's great accomplishments, in fact, was to defend historical Christianity against the attacks of Gnosticism without falling into the anti-intellectualism or fundamentalism that many Christians of his day had retreated to.

But the literal sense itself did not make the Old Testament a Christian book. For this Origen invoked another sense, a spiritual sense. The terms "spiritual sense" or "spiritual exegesis" describe any interpretation that Origen does not call literal or historical or corporeal. "Spiritual exegesis," Henri Crouzel writes so well, "is in a kind of way the reverse process of prophecy: the latter looks to the future, but the former looks back from the future to the past. Prophecy follows the course of time forwards and in a historical or contemporary event sees darkly the messianic or eschatological fact that is prefigured. Spiritual exegesis follows the course of time backwards and, starting from the Messiah already given to the People of God, recognizes in the old Scriptures the preparations and the seeds of what is now accomplished."[8]

There is no time, nor is this the place, to study Origen's spiritual exegesis in detail. But one sentence from the *Homilies on Genesis* exemplifies his approach. Genesis 18:8 reads, "[Abraham] stood under the tree." Origen comments, "What does it help me who have come to hear what the Holy Spirit teaches the human race, if I hear that 'Abraham was standing under a

---

7. Henri Crouzel, *Origen*, trans. A. S. Worrall (Edinburgh, 1989), 61.
8. Crouzel, *Origen*, 71.

tree'"? In other words, the Scripture must speak the saving truth to me now. No detail is insignificant. Numbers delight Origen. Two suggests matter, three suggests the Trinity, four suggests the Gospels, five suggests the senses, six suggests creation. Etymologies—some of them correct, others wrong or even fantastic—also delight Origen. In a tour de force, he interprets the Hebrew names of the Israelites' forty-two stopping places in the desert as the stages of spiritual growth. Material things also light up with inner significance: water suggests baptism, wood suggests the cross, manna suggests the Eucharist. But all of these details are subordinate to a controlling conviction: Origen is convinced, in faith, that the whole Old Testament is a prophecy of Christ and of all that Christ signifies, and that Christ is the key to understanding the Old Testament. The world of spiritual exegesis is the world of prayer and contemplation, but also a world in which the Holy Scriptures were a source of endless delight. And Origen's delight in studying the Scriptures is, perhaps, the element most often missed by his critics.

Henri de Lubac beautifully summarizes Origen's accomplishment.[9] Judaizers and Gnostics were both dangerous enemies of the church. Happily, both could be defeated with the same weapon. Thanks to spiritual interpretation, the church freed itself from Judaism without having to reject the Old Testament, like those who did not find the Father of Jesus Christ there. The whole of the Scripture is worthy of God, and the freedom of the Christian did not have to be sacrificed to affirm

---

9. Henri de Lubac, *Geist aus der Geschichte: Das Schriftverständnis des Origenes*, trans. Hans Urs von Balthasar (Einsiedeln, 1968), 69–70.

that. All the books of the Bible together, from the first to the last, form a harmonious whole. Christianity is both old and new at once: as old as the world, and as new as the light of dawn; as old and as new as Christ himself. Christianity is no longer a sudden and unexpected innovation; nor is it indentured through the letter to the past. The Bible is preserved not merely as a founding document, as archival material that contains some noble titles for Christ and some wonderful prophecies; it is truly, and in its entirety, Holy Scripture, the living word of the living God, without remaining a legal codex. Everything in it is still addressed to us, still valid for us. *Etiam nunc*, Origen repeats again and again, *etiam nunc*, "even now," for everything in the Scriptures is understood in accord with the one plan that was revealed from the beginning, as the apostle Paul teaches Timothy: "The aim of the Law is love that issues from a pure heart and unfeigned faith" (1 Tim. 1:5). The Scriptures are the book of today and of yesterday. Each day the Scripture feeds Christ's faithful with its eternal nourishment.

Thus Origen began a quest—and this is the best way to put it. His work made it certain that the church would retain the Old Testament as part of its Bible. He also provided the first real Christian interpretation of that Old Testament. His interpretation influenced other interpretations for centuries. Nevertheless, what Origen began is only a quest, and the quest must go on.

Conclusion

I suggested at the beginning that the problem raised is not completely solved, and perhaps never will be. To give one concrete example: for the past thirty years, since the First Sunday of Advent in 1969, Catholics have heard three readings from the Bible at Sunday Mass. Other Christian churches have similar lectionaries. And, apart from the fifty days of Easter, the first reading on Sunday is from the Old Testament. But the Old Testament reading is chosen for its relation to the reading from the Gospels. This usage implies that, on the one hand, the Old Testament is just as much the word of the Lord as the New Testament is, but, on the other hand, it is somehow subordinated to the gospel, at least in its interpretation. This fact raises anew the question of the place and interpretation of the Old Testament in the Christian church.

Some general principles are clear. The primary locus or home of Scripture in Christianity is the liturgy. Theologians write books about the Bible because it is proclaimed in the liturgy; the Bible is not proclaimed in the liturgy because theologians write books about it. Further, for Christians, the fullness of God's self-revelation is a person, not a book. Hence the book is read in the light of the person, Jesus the Christ. It is believers who celebrate the liturgy, and theology is faith seeking understanding. If this is the case, then in some way—and I would be the last to say that it is easy—the church must maintain the double interpretation of the Old Testament, literal and spiritual.

Finally, we are dealing with a mystery. In a beautiful passage, St. Augustine reminds us that the Scriptures accompany us on our way; they are not the goal. Writing of the end time, he says: "When, therefore, our Lord Jesus Christ shall come and, as the apostle Paul says, 'bring to light things hidden in darkness and make plain the secrets of the heart, so that everyone may receive his commendation from God,' then lamps will no longer be needed. When that day is at hand, the prophet will not be read to us, the book of the Apostle will not be opened, we shall not require the testimony of John, we shall have no need of the Gospel itself. Therefore all Scriptures will be taken away from us, which in the night of this world burned like lamps so that we might not remain in darkness."[10]

10. Augustine, *Tractates on the Gospel of John* 35, 9, cited from *The Liturgy of the Hours,* Office of Readings for Tuesday of the Thirty-Fourth Week in Ordinary Time.

LIVING BY *LEAR*

(From beliefnet.com)

Shakespeare's *King Lear* may be the greatest work of art in the English language, and it is surely among a handful of the most important dramas ever written. With amazing acuity, this play plumbs the depths of suffering, explores the labyrinth of human identity, and maps the modern moral landscape. But when I first read *Lear*, I knew little about its stature. Instead, the play's spare but riveting story drew me into a strange yet somehow familiar world. Though it has an epic subject of a ruler and the loss of his kingdom, *Lear* is also a most personal story about a family being torn apart by death and deception. This was a story that I knew all too well.

At the age of eighteen, I had been prepared for *King Lear* by events in my family's life. Three years earlier, my only brother, Gordon, had died suddenly in the middle of the night. The next morning, for some reason, I decided to go to school and keep the news to myself. I remember little about that day, except for my disappointed wonder that the world went on its way, regardless of Gordie's death. I watched janitors sweep the floor, cafeteria workers scoop vegetables, and classmates joke and jostle in the halls, and I asked, "How can you carry on this way, when the person who matters most to me in the world has died? Why should you be alive, when my brother is dead?"

My astonishment that day gave way to a more general sadness in the weeks that followed. In different ways, each of us who remained in the family—my mother, my father, and I—retreated into separate regions of isolated grief. We lived beneath the same roof but rarely spoke of our private anguish, and over time our self-deception and quiet anger tore at the already tattered fabric of our life together. Unchurched and not widely read, I had neither scriptural nor fictional points of reference to make sense of my life's confusion.

When I came to *King Lear*, the play seemed like a gift that mysteriously explained my life. Shakespeare's treatment of the corrosive power of self-deception and sorrow in a family's life seemed more truthful than anything I had learned from the television shows I had consumed, in the high-school classrooms where I had been taught, or on the streets of the city in which I lived. As I read, for example, of Lear staggering under the weight of his daughter Cordelia's body, I recognized his grief and remembered my own resentful amazement on the day my brother had died. Lear howled in protest, and I felt for the first time that someone understood my own hidden sorrow: "And my poor fool is hanged: no, no, no life? / Why should a dog, a horse, a rat, have life, / And thou no breath at all? Thou'lt come no more, / Never, never, never, never, never."

But it was not only my grief that Shakespeare expressed, for his play also gave me a hint of that Christian hope which I would shortly claim as my own. As the tragic events of the drama draw to a climax, Lear and Cordelia are captured and are about to be led away. Cordelia resists, but Lear quiets her with a miraculous vision of reconciliation and glory: "Come, let's away to prison, / We two alone will sing like birds i' th' cage; / When thou dost ask me blessing, I'll kneel down / And ask of thee forgiveness."

Feeling myself both cursed and guilty, I took solace in this image of endless blessing and forgiveness. And within a year of reading that play for the first time, I came to believe that because of the crucifixion and resurrection of Jesus Christ, I could trust God to forgive my sins and raise me from the dead.

Over the years, I have reread and taught *Lear* more than fifteen times, have seen it performed on stage several times, and have watched every available filmed version of it. The play's language has burrowed its way deep into my consciousness, and its depictions of love and suffering have shaped my spiritual experience, family life, and professional career in incalculable ways. Like other great works of literature, it has taken the homeless grief within me and provided it with a name, relations, and a place to abide.

However vast becomes the intellectual and cultural terrain occupied by *Lear,* I will always think of it as a work that is, in the end, no larger than a father's arms or a daughter's heart. Such an understanding of *King Lear* seems consistent with the Christian faith and its doctrine of the incarnation. The Gospels speak of the God of the universe coming into the world as an infant, and in Shakespeare's play, universal themes are embodied in mundane deeds and family relationships. Though a pagan sense hovers over the world of *King Lear,* there is at the heart of this play a sublime representation of that greatest of all stories about a child's death and a father's love. In different ways, *King Lear* and the Gospels have done more than change my life. They have saved it.

ALICE MCDERMOTT

CONFESSIONS OF A RELUCTANT CATHOLIC

(From *Commonweal*)

I am a Catholic by birth, third child and only daughter of two first-generation New York Irish Catholics who never paused to think twice (as they would have put it) about where or when or whether I should be baptized into the Catholic church (St. Catherine of Siena, St. Albans, Queens, two weeks after my birth) or sent to Catholic schools (St. Boniface School, Elmont, Long Island; Sacred Heart Academy, Hempstead), or whether Catholicism would ever become something less than essential in my life.

My family attended ten o'clock Mass every Sunday without fail and confession once a month on Saturday if the nuns hadn't taken care of it at school (or if our behavior required additional penance), and my brothers and I collected our sacraments—First Communion, First Confession, Confirmation—without hesitation or dissent, or, for that matter, discussion. We were instructed to say our prayers every night, although we only got down on our knees together when one of us carted home the big plastic statue of Mary with the glow-in-the-dark rosary beads in its base and a family rosary was part of the homework. We each had our own set of beads, usually kept under our pillow, and there was a crucifix on the wall of my parents' bedroom, a small statue of St. Joseph on the server in the dining room, another of the Blessed Virgin on my mother's dresser, and one on my own. My father carried a worn scapular. My mother put a holy card of St. Jude in the back window whenever she was praying for good weather. One of my brothers was an altar boy, the other spoke about becoming a priest. We ate spaghetti with tomato sauce on Friday nights. We were Catholics as inevitably as we were ourselves: the McDermott family on Emily Avenue, and with about as much self-consciousness and, it seemed, volition.

When the changes in the church began, when Latin was dropped and the altar turned around and fasting discarded and the nuns started showing up in street clothes, my parents accepted it all with good humor. These were not essential things, they seemed to understand and seemed to convey to us without ever quite saying it. These were not things worth getting riled up about, as so many of our friends and neighbors seemed to be doing.

When my brothers and I began to rebel, in high school, driving to Dunkin' Donuts for an hour when my parents thought we were all going to Mass, throwing around words like "hypocrisy," "irrelevant," and "outdated" and phrases like "opiate of the masses," throwing around arguments that began, "If God really existed. . . ," or, "If you look at Jesus as just a historical figure. . . ," or, "Who really cares. . . ," my parents formed two lines of defense.

My father, in the great tradition of Catholic fathers everywhere, proclaimed, "As long as you're living in my house, you'll go to Mass on Sunday," and then added, always, in a softer, wearier, but so much more effective tone, "Trust me. You'll need the church as you get older. You don't think you need it now, but as you live, you'll see. Trust me." An argument that was effective not so much because it made us return to the rituals of the church—it didn't, or at least it didn't for more than a Sunday or two—but because it was the only indication we had of what was at the heart of his determination to keep the laws of the church. My father had been orphaned at a young age and had fought in the war. This was the only indication we ever had of what, other than rules for living, the church may have provided him.

My mother, on the advice of a young priest from our parish and in deference to her own peace-at-any-price nature, simply told us that she would pray we'd go back to the church eventually, but she would not let the issue cause anger and unrest in our family.

Through our college years and in the years after, whenever we returned home, we were allowed to sleep in on Sunday mornings, if we chose, while my parents, still, went to ten o'clock Mass, their disappointment in us mostly disguised.

My brothers never did return to the church. And I, after years of semi-indifference, occasional rejection, political objection, and unshakable associations (no other cure for a sleepless night than a rosary counted off on your fingers, no better solace for unnamed sorrows than a candle lit in an empty church), find myself at middle age a practicing Catholic. A reluctant, resigned, occasionally exasperated but nevertheless practicing Catholic with no thought, or hope, of ever being otherwise.

I must confess (it's a genetic thing, no doubt) that it occurs to me that it doesn't bode well for our church at this millennium to have the likes of me as any kind of standard-bearer, and I offer this account of my own religious history only because it strikes me that it is similar to the religious history of many of us now middle-agers born into the Catholic faith. I offer you my own religious evolution not because it illustrates a triumph of faith, but because it provides, perhaps, a place from which to talk about what brings us back, what leads us middle-aged born Catholics finally to choose the faith we were given from the very first moment of our lives. To a church we have, at various times in our lives, seen as flawed, irrelevant, out-dated, impossible, and impossible to leave behind.

And I must admit—the confession thing again—that I come to the discussion itself somewhat reluctantly. Except when I am reading fiction—where the *I* is a creation all its own—the sight of too many first-person pronouns dribbling down a page tends to affect my reading mind in much the same way too many ice cubes dropped down my back affect my spine. I can hardly stand it. And when those first-person pronouns are put to the task of describing clichéd Catholic experiences (and at this point they're almost all clichés: mad nuns and dithering priests, glow-in-the-dark rosary beads, ridiculous moral and physical acrobatics performed in order to maintain and defy the letter of church law), I am most likely to close the book. I am most likely to throw the book across the room when these relentless "I's" are employed to describe a religious experience whose authenticity would be better confirmed if the author had faith enough to leave the experience out of the public venue, to leave it as a personal, unspoken thing between the believer and the believed-in.

But I recognize that my writer's life, my Catholic writer's life, carries certain obligations, and while I would much prefer wielding this unwieldy pronoun in a work of fiction, I proceed with the hope that something of my personal experience as a reluctant Catholic will be of value.

Flannery O'Connor wrote (in a letter, by the way, to a young writer who had reviewed *A Good Man Is Hard to Find* for *Commonweal* in 1955): "I feel myself that being a Catholic has saved me a couple of thousand years in learning to write." I love the sentiment, but I find my own experience is both parallel and opposite. I find that learning to be a writer has saved me a couple of thousand years (in purgatory, no doubt) of being a Catholic.

As I hope I've made clear, learning to be a Catholic was not something that ever seemed to require much energy on my part. Learning to be a writer, however, had seemed to me from the outset to be an impossible pursuit, one for which I had no preparation or training, or even motive, except for a secret and undeniable urge to do so. In the initial days of my quest, when I was casting about for any kind of guidance, I came across a recording of William Faulkner reading from his novel *As I Lay Dying*. I loved Faulkner's work and knew I would benefit in my reading of it by hearing the author's own tone and inflections ("My mother is a fish"). I listened avidly, and then continued listening as he went on to recite his Nobel prize acceptance speech.

The speech is so familiar to me now, and so often quoted, that it is hard to convey what a revelation it seemed to me then, the very first time I heard it. Here was the master novelist saying concisely and precisely what I must do in order to learn to be a writer.

The young writer, Faulkner said, "must teach himself that the basest of all things is to be afraid, and teaching himself that, forget it forever, leaving no room in his workshop for anything but the old verities and truths of the heart—the authorities and truths without which any story is ephemeral and doomed."

Faulkner's injunction became the incentive and the goal for everything else I learned about fiction in those years—the incentive and goal for all matters of craft: how to create characters, how to use detail, how to set scenes, advance plot, write dialogue, all the writing-workshop hints, bits of advice, tricks of the trade. All of it ephemeral and doomed if not put to the purpose of seeking out the verities and truths of the human heart.

Ironically, or perhaps predictably, I was not a practicing Catholic in those days, and when a novelist in one of my graduate classes proclaimed that fiction was the only altar at which he was willing to worship, I wholeheartedly identified. Because it seemed to me then that my reading life, and my nascent writing life, had indeed provided for me an altar as glorious, as complex, and as worthy as any I had known. It had seemed to me that through literature all the questions my Catholic upbringing had taught me to ask were raised and explored and illustrated in a far more compelling and intelligent way than ever I had heard in the old familiar gospel or from a Sunday morning pulpit: Who are we and why are we here? How should we behave toward one another? How should we think about ourselves? What are we to make of love and loss, our happiness and our sorrow?

Literature, it seemed to me, spoke of the undeniable fears and longings of being human: the fear that we are, ultimately, lost, ineffectual, trumped in all our pursuits and passions by death, though longing to discover otherwise. Fiction made the chaos bearable, fiction transformed the absurdity of our brief lives by giving context and purpose and significance to every gesture, every desire, every detail. Fiction transformed the meaningless, fleeting stuff of daily life into the necessary components of an enduring work of art. Fiction, if only briefly, if only in the space of the novel or the story itself, gave form to our existence, the form that it seemed our hearts so persistently desired.

But fiction revealed something else as well, something that I found I was stumbling on again and again in my own pursuit, and that was the very simple notion that fiction revealed our human heart's need for it. Fiction itself, even the most pessimistic fiction, the most absurdist fiction, revealed our need to see the stuff of life made into something that stands against time. Fiction itself—the making of stories and novels—revealed our determination not to be trumped by death. It revealed our determination to be redeemed.

It would be easy enough to dismiss as inevitable the eventuality that anyone with my background and upbringing would sooner or later start writing about Catholics, but as I remember it, it was Faulkner who got me there, not St. Boniface School or Sacred Heart Academy. Because as far as I could see, there was enough being said in fiction about Catholics, and most of it was being said by writers who had actually read Augustine and Aquinas and who had, at some point in their lives, had priests over to dine. I had not. I had no particular interest in railing against the church or defending it. I had no reason to claim it had enhanced my life or done me irreparable harm. I had a good supply of mad-nun stories in my experience, and all kinds of Catholic anecdotal ironies—my high school years were full of them—but so did most of my friends. None of it much interested me as material for fiction.

What did interest me was this need for fiction, this need for the transforming power of art that seemed to me to be one of Faulkner's verities and truths of the human heart, and, slowly, I began to discover that the church, Catholicism, gave certain of my characters a language they could use in order to talk about, and to think about, this longing. So for me, at first, it was simply a matter of craft: The language of Catholicism, a language I knew, had readily at hand, was a language I could use in order to pursue something I saw as enduring about the human spirit. I had to be very careful about it. I had to pare down the language of Catholicism, as I knew it, to what I saw as its essentials, in order to avoid getting caught up in the nonessentials, much as our Latin/fasting/priest with his back to the people and nuns-who-look-like-nuns neighbors had done those many years ago. But I knew that the questions I most wanted to ask as a novelist were the questions the church had already given language to. What I was not prepared to discover, or to rediscover, was that they were questions for which the church also provided answers.

There comes a time in the composition of a work of fiction when the writer must put aside all plans and intentions and preconceived notions of the work at hand and simply proceed, blindly, if you will, with the writing itself. It is the most difficult aspect of craft for a young writer to learn—this letting go—and it is linked in my mind to Faulkner's advice that the "basest" of all things is to be afraid, and teaching himself this, the young writer must "forget it forever." Seamus Heaney puts it another way: "We must teach ourselves to walk on air against our better judgment." Both writers, of course, are talking about faith. They're talking about the faith it takes to write, to lay down words upon the page even before we know the precise extent of their meaning, to forge ahead blindly into what we do not yet know or fully understand, to forge ahead in the hope that the pattern will reveal itself, that what we intuit will prove as valuable as what we have already confirmed.

The experience of my writing life and my reading life had taught me to pay attention to what appears at first to be only intuitive, to pay attention to repeated allusions, metaphors, and recurring themes even before I understood their meaning. There is some risk here. Not everything that appears on the page in the course of composition is useful or fully meaningful, and every writer has had the experience of eventually tossing out some theme, some narrative line, some gesture or detail that had once been avidly pursued but had finally proven irrelevant to the work as a whole. And yet, at the moment of composition, we must forget that possibility, we must walk on air, we must trust that somehow we will discover what we need, what our story needs; we must trust that through the persistent working at words we will discover something we would not have known otherwise.

Gradually, as the pattern of my own work began to come clear, I began to understand that this repetition of what might be called Catholic themes, Catholic language, had meaning that I did not at first recognize, meaning that went far beyond matters of craft and convenience and material at hand. Gradually— no lightning bolts here—I began to realize that the language

of the church, my church, was not only a means to an end in
my fiction, but an essential part of my own understanding of
the world. In my own understanding of the world, the authority and truth of the human heart revealed again and again our
insatiable longing to prove that we will not be trumped by
death, that our spirits endure, that our love for one another
endures, and it is because of our love for one another that our
hearts most rail against meaninglessness.

Time and again I discovered for myself, if not always for my
characters, that the promises of my faith, of Christ, gave perfect
answers to the questions my own work had raised. Proceeding
blindly, walking on air, I had come to see a pattern emerge. I
had come to see that the life of Christ, the Son of God whose
death redeemed our lives, redeemed from absurdity our love for
one another, made of our existence a perfect, artistic whole that
satisfied, in a way that great art could only briefly satisfy, our
hearts' persistent, insatiable need for meaning, for redemption.

Of course I'm referring here to faith in Christianity in general, not Catholicism in particular. But my writing life, life
itself, had also begun to reveal to me a healthy sense of inevitability. There is also a time in the composition of a work of fiction
when the writer realizes that he or she is committed to the
work, to the completion of the work, come what may. It is a
sense of both resignation and delight: This is my material, this
is the story I have chosen to tell, this is the language I must use
because the language itself, my own particular choice of words,
has been shaped by the particular and cumulative experiences
of my life and I would have to live another lifetime in order to
discover an alternative. And while another lifetime, another
writer, for that matter, with another life, another set of words,

another story, may well produce another work that is far more entertaining or compelling or intelligent, this is mine, inevitably, and I am obliged only to make the best of it.

Catholicism, I began to see, was also mine, inextricably mine, the fabric of my life and my thoughts. It was the native language of my spirit, the way in which I had from the beginning thought about faith. And though I could acknowledge that there were indeed other languages for faith and that it may well be that those languages were more effective, less burdened by nonessentials, perhaps even superior to the language the Catholic church had provided me, I would have to live another life entirely in order to know them and to feel them as deeply or as inevitably as I knew and felt my Catholic faith. Resignation and delight: I am a Catholic after all. My only obligation, my profound obligation, is to make the best of it.

I do not want to give the impression that none of this would have happened if I had not had that initial, secret urge to write fiction. Learning to be a writer did not lead me back to the church, it merely helped me to understand what place the church has always had in my heart. Nor do I want to give the sense that life itself, life lived outside my writing life, had nothing to do with it.

As is the case with so many of my peers, my return to the church also coincided with the birth of my own children and the inevitable questions the birth of children raises: How will they be educated? How will they learn to be good people? How is it I took so long to realize my parents did a pretty decent job after all? Twenty years ago no one could have convinced me that I would send my children to Catholic schools, but of course, now, that's where they are. Because I want them to have the ballast of faith, because I want them to understand the importance of the life of the spirit, because I want their moral education to have a context that exceeds human logic and understanding and gives to the whole of life that shapeliness that I had thought once could only be achieved, momentarily, by art. Because I know there will be times in their lives when they will need the church.

The last thing my father did in his life was to attend Mass on Easter Sunday. He collapsed leaving the church and died five days later. The novelist in me cherishes the significance of the details, the consistency and completion of the theme. The daughter finds comfort. The Catholic a strengthening of faith.

But neither do I want to convey that my recognition of the inevitability of my Catholicism frees me from any of the old doubts and dissents. Still I often feel when in the midst of things Catholic like a teenager trapped in a endless gathering of extended family. My church reiterates its insistence that women must never be priests and I metaphorically roll my eyes like some sixteen-year-old listening to the petrified logic of a doddering, but beloved, old uncle. A dynamic and inspiring parish priest is made secretary to the archbishop and I want to howl a childish objection at the sight of a talented young minister kept apart from the people so that he might hold an old man's cap. I find myself involved in a heated discussion with my fellow Catholic mothers about whether a priest was right or wrong to tell a woman she could receive Communion twice in one day and I hear my inner adolescent ask, "Excuse me, like, what century are we in?"

Pro-life comes up; pro-life, pro-choice, pro-family, pro-child, and those among us who shrilly politicize, sloganize, bumper-stickerize this complex, personal, and heartbreaking moral issue make me want to bolt for the door. Stop shouting, marching, lobbying, I want to say. Try teaching. The incredible notion of the Redemption, the incredible notion of God made flesh, of one solitary human being, one ordinary death out of the billions of ordinary deaths the earth has witnessed, changing forever the fate of humankind, cannot be sustained, cannot logically be sustained, if any single life forever after becomes expendable. Any life, under any circumstances. The feminist in me wishes it were not so—a simple, uncomplicated vote for pro-choice is my political preference—but the novelist bows to the need for logical consistency, for connectedness. If any one life can be dismissed as meaningless, so too can the life of Christ.

Like a teenager at some extended family gathering—like any of us, let's face it, at some extended family gathering—I have come to realize that it is not always easy to be a part of this family of the Catholic church. It is not always easy to have a sense of humor and a sense of irony and still be a part of this church. It is not always easy to escape the constrictions and the narrow-mindedness that the church has been responsible for. It is not always easy to feel hip and intelligent and modern while a part of this church. (I have silenced intrepid reporters with the news that I am a practicing Catholic. I have ended hip and intelligent and modern conversations simply by admitting that I still believe in my church.) It is not always easy to love the church, but then again, in my experience, it is not always easy to love anyone.

I suppose it's another lesson from my writing life. Or perhaps it's another inheritance from my Catholic parents, who knew what was essential about their Catholicism and what was not, but I find I can dismiss my occasional impatience and annoyance with the church more easily these days. While my writing life has revealed to me something about the longing for rightness, for wholeness, for perfection of form, it has also shown me that this is a yearning for the unattainable. Our means, after all, are limited, our language flawed. Our art strains to define the indefinable. We approach, we may, momentarily, catch a glimpse, but we cannot sustain the vision. We fail, we try again. Faulkner himself said an author writes a second novel only because he didn't get it right the first time, and then another for the same reason, and another.

The church, as a human institution, isn't always going to get it right either. Its means are limited, its language imperfect. What the heart knows by intuition cannot always be fully expressed or defined by sermon or law. The heart knows the rightness of its yearning for eternal life; the heart, in its persistent desire for redemption, understands the power of God's love. Reluctantly, we submit to what it seems we have always known. We teach ourselves that the "basest" of all things is to be afraid, and teaching ourselves this, we forget it forever. Against our better judgment, we walk on air. We return to the faith that has always been our own.

DIVINE SUMMONS

(From *Christian Century*)

I have learned over the years that students wearily carrying out a writing assignment, often have recourse to the dictionary. Assigned to write on a specific topic, they will begin with a dictionary definition. Let it never be said that I have learned nothing from reading their papers all these years. Look up the word *vocation* in a dictionary, and you will find that the first two meanings given will be something like the following: "(1) a summons or strong inclination to a particular state or course of action: esp. a divine call to the religious life; (2) the work in which a person is regularly employed: occupation."

It was in part the genius and in part the danger of the Reformations of the sixteenth century that they tended to collapse the first of these into the second. One's vocation became simply one's work. To be sure, for the Reformers this was a wider concept than what we have come to mean by work— which is, roughly, a job for the doing of which one is paid, a way to make a living. For example, familial responsibilities, though they do not belong to the sphere of work, were clearly understood by the Reformers to be part of one's vocation.

Hence, a man could be very conscientious in the duties of his occupation and still fail terribly in his calling as a father.

Even granting such qualifications, however, it is true to say that for the Reformers vocation came to be associated with the responsibilities of everyday life rather than with a divine summons to do something extraordinary. To that sanctification of everyday work—and to the dangers of such sanctification—I will return in a little while. It is one of the tensions built into our concept of vocation.

Even if we connect vocation not only with work, but also with the domestic and familial responsibilities so essential to life, there may be other duties that call us as well. When Ken Burns produced his much-acclaimed series of public television shows on the Civil War, one of the most powerful moments for many listeners was the reading of a letter written by Major Sullivan Ballou of the Second Rhode Island regiment to his wife, Sarah. Believing that his regiment would engage in battle within a few days, and reckoning with the fact that he might not return alive to her or to his sons, he wrote to Sarah, using quite naturally the language of vocation: "I have sought most closely and diligently, and often in my breast, for a wrong motive in thus hazarding the happiness of those I loved and could not find one. A pure love of my Country and the principles I have often advocated before the people, and 'the name of honor that I love more than I fear death' have called upon me, and I have obeyed." In such an instance we may find it harder to say whether we are still talking about the duties of everyday life, or whether a sense of vocation is here associated with something more heroic and extraordinary. In any case, this example begins to push us in the direction of the first—and deeper—tension I want to explore.

Students writing their papers tend to look simply at the several dictionary definitions of a word, but an unusually diligent student might also find ways to make use of the etymological information supplied in a dictionary entry. In the instance of the word *vocation,* this is not very complicated. Our English word has its root in the Latin *vocare*—"to call" or "to summon." A vocation is a calling—which implies a Caller. It is a summons. Taking this seriously will, I think, draw us into reflection upon a disturbing problem built into the idea of vocation. It reminds us also that—however often the concept of vocation has been connected especially to the Reformers Luther and Calvin—the concept also has other important roots in Western culture.

It is, after all, Aeneas, depicted by Vergil as the destined founder of Rome, who says, in Robert Fitzgerald's translation: "I am the man / Whom heaven calls." The *Aeneid* is, among other things, a poem about vocation. In their recent book, *Heroism and the Christian Life,* Brian Hook and Russell Reno have noted how Vergil's poem, certainly one of the formative epics of our culture, compels us to ponder what is the deepest problem in the idea of a vocation—namely, whether obedience to a divine summons diminishes or enhances the one who has been called. So I begin there.

Of the *Aeneid* C. S. Lewis once wrote that no one "who has once read it with full perception remains an adolescent." What he had in mind was the Vergilian sense of vocation, which distinguishes the *Aeneid* from Homer's equally great epic, the *Iliad.* Homer's subject is not really the great contest between Greeks and Trojans; it is the personal story of Achilles' refusal to fight and of the events that bring him, finally, to change his mind. It is a story about the personal glory and honor of a heroic figure, and in such a story there may be fate, but not vocation. There are personal triumphs and personal tragedies, but not a calling or a destiny in service of which greatness is exhibited. There is fate, but she is blind and, in her blindness, establishes a kind of equity among the warring parties. Both the nobility and the tragedy of heroes such as Achilles and Hector are set against a background of meaningless flux. Thus, Simone Weil writes that "the progress of the war in the *Iliad* is simply a continual game of seesaw." What is absent is divine purpose—and, therefore, as Lewis notes, none of the events in the *Iliad* can have the kind of significance that the founding of Rome has in the *Aeneid*.

Aeneas's story is quite different. He is, Vergil tells us at the very outset, one who "came to Italy by destiny." Suffering countless setbacks both on land and sea—"so hard and huge / A task it was to found the Roman people"—still he was "a man apart, devoted to his mission." To be the man whom heaven calls exacts a great price. Having already endured the ten-year siege of Troy and its fall, having lost his wife while making his escape with a small band of surviving Trojans, Aeneas must still suffer the wrath of Juno—storm, plague, and warfare—as he journeys from the ruins of Troy (on the western coast of modern Turkey) to Italy.

Seven summers after Troy's fall, Aeneas's company—still on the way—takes refuge from a storm at a port in Sicily. There they hold a festival to commemorate the death of Aeneas's father, Anchises. But in the midst of these games the

Trojan women are moved to consider how long they have been wandering and how many hardships they have suffered.

> But on a desolate beach apart, the women
> Wept for Anchises lost as they gazed out
> In tears at the unfathomable sea.
> "How many waves remain for us to cross,
> How broad a sea, though we are weary, weary?"

> All had one thing to say: a town and home
> Were what they dreamed of, sick of toil at sea.

The women set fire to the ships, hoping—though unsuccessfully, of course—to compel the company to settle permanently in Sicily. They force Aeneas himself to wrestle with "momentous questions."

> Should he forget the destiny foretold
> And make his home in Sicily, or try
> Again for Italy?

Finally, he accepts the advice of Nautes that those "too weary of your great quest" should be permitted to remain behind and settle in Sicily. "Set them apart, and let them have their city / Here in this land, the tired ones."

A vocation exacts a price, and not all can pay it. Even though it may seem to draw us, its point is not happiness. It is, as C. S. Lewis notes, the nature of vocation to appear simultaneously both as desire and as duty. "To follow the vocation does not mean happiness; but once it has been heard, there is no

happiness for those who do not follow." The price of a calling
had been made clear to Aeneas himself even earlier. In one of
the most famous books of the *Aeneid*, Vergil recounts the love
affair of Aeneas and Dido. Their ships buffeted by a tremendous storm at sea, the Trojan company has made it to shore on
the coast of North Africa, where the new colony of Carthage
is being founded by a group of immigrants from Tyre and their
queen, Dido.

Weary of the endless journeying to which Aeneas's destiny
has committed them, the Trojans are glad to stay for a time at
Carthage while they repair their ships. Aeneas, in particular,
finds happiness and seeming fulfillment in overseeing the work
of building Carthage, and, ominously, he and Dido fall pas-
sionately in love. But when Jupiter learns this, he commands
Mercury to remind Aeneas of the task he has been given.

What has he in mind? What hope, to make him stay
Amid a hostile race, and lose from view
Ausonian progeny, Lavinian lands?
The man should sail: that is the whole point.
Let this be what you tell him, as from me.

"The man should sail." In the Latin, one word: *naviget!* The
divine summons—which wounds even as it lures.

Mercury delivers the message; Aeneas hears and obeys. He
gives orders to prepare the ships to sail, but, of course, Dido
learns what is happening and begs him to stay.

Duty bound,
Aeneas, though he struggled with desire
To calm and comfort her in all her pain,

To speak to her and turn her mind from grief,
And though he sighed his heart out, shaken still
With love of her, yet took the course heaven gave him
And went back to the fleet.

Her sister Anna brings Dido's pleas to Aeneas, asking him
at least to postpone his departure and not to leave so abruptly.
"But no tears moved him. . . . God's will blocked the man's
once kindly ears." Aeneas has for the first time in a long time
been happy and content in Carthage—sharing Dido's love,
overseeing the work of construction. Dido seems finally to
have found new love, years after the death of her husband
Sychaeus. The Trojan company seems to have found a place
to settle.

But it is not the homeland to which they are called, and it
is not the city Aeneas has been summoned to found. This is
not his calling. "The man should sail." As Hook and Reno
write, Vergil "does not wish us to cast our lot with Dido and
our anachronistic ideas of authenticity." Do you want to know
what is your vocation? Then the first question to ask is not,
"What do I want to do with my life?" It is not as if I first come
to know myself and then choose a vocation that fulfills and
satisfies me, for it is only by hearing and answering the divine
summons, by participating in my calling, that I can come to
know who I am. We are not who we think we are; we are who
God calls us to be. "The man should sail."

And sail he does—away from Carthage, willing to participate in his destiny. But perhaps for all readers, and certainly, I
suspect, for at least some, a question presses insistently upon
us. Hook and Reno sharpen the point when they write: "Aeneas
sails away from Carthage changed, a greater hero in potential,

but in most ways obvious to him and to us, a lesser man." That's the issue: Does obedience to his calling enhance or diminish Aeneas? That calling has drawn him away from ordinary human loves, it has compelled him to harden himself against quite natural emotions, and it has brought upon him and those who accompany him countless hardships. That calling requires not that he seek to be himself, not that he ask first what he wants to do, not that he authentically determine his being—but that he obey. He says to Dido: "I sail for Italy not of my own free will" (*"Italiam non sponte sequor"*). One way to put all this is to note that for many readers Aeneas seems to become an almost divine figure, more than human, as his person is folded into his calling as founder of Rome. The other way to put it is to note that it can sometimes be hard to distinguish between one who is more than human and one who is, simply, inhuman. Especially for us, devoted as we are to authenticity and autonomy, the divine summons to obedience may seem to have left Aeneas diminished rather than enhanced. Such may be the price of a calling.

Is the price too great? Has Aeneas, in turning from authenticity to obedience, diminished his humanity? How we answer that question will tell us a good bit about ourselves. "I have read," C. S. Lewis writes, "that

> his [Vergil's] Aeneas, so guided by dreams and omens, is hardly the shadow of a man beside Homer's Achilles. But a man, an adult, is precisely what he is: Achilles had been little more than a passionate boy. You may, of course, prefer the poetry of spontaneous passion to the poetry of passion at war with vocation, and finally reconciled. Every man to

his taste. But we must not blame the second for not being the first. With Virgil European poetry grows up.

In an effort to understand, make sense of, and confirm Lewis's judgment, we may recall another reader of Vergil.

In Book I of his *Confessions*, Augustine remembers how, as a boy, "I was forced to learn all about the wanderings of a man called Aeneas, while quite oblivious of my own wanderings." How sinful must he not have been, Augustine suggests, to care more about the wanderings of Aeneas in search of a homeland than about the wanderings of his own soul away from the One for whom he was made. "What indeed can be more pitiful than a wretch with no pity for himself, weeping at the death of Dido, which was caused by love for Aeneas, and not weeping at his own death, caused by lack of love for you, God?" And yet, at a deeper level, we must suppose that what Augustine learned from Vergil may have reinforced what he was eventually to learn from the Scriptures, from his mother Monica and from Ambrose.

The wanderings of Augustine's soul find their pattern in the story of Aeneas. "I came to Carthage," Augustine writes at the outset of Book III, conscious certainly that this was Dido's Carthage, "and all around me in my ears were the sizzling and frying of unholy loves." And years later, having decided to teach rhetoric in Rome rather than Carthage, a decision opposed by his mother, Augustine stole away on ship at night, going—like Aeneas—from Carthage to Rome, and leaving a weeping woman behind. This is the Augustine of whom, in that great scene in the garden, Lady Continence asks what is essentially a vocational question: "Why do you try and stand by yourself and so not stand at all? Let him [God] support you." This is the Augustine who, having been converted from the false ideal of personal authenticity and having handed over to God his broken will, torn between desire and duty, concludes that he can be an authentic self only in submission to God's call—concludes, indeed, that only God can catch the heart and hold it still, that only God can know him as he truly is. "There is still something of man, which even the spirit of man that is in him does not know. But you, Lord, know all of him, you who made him."

Thus, Augustine learned—more from the story of Jesus than from that of Aeneas—"what the difference is between presumption and confession, between those who see their goal without seeing how to get there and those who see the way which leads to that happy country." That way was not anything Augustine had done, his own hard and huge task; it was something that had been done for him. What he found in the story of Jesus that he had not found elsewhere was "the face and look of pity, the tears of confession, your sacrifice." The story of Jesus' own obedience makes clear that what looks like an annihilation of the self may, in fact, be its enlargement. We flourish as we answer obediently God's call. And this, in turn, has an important effect on our understanding of vocation. As Hook and Reno observe, the more we believe that God has himself done whatever needs to be done and that our task is simply to answer his call, "the less room appears to be left for our greatness, our achievement, and accomplishment." Vocation, it seems, need no longer be heroic—which brings us back to the other issue I identified at the outset.

Consider, for example, the following passage from John Galsworthy's novel *One More River*, in which a character named Dinny reflects on the death of old Betty Purdy.

Death! At its quietest and least harrowing, but yet—death! The old, the universal anodyne; the common lot! In this bed where she had lain nightly for over fifty years under the low sagged ceiling, a great little old lady had passed. Of what was called "birth," of position, wealth and power, she had none. No plumbing had come her way, no learning and no fashion. She had borne children, nursed, fed and washed them, sewn, cooked and swept, eaten little, traveled not at all in her years, suffered much pain, never known the ease of superfluity; but her back had been straight, her ways straight, her eyes quiet and her manners gentle. If she were not the "great lady," who was?

Perhaps there is something heroic here, but nothing extraordinary. There is no quest for the great deed required by God. There are only the everyday tasks, infused with the sense of duty and dignity that may make it appropriate to describe them as a calling.

When less room is left for our greatness and our achievement, this is what ultimately happens to the idea of vocation. If the seeds were already there in Augustine's rereading of the story of Aeneas, it took centuries for this leveling or democratizing of vocation to work itself out in the thought of the sixteenth-century Reformers. "The affirmation of ordinary life finds its origin," Charles Taylor writes, "in Judaeo-Christian spirituality, and the particular impetus it receives in the modern era comes first of all from the Reformation. . . . The highest can no longer be defined by an exalted *kind* of activity; it all turns on the *spirit* in which one lives whatever one lives, even the most mundane existence." That spirit is eloquently captured in George Herbert's poem "The Elixir," which reads in part:

> Teach me my God and King,
> In all things thee to see,
> And what I do in anything,
> To do it as for thee. . . .
>
> A servant with this clause
> Makes drudgery divine;
> Who sweeps a room, as for thy laws,
> Makes that and th' action fine.
>
> This is the famous stone
> That turneth all to gold:
> For that which God doth touch and own
> Cannot for less be told.

This sentiment, both beautiful and powerful, intensifies our sense of vocation not by drawing us away from ordinary duties to some great quest, but by drawing us more deeply into them. The strength—or, at least, one strength—of this shift is that the demands and the blessings of a calling are placed on every person. When a vocation is something as extraordinary and heroic as the huge labor of founding Rome—or, even, to take the example that more concerned the Reformers, something as extraordinary as the monastic life—it cannot be generally accessible. So, for example, in his well-known essay "Our Call-ing," Einar Billing, a Swedish Lutheran theologian of the early twentieth century, wrote:

> The more fully a Catholic Christian develops his nature, the more he becomes a stranger to ordinary life, the more he departs from the men and women who move therein. But in the evangelical [he means Lutheran] church it can-not, it should and may not be. The evangelical church does not seek to create religious virtuosos, but holy and saintly men and women in the call.

Now, Billing writes, "the demand to become a unique Christian character is put on each and every individual."

As those who have read Gustaf Wingren on Luther or Max Weber and Ernst Troeltsch on "inner-worldly asceticism" will know, the power of such an understanding of vocation—sanc-tifying the work of every life, however humble—is undeni-able, but it is by no means free of danger. The beauty of Herbert's poem notwithstanding, we should be hesitant to sanctify drudgery—as if one should not retire from it if one could. Still more, there is sometimes backbreaking and dan-gerous labor, or tedious and boring work, that must be done if we or our loved ones are to live, but the language of vocation imbues such work with a kind of meaning and significance that may seem unbelievable to those who must actually do it. They work to live; they do not live to work. Taken seriously, the sanctification of such laborious or tedious work with the language of vocation would suggest that we should struggle to find more time for it, not plot ways to escape it.

More important still, this sanctifying of ordinary work, this sense that it becomes exalted if only approached in the right spirit, may cause us to forget that a divine summons must not only hallow but also transform whatever we do. When the difference between a carpenter and a Christian carpenter, a historian and a Christian historian, a father and a Christian father, an artist and a Christian artist, a soldier and a Christian soldier—when all these differences are reduced to a matter of the "spirit" in which the work is done, we are well on our way to making the divine summons largely irrelevant. Whatever work we want to do—we'll just call that our vocation.

This is to nod at the call of God and go on our way; it is to lose the infinite, transforming horizon of God's call. To the degree that we collapse the divine call into the work we regularly do, work pretty much like that done by many others, we really collapse the two love commandments into one. We suppose that in loving the neighbor—and in no more than that—the love of God consists, as if we were made, ultimately, for work and not for rest in God.

If we try to unify our lives through the idea of vocation— by supposing that God summons us only to good work pretty much like everyone else's work—we lose the infinite horizon of God's call. It was Augustine—again—who saw clearly that such a unified life cannot be ours in this world. When, at the beginning of Book XIX of his *City of God*, Augustine enumerates Varro's 288 possible answers to the question, "What is the good life?" and rejects them all, his rejection, as Peter Brown has written, "marks the end of classical thought." In place of the classical ideal of a unified life actually available to us here and now, Augustine substitutes the image of a pilgrim who must live in hope.

We should be equally clear that a life faithfully committed to the responsibilities of our vocation is not itself "the good life." God calls us not just to that, but to himself—beyond every earthly joy or responsibility, beyond any settled worldliness that places its hope for meaning in those we love or the work we do. This lesson is taught unforgettably in Dante's *Divine Comedy*.

The engine that drives Dante's desire for the beatific vision is not simply love for God. It is love for that particular woman, Beatrice, whose beauty has drawn him every step of the way and through whose beauty he is being summoned beyond himself and toward the One who is Beauty itself. On his journey through hell and purgatory Dante has had Vergil as his guide. By the time we come to the end of the *Purgatorio*, in fact, Vergil has come to seem a permanent fixture on Dante's way. Then, in Canto XXX of the *Purgatorio*, Beatrice finally appears. And instantly, Dante writes,

> There came on me, needing no further sight,
> Just by that strange, outflowing power of hers,
> The old, old love in all its mastering might.

Overcome by emotion, Dante turns, as he has so often along the way, to Vergil for reassurance—and Vergil is gone. He has taken Dante as far as he may, as far as human wisdom is able, but now love—love for that particular woman Beatrice as the image of a still greater Beauty—must take Dante the rest of the way. Tears come unbidden to his eyes, and Beatrice says:

Dante, weep not for Vergil's going—keep
As yet from weeping, weep not yet, for soon
Another sword shall give thee cause to weep. . . .

Look on us well; we are indeed, we are
Beatrice. How hast thou deigned to climb the hill?
Didst thou not know that man is happy here?

   The loss of Vergil, his master and guide, is a sword that
pierces Dante's soul—a necessary pain if he would see God.
But an even greater renunciation awaits Dante in Canto XXXI
of the *Paradiso*. In preparation for that renunciation we might
recall the scene in Book VI of the *Aeneid*, when Aeneas, journeying in the underworld to see his father Anchises, confronts
Dido among the souls of those who have taken their own life.
He weeps as he speaks to her:

I left your land against my will, my queen,
The gods' commands drove me to do their will,. . .
And I could not believe that I would hurt you
So terribly by going. Wait a little.
Do not leave my sight. . . .

                         But she had turned
With gaze fixed on the ground as he spoke on,
Her face no more affected than if she were
Immobile granite or Marpesian stone.
At length she flung away from him and fled,
His enemy still, into the shadowy grove
Where he whose bride she once had been, Sychaeus,
Joined in her sorrows and returned her love.

Dido turns away from Aeneas—but not in hope for any new and greater love. Instead, she returns to an old love, and Aeneas takes up again his huge and hard task.

Not so for Dante as he journeys toward the vision of God. Beatrice has now taken him as far as she is able. She has brought him to the very brink of that final mystical vision shared by all the redeemed; she has prepared him to look upon the face of God. And now, if he is to answer the divine summons, he must turn from image to reality. As Dante gazes at the snow-white rose that is filled with rank upon rank of the redeemed who look upon God, he turns to Beatrice that she may explain it to him.

And she is gone—returned to her place within those heavenly ranks. Looking up, Dante sees her "in her glory crowned, / Reflecting from herself the eternal rays," and he utters a plea that she continue to pray for him.

> Such was my prayer and she, so distant fled,
> It seemed, did smile and look on me once more,
> Then to the eternal fountain turned her head.

The austerity of that moment is overpowering. When we consider all that Dante has endured to find her, when we consider that it was she who had charged Vergil to be his guide, she who, as Dante says, "to bring my soul to Paradise, / Didst leave the imprint of thy steps in Hell," and when we consider that now—at last—he has come to her . . . seeing all that, we must see yet one thing more. It has, finally, been the beauty not of Beatrice, but of God through Beatrice that has been summoning Dante all along the way. Having accomplished that, she turns her face away from him, once more to the eternal fountain. She does not leave him, nor does he leave her behind, but together they are to gaze at the love that moves the sun and the other stars. It is not simply the beauty of Beatrice that has been summoning and drawing Dante, but God, and in looking away from him to God she does no harm to his joy or her own. "Didst thou not know that man is happy here?"

C. S. Lewis's *A Grief Observed*, written after the death of his wife Joy, ends with an evocation of this scene from the *Paradiso*. Lewis writes: "She said not to me but to the chaplain, 'I am at peace with God.' She smiled, but not at me." Likewise, in his powerful and astringent chapter on charity in *The Four Loves*, Lewis writes that

> there is no good applying to Heaven for earthly comfort. Heaven can give heavenly comfort; no other kind. . . . We were made for God. Only by being in some respect like Him, only by being a manifestation of His beauty, loving-kindness, wisdom or goodness, has any earthly Beloved excited our love. . . . It is not that we shall be asked to turn from them, so dearly familiar, to a Stranger. When we see the face of God we shall know that we have always known it.

Beyond and through every earthly love and every earthly duty, we are to hear the call of God. On the one hand, we are called to the God who can put an end to our work and bring fulfillment to our loves and labors. "Didst thou not know that man is happy here?" But on the other hand, this call will often exact a price along the way—the price of renunciation, of huge and hard labor. At times, to be sure, by God's grace, our calling may bring considerable joy and satisfaction, but it cannot offer settled contentment. As Augustine says, "It is one thing to see from a mountaintop in the forests the land of peace in the distance . . . and it is another thing to hold to the way that leads there." Which is to say: for now, "The man should sail."

RICHARD JOHN NEUHAUS

BORN TOWARD DYING

(From *First Things*)

We are born to die. Not that death is the purpose of our being born, but we are born toward death, and in each of our lives the work of dying is already under way. The work of dying well is, in largest part, the work of living well. Most of us are at ease in discussing what makes for a good life, but we typically become tongue-tied and nervous when the discussion turns to a good death. As children of a culture radically, even religiously, devoted to youth and health, many find it incomprehensible, indeed offensive, that the word "good" should in any way be associated with death. Death, it is thought, is an unmitigated evil, the very antithesis of all that is good.

Death is to be warded off by exercise, by healthy habits, by medical advances. What cannot be halted can be delayed, and what cannot forever be delayed can be denied. But all our progress and all our protest notwithstanding, the mortality rate holds steady at 100 percent.

Death is the most everyday of everyday things. It is not simply that thousands of people die every day, that thousands will die this day, although that too is true. Death is the warp and woof of existence in the ordinary, the quotidian, the way things are. It is the horizon against which we get up in the morning and go to bed at night, and the next morning we awake to find the horizon has drawn closer. From the twelfth-century *Enchiridion Leonis* comes the nighttime prayer of children of all ages: "Now I lay me down to sleep, I pray thee Lord my soul to keep; if I should die before I wake, I pray thee Lord my soul to take." Every going to sleep is a little death, a rehearsal for the real thing.

Such is the generality, the warp and woof of everyday existence with which the wise have learned to live. But then our wisdom is shattered, not by a sudden awareness of the generality but by the singularity of *a* death—by the death of someone we love with a love inseparable from life. Or it is shattered by the imminent prospect of our own dying. With the cultivated complacency of the mass murderer that he was, Josef Stalin observed, "One death is a tragedy; a million deaths is a statistic." The generality is a buffer against both guilt and sorrow. It is death in the singular that shatters all we thought we knew about death. It is death in the singular that turns the problem of death into the catastrophe of death. Thus the lamentation of Dietrich von Hildebrand: "I am filled with disgust and emptiness over the rhythm of everyday life that goes relentlessly on—as though nothing had changed, as though I had not lost my precious beloved!"

It used to be said that the Victorians of the nineteenth century talked incessantly about death but were silent about sex, whereas today we talk incessantly about sex and are silent about death. In 1973, Ernest Becker's *The Denial of Death* contended that Freud had gotten it exactly backwards. It is not true, said Becker, that our fear of death is rooted in our denial of sex, but, rather, that our fear of sex is rooted in our denial of death. Throughout history, and in many cultures, sex and death have been engaged in a *danse macabre*, and not simply at the shadowed margins of erotic fantasy where dwell the likes of the Marquis de Sade.

In sex and death are joined beginning and ending, the generative and the destructive. In today's culture we chatter incessantly about both sex and death. They are subjected to the specialization of experts, of therapists, ethicists, and the like. Sex and death have been "problematized," and problems are to be "solved" by sexual technique and the technology of dying. Victorian reticence about sex and our former reticence about death may have mystified both, although the probable intent was simply to put them out of mind. In any event, we have now embarked with a vengeance upon a course of demystification. Now there is nothing we cannot talk about in polite company. It is a great liberation. And a great loss, if in fact both sex and death partake of mystery. Mystery is attended by a fitting reticence.

Death and dying has become a strangely popular topic. "Support groups" for the bereaved crop up all over. How to "cope" with dying is a regular on television talk shows. It no doubt has something to do with the growing number of old people in the population. "So many more people seem to die these days," remarked my elderly aunt as she looked over the obituary columns in the local daily. Obituaries routinely include medical details once thought to be the private business of the family. Every evening without fail, at least in our cities, the television news carries a "sob shot" of relatives who have lost someone in an accident or crime. "And how did you feel when you saw she was dead?" The intrusiveness is shameless, and taboos once broken are hard to put back together again.

Evelyn Waugh's *The Loved One* brilliantly satirized and Jessica Mitford's *The American Way of Death* brutally savaged the death industry of commercial exploitation. Years later it may be time for a similarly critical look at the psychological death industry that got under way in 1969 when Elisabeth Kübler-Ross set forth her five stages of grieving—denial, anger, bargaining, depression, and acceptance. No doubt many people feel they have been helped by formal and informal therapies for bereavement and, if they feel they have been helped, they probably have been helped in some way that is not unimportant. Just being able to get through the day without cracking up is no little thing. But neither, one may suggest, is it the most important thing. I have listened to people who speak with studied, almost clinical, detail about where they are in their trek through the five stages. Death and bereavement are "processed." There are hundreds of self-help books on how to cope with death in order to get on with life. This essay is not of that genre.

A measure of reticence and silence is in order. There is a time simply to be present to death—whether one's own or that of others—without any felt urgencies about doing something about it or getting over it. The Preacher had it right: "For everything there is a season, and a time for every matter under heaven: a time to be born, and a time to die . . . a time to mourn, and a time to dance." The time of mourning should be given its due. One may be permitted to wonder about the wisdom of contemporary funeral rites that hurry to the dancing,

displacing sorrow with the determined affirmation of resurrection hope, supplying a ready answer to a question that has not
been given time to understand itself. One may even long for
the *Dies Irae*, the sequence at the old Requiem Mass. *Dies irae,
dies illa / Solvet saeclum in favilla / Teste David cum Sibylla*: "Day of
wrath and terror looming / Heaven and earth to ash consuming / Seer's and Psalmist's true foredooming."

The worst thing is not the sorrow or the loss or the heart-
break. Worse is to be encountered by death and not to be
changed by the encounter. There are pills we can take to get
through the experience, but the danger is that we then do not
go through the experience but around it. Traditions of wisdom
encourage us to stay with death a while. Among observant
Jews, for instance, those closest to the deceased observe shiva
for seven days following the death. During shiva one does not
work, bathe, put on shoes, engage in intercourse, read Torah,
or have his hair cut. The mourners are to behave as though
they themselves had died. The first response to death is to
give inconsolable grief its due. Such grief is assimilated during
the seven days of shiva, and then tempered by a month of
more moderate mourning. After a year all mourning is set
aside, except for the praying of kaddish, the prayer for the
dead, on the anniversary of the death.

In *The Blood of the Lamb*, Peter de Vries calls us to "the recognition of how long, how very long, is the mourners' bench
upon which we sit, arms linked in undeluded friendship—all
of us, brief links ourselves, in the eternal pity." From the pity
we may hope that wisdom has been distilled, a wisdom from
which we can benefit when we take our place on the mourners'
bench. Philosophy means the "love of wisdom," and so some

may look to philosophers in their time of loss and aloneness. George Santayana wrote, "A good way of testing the caliber of a philosophy is to ask what it thinks of death." What does it tell us that modern philosophy has had relatively little to say about death? Ludwig Wittgenstein wrote, "What can be said at all can be said clearly; and whereof one cannot speak thereof one must be silent." There is undoubtedly wisdom in such reticence that stands in refreshing contrast to a popular culture sated by therapeutic chatter. But those who sit, arms linked in undeluded friendship, cannot help but ask and wonder.

All philosophy begins in wonder, said the ancients. With exceptions, contemporary philosophy stops at wonder. We are told: don't ask, don't wonder about what you cannot know for sure. But the most important things of everyday life we cannot know for sure. We cannot *know* them beyond all possibility of their turning out to be false. We order our loves and loyalties, we invest our years with meaning and our death with hope, not knowing for sure, beyond all reasonable doubt, whether we might not have gotten it wrong. What we need is a philosophy that enables us to speak truly, if not clearly, a wisdom that does not eliminate, but comprehends our doubt.

A long time ago, when I was a young pastor in a very black and very poor inner-city parish that could not pay a salary, I worked part-time as chaplain at Kings County Hospital in Brooklyn. With more than three thousand beds, Kings County boasted then of being the largest medical center in the world. It seems primitive now, but thirty-five years ago not much of a fuss was made about those who were beyond reasonable hope of recovery. They were almost all poor people, and this was before Medicare or Medicaid, so it was, as we used to say, a charity hospital. They were sedated, and food was brought for those who could eat. The dying, male and female, had their beds lined up side by side in a huge ward, fifty to a hundred of them at any given time. On hot summer days and without air-conditioning, they would fitfully toss off sheets and undergarments. The scene of naked and half-naked bodies groaning and writhing was reminiscent of Dante's *Purgatorio*.

Hardly a twenty-four-hour stint would go by without my accompanying two or three or more people to their death. One such death is indelibly printed upon my memory. His name was Albert, a man of about seventy and (I don't know why it sticks in my mind) completely bald. That hot summer morning I had prayed with him and read the Twenty-Third Psalm. Toward evening, I went up again to the death ward— for so everybody called it—to see him again. Clearly the end was near. Although he had been given a sedative, he was entirely lucid. I put my left arm around his shoulder and together, face almost touching face, we prayed the Our Father. Then Albert's eyes opened wider, as though he had seen something in my expression. "Oh," he said, "oh, don't be afraid." His body sagged back and he was dead. Stunned, I realized that, while I thought I was ministering to him, his last moment of life was expended in ministering to me.

There is another death that will not leave me. Charlie Williams was a deacon of St. John the Evangelist in Brooklyn. (We sometimes called the parish St. John the Mundane in order to distinguish it from St. John the Divine, the Episcopal cathedral up in Morningside Heights.) Charlie was an ever ebullient and sustaining presence through rough times. In the face of every difficulty, he had no doubt but that "Jesus going to see us through." Then something went bad in his chest, and the doctors made medically erudite noises to cover their ignorance. I held his hand as he died a painful death at age forty-three. Through the blood that bubbled up from his hemorrhaging lungs he formed his last word. Very quietly, not complaining but deeply puzzled, he looked up at me and said, "Why?"

Between Albert's calm assurance and Charlie's puzzlement, who is to say which is the Christian way to die? I have been with others who screamed defiance, and some who screamed with pain, and many who just went to sleep. Typically today the patient is heavily sedated and plugged into sundry machines. One only knows that death has come when the beeping lines on the monitors go flat or the attending physician nods his head in acknowledgment of medicine's defeat. It used to be that we accompanied sisters and brothers to their final encounter. Now we mostly sit by and wait. The last moment that we are really with them, and they with us, is often hours or even many days before they die. But medical technology notwithstanding, for each one of them, for each one of us, at some point "it" happens.

It has often been said that each death is unique, that each of us must die our own death. Enthusiasts such as Walt Whitman gild the inevitable. "Nothing can happen more beautiful than death," he wrote in *Leaves of Grass*. In "Song of Myself" he trumpets: "Has anyone supposed it lucky to be born? / I hasten to inform him or her, it is just as lucky to die, and I know it." Good for him. "Why fear death?" asked Charles Frohman as he went down with the sinking *Lusitania*. "Death is only a beautiful adventure." Fare thee well, Mr. Frohman. If each life is unique, and it is, then it would seem to follow that each death is unique. I will not dispute the logic of that. And there is no doubt an element of adventure in moving into the unknown. But in my own experience of dying, it struck me as so very commonplace, even trite, that this life should end this way. Perhaps I should explain.

Several lawyers have told me that it would make a terrific malpractice suit. All I would have to do is give a deposition and then answer a few questions in court, if it ever came to trial, which it probably wouldn't since the insurance companies would be eager to settle. It would be, I was assured, a very big settlement. The statute of limitations has not run out as of this writing. But I will not sue, mainly because it would somehow sully my gratitude for being returned from the jaws of death. Gratitude is too precious and too fragile to keep company with what looks suspiciously like revenge.

The stomach pains and intestinal cramps had been coming on for almost a year. My regular physician, a Park Avenue doctor of excellent reputation, had told me long ago how pleased he was with the new techniques for colonoscopy. It meant, he said, that none of his patients need die of colon cancer. His partner, the specialist in these matters, did one colonoscopy and, some weeks later, another. After each mildly painful probing up through the intestines, he was glad to tell me that there was nothing there. Then, on Sunday afternoon, January 10, 1993, about five o'clock, after four days of intense discomfort in which there was yet another probe and yet another X-ray, I was at home suddenly doubled over on the floor with nausea and pain. The sensation was of my stomach exploding.

My friend George Weigel was visiting and he phoned the doctor's office, but the doctor was on vacation. The doctor covering for him listened to the symptoms and prescribed a powerful laxative. (I said that this story would smack of the commonplace.) Much later, other doctors said that the prescription might, more than possibly, have been fatal. They said they never heard of several colonoscopies not detecting a tumor, and shook their heads over a physician who would prescribe a laxative after being apprised of symptoms indicating something much more seriously wrong.

Weigel had the presence of mind to bundle me off—pushing, pulling, half carrying me—to the nearest emergency room, which, fortunately, was only a block from the house. The place was crowded. I strongly recommend always having with you an aggressive friend or two when you go to a hospital and are really sick. A large and imperiously indifferent woman at the desk was not about to let anyone jump the line of waiting cases, relenting only when Weigel gave signs that he was not averse to the use of physical violence. She then sat me down to answer a long list of questions about symptoms and medical insurance, which I tried to answer until I fell off the chair in a faint, at which point she surmised she had an emergency on her hands. The experience so far did not instill confidence in the care I was likely to receive.

Very soon, however, I was flat on my back on a gurney, surrounded by tubes, machines, and technicians exhibiting their practiced display of frenetic precision, just like on television. The hospital's chief surgeon, who happened to be on duty that night, ordered an X-ray that showed a large tumor in the colon and declared there was no time to lose. I was wheeled at great speed down the halls for an elevator to the operating room, only to discover the elevators were out of order. By then I had been sedated and was feeling no pain. In fact, I was somewhat giddy and recall trying to make a joke about the contrast between the high-tech medicine and the broken-down elevators. A guard showed up who said he knew how to get the number-six elevator working, and then I was looking up at the white water-stained ceiling of the operating room, and then there was someone putting a mask over my face and telling me to breathe deeply, and then there was "Now I lay me down to sleep. . . ," and then there was the next morning.

The operation took several hours and was an unspeakable mess. The tumor had expanded to rupture the intestine; blood, fecal matter, and guts all over the place. My stomach was sliced open from the rib cage down to the pubic area, then another slice five inches to the left from the navel for a temporary colostomy. I've noticed that in such cases the doctors always seem to say that the tumor was "as big as a grapefruit," but my surgeon insists the blackish gray glob was the size of "a big apple." After they had sewed me up, the hemorrhaging began, they knew not from where. Blood pressure collapsed and other vital signs began to fade. What to do? The surgeon advised my friend to call the immediate family and let them know I would likely not make it through the night. The doctors debated. To open me up all over again might kill me. On the other hand, if they didn't find and stop the hemorrhaging I was surely dead.

Of course they went in again. The source of the effusion of blood was the spleen, "nicked," as the surgeon said, in the ghastliness of the first surgery. Given the circumstances, I'm surprised that parts more vital were not nicked. The spleen removed and the blood flow stanched, they sewed me up again and waited to see if I would live. The particulars of that night, of course, I was told after the event. "It was an interesting case," one doctor opined in a friendly manner. "It was as though you had been hit twice by a Mack truck going sixty miles an hour. I didn't think you'd survive."

My first clear memory is of the next morning, I don't know what time. I am surrounded by doctors and technicians talking in a worried tone about why I am not coming to. I heard everything that was said and desperately wanted to respond, but I was locked into absolute immobility, incapable of moving an eyelash or twitching a toe. The sensation was that of being encased in marble; pink marble, I thought, such as is used for gravestones. The surgeon repeatedly urged me to move my thumb, but it was impossible. Then I heard, "The Cardinal is here." It was my bishop, John Cardinal O'Connor. He spoke directly into my right ear, repeatedly calling my name. Then, "Richard, wriggle your nose." It was a plea and a command, and I wanted to do it more urgently than anything I have ever wanted to do in my life. The trying, the sheer exercise of will to wriggle my nose, seemed to go on and on, and then I felt a twinge, no more than a fraction of a millimeter, and the Cardinal said, "He did it! He did it!" "I didn't see anything," said the surgeon. So I tried again, and I did it again, and everybody saw it, and the Cardinal and the doctors and the technicians all began to exclaim what a wonderful thing it was, as though one had risen from the dead.

The time in the intensive-care unit was an experience familiar to anyone who has ever been there. I had never been there before, except to visit others, and that is nothing like being

there. I was struck by my disposition of utter passivity. There
was absolutely nothing I could do or wanted to do, except to
lie there and let them do whatever they do in such a place.
Indifferent to time, I neither knew nor cared whether it was
night or day. I recall counting sixteen different tubes and other
things plugged into my body before I stopped counting. From
time to time—it seemed several times an hour but surely could
not have been—a strange young woman with a brown wool
hat and heavy gold necklace would come by and whisper, "I
want blood." She stuck in a needle and took blood, smiling
mysteriously all the time. She could have said she wanted to
cut off my right leg and I would probably have raised no objection, so busy was I with just being there, with one thought that
was my one and every thought: "I almost died."

Astonishment and passivity were strangely mixed. I confess
to having thought of myself as a person very much in charge.
Friends, meaning, I trust, no unkindness, had sometimes
described me as a control freak. Now there was nothing to be
done, nothing that I could do, except be there. Here comes a
most curious part of the story, and readers may make of it
what they will. Much has been written on "near-death" experiences. I had always been skeptical of such tales. I am much less
so now. I am inclined to think of it as a "near-life" experience,
and it happened this way.

It was a couple of days after leaving intensive care, and it
was night. I could hear patients in adjoining rooms moaning
and mumbling and occasionally calling out; the surrounding
medical machines were pumping and sucking and bleeping as
usual. Then, all of a sudden, I was jerked into an utterly lucid
state of awareness. I was sitting up in the bed staring intently

into the darkness, although in fact I knew my body was lying flat. What I was staring at was a color like blue and purple, and vaguely in the form of hanging drapery. By the drapery were two "presences." I saw them and yet did not see them, and I cannot explain that. But they were there, and I knew that I was not tied to the bed. I was able and prepared to get up and go somewhere. And then the presences—one or both of them, I do not know—spoke. This I heard clearly. Not in an ordinary way, for I cannot remember anything about the voice. But the message was beyond mistaking: "Everything is ready now."

That was it. They waited for a while, maybe for a minute. Whether they were waiting for a response or just waiting to see whether I had received the message, I don't know. "Everything is ready now." It was not in the form of a command, nor was it an invitation to do anything. They were just letting me know. Then they were gone, and I was again flat on my back with my mind racing wildly. I had an iron resolve to determine right then and there what had happened. Had I been dreaming? In no way. I was then and was now as lucid and wide awake as I had ever been in my life.

Tell me that I was dreaming and you might as well tell me that I was dreaming that I wrote the sentence before this one. Testing my awareness, I pinched myself hard, ran through the multiplication tables, and recalled the birth dates of my seven brothers and sisters, and my wits were vibrantly about me. The whole thing had lasted three or four minutes, maybe less. I resolved at that moment that I would never, never let anything dissuade me from the reality of what had happened. Knowing myself, I expected I would later be inclined to doubt it. It was an experience as real, as powerfully confirmed by the senses, as anything I have ever known. That was some seven years ago. Since then I have not had a moment in which I was seriously tempted to think it did not happen. It happened—as surely, as simply, as undeniably as it happened that I tied my shoelaces this morning. I could as well deny the one as deny the other, and were I to deny either I would surely be mad.

"Everything is ready now." I would be thinking about that incessantly during the months of convalescence. My theological mind would immediately go to work on it. They were angels, of course. *Angelos* simply means "messenger." There were no white robes or wings or anything of that sort. As I said, I did not see them in any ordinary sense. But there was a message; therefore there were messengers. Clearly, the message was that I could go somewhere with them. Not that I must go or should go, but simply that they were ready if I was. Go where? To God, or so it seemed. I understood that they were ready to get me ready to see God. It was obvious enough to me that I was not prepared, in my present physical and spiritual condition, for the beatific vision, for seeing God face to face. They were ready to get me ready. This comports with the doctrine of purgatory, that there is a process of purging and preparation to get us ready to meet God. I should say that their presence was entirely friendly. There was nothing sweet or cloying, and there was no urgency about it. It was as though they just wanted to let me know. The decision was mine as to when or whether I would take them up on the offer.

There is this about being really sick: you get an enormous amount of attention. I cannot say that I did not enjoy it. In the pain and the nausea and the boredom without end, there were times when I was content to lie back and enjoy the attention.

It was a kind of compensation. Over these days there were hundreds of cards and letters and phone calls and, later, brief visits—the last by people who sometimes betrayed the hope of having a final word with what they took to be their dying friend. Some of those who checked in I had not seen in years. Nor have I seen them since, so busy are we with our several busynesses. Sickness is an enforced pause for the counting up of our friends, and being grateful.

In all the cards and letters assuring me of prayer, and almost all did offer such assurance, there were notable differences. Catholics say they are "storming the gates of heaven" on your behalf and have arranged to have Masses said. Evangelical Protestants are "lifting you up before the throne." Mainline Protestants, Jews, and the unaffiliated let it go with a simple "I am praying for you" or "You are in my prayers." One gets the impression that Catholics and evangelicals are more aggressive on the prayer front.

Then there were longer letters laying out the case for my getting better. A friend who is a constitutional scholar at an Ivy League university wrote a virtual lawyer's brief summing up the reasons for dying and the reasons for living, and came down strongly on the side of my living. It was very odd, because after that there were a number of similar letters, all arguing that I should stay around for a while and assuming that I was undecided about that. I was undecided. This struck me as strange: at the time of crisis and in the months of recovery following, I was never once afraid. I don't claim it as a virtue; it was simply the fact. It had less to do with courage than with indifference. Maybe this is "holy indifference," what the spiritual manuals describe as "a quality in a person's love for God above all that excludes preferences for any person, object, or condition of life." Aquinas, St. John of the Cross, and Ignatius of Loyola all write at length about such holy indifference. All I know is that I was surprisingly indifferent to whether I would live or die. It probably had less to do with holiness than with my knowing that there was nothing I could do about it one way or the other.

On the other hand, there was the message: "Everything is ready now." As though the decision were mine, to stay or to go. A friend who had written with his son the story of his son's several years of waging a heroic battle against a horrific series of cancers sent me their book, inscribed with the admonition "to fight relentlessly for life." It was very kind, but I was not at all disposed to fight. More to the point were those letters calmly laying out the reasons why it would be better for others, if not for me, were I to live rather than to die. Over the slow weeks and slower months of recovery, I gradually came to agree. But still very tentatively.

When I was recuperating at home and could take phone calls, those calls became a staple of everyday existence. There were dozens of calls daily; closer friends called every day. Somebody was always on call-waiting. I enjoyed it shamelessly. Although I was often too tired to talk, when I had the energy I related in detail, over and over again, every minuscule change in my condition. With a credible display of intense interest, people listened to the problems with colostomy bags and the latest wrinkle in controlling the nausea that came with chemotherapy. And always in my talking, I was on the edge of tears. I, who had seldom cried in my adult life, was regularly, and without embarrassment, blubbering. Not in sadness. Not at all. But in a kind of amazement that this had happened to me, and maybe I was going to die and maybe I was going to live, and it was all quite out of my control. That was it, I think: I was not in charge, and it was both strange and very good not to be in charge.

Tentatively, I say, I began to think that I might live. It was not a particularly joyful prospect. Everything was shrouded by the thought of death, that I had almost died, that I may still die, that everyone and everything is dying. As much as I was grateful for all the calls and letters, I harbored a secret resentment. These friends who said they were thinking about me and praying for me all the time, I knew they also went shopping and visited their children and tended to their businesses, and there were long times when they were not thinking about me at all. More important, they were forgetting the primordial, overwhelming, indomitable fact: we are dying! Why weren't they as crushingly impressed by that fact as I was?

After a month or so, I could, with assistance, walk around the block. Shuffle is the more accurate term, irrationally fearing with every step that my stomach would rip open again. I have lived in New York almost forty years and have always been a fierce chauvinist about the place. When you're tired of London, you're tired of life, said Dr. Johnson. I had always thought that about New York, where there is more terror and tenderness per square foot than any place in the world. I embraced all the clichés about the place, the palpable vitality of its streets, the electricity in the air, and so forth and so on. Shuffling around the block and then, later, around several blocks, I was tired of it. Death was everywhere. The children at the playground at 19th Street and Second Avenue I saw as corpses covered with putrefying skin. The bright young model prancing up Park Avenue with her portfolio under her arm and dreaming of the success she is to be, doesn't she know she's going to die, that she's already dying? I wanted to cry out to everybody and everything, "Don't you know what's happening?" But I didn't. Let them be in their innocence and ignorance. It didn't matter. Nothing mattered.

Surprising to me, and to others, I did what had to be done with my work. I read manuscripts, wrote my columns, made editorial decisions, but all listlessly. It didn't really matter. After some time, I could shuffle the few blocks to the church and say Mass. At the altar, I cried a lot, and hoped the people didn't notice. To think that I'm really here after all, I thought, at the altar, at the *axis mundi*, the center of life. And of death. I would be helped back to the house, and days beyond numbering I would simply lie on the sofa looking out at the back yard. That birch tree, which every winter looked as dead as dead could be, was budding again. Would I be here to see it in full leaf, to see its leaves fall in the autumn? Never mind. It doesn't matter.

When I was a young man a parishioner told me, "Do all your praying before you get really sick. When you're sick you can't really pray." She was right, at least in largest part. Being really sick—vomiting, and worrying about what will show up on the next blood test, and trying to ignore the pain at three o'clock in the morning—is a full-time job. At best, you want to recede into relatively painless passivity and listen to your older sister reading Willa Cather, as my sister read to me. During those long nights, *My Antonia, Death Comes for the Archbishop, Shadows on the Rock,* and at those times I could have wished it to go on and on. Not that it mattered, but it was ever so pleasant being ever so pampered.

People are different around the very sick, especially when they think they may be dying. In the hospital, bishops came to visit and knelt by my bedside, asking for a blessing. A Jewish doctor, professing himself an atheist, asked for my prayers with embarrassed urgency. His wife had cancer, he explained, "And you know about that now." Call it primitive instinct or spiritual insight, but there is an aura about the sick and dying. They have crossed a line into a precinct others do not know. It is the aura of redemptive suffering, of suffering "offered up" on behalf of others, because there is nothing else to be done with it and you have to do something with it. The point is obvious, but it impressed me nonetheless: when you are really sick it is impossible to imagine what it is like to be really well; and when you are well it is almost impossible to remember what it was like to be really sick. They are different precincts.

I had lost nearly fifty pounds and was greatly weakened. There was still another major surgery to come, to reverse the colostomy. You don't want to know the details. It was not the most dangerous surgery, but it was the third Mack truck, and for a long time afterward I barely had strength to lift my hand. Then, step by almost imperceptible step, I was recovering and dared to hope that I would be well again, that I would stride down the street again, that I would take on new projects again. Very little things stand out like luminous signposts. The first time I was able to take a shower by myself. It was dying and rising again in baptismal flood. When one day I was sent home from the hospital after another round of tests, I was told that, if I did not urinate by five o'clock, I should come back to the emergency room and someone would put the catheter back in. My heart sank. It was quite irrational, but going back to the emergency room would have been like recapitulating the entire ordeal of these last several months. I could not endure the thought. When at four o'clock I peed a strong triumphant pee, my heart was lifted on high, and with tears of gratitude I began to sing with feeble voice a Te Deum. I thought, "I am going to get better." And I allowed myself, ever so tentatively, to be glad.

That was seven years ago. I feel very well now. They tell me I might be around for another twenty years or so. Medical science, perhaps arbitrarily, says five years is the point of complete recovery when you are reassigned to your age slot on the actuarial chart. But just to be safe, the tests continue on a regular basis. Next Monday we get the latest report on the CEA (carcinoembryonic antigen), the blood indicator of cancerous activity, although the doctor says the test is really not necessary. But I think I am well now. It took a long time after the surgeries, almost two years, before the day came when I suddenly realized that the controlling thought that day had not been the thought of death. And now, in writing this little essay, it all comes back. I remember where I have been, and where I will be again, and where we will all be.

There is nothing that remarkable in my story, except that we are all unique in our living and dying. Early on in my illness a friend gave me John Donne's wondrous *Devotions Upon Emergent Occasions*. The *Devotions* were written a year after Donne had almost died, and then lingered for months by death's door. He writes, "Though I may have seniors, others may be elder than I, yet I have proceeded apace in a good university, and gone a great way in a little time, by the furtherance of a vehement fever." So I too have been to a good university, and what I have learned, what I have learned most importantly, is that, in living and in dying, everything is ready now.

DEATH AND TEXAS

(From *Books & Culture*)

The brochure from our local museum had described its new exhibit as an "installation," a term that, in our town, we usually apply to dishwashers, church officers, or, more recently, computer software. My husband declined the invitation to the opening, preferring to spend the afternoon laying bricks for a new patio, so I went alone the following Saturday to "The Waiting Room," a multimedia production by San Francisco artist Richard Kamler.

"What was it like?" my husband asked when I got home, looking up from a patch of sand he was leveling.

"Big," I said. "It took up two rooms."

In the main gallery, ten gray posters, each about twelve feet long, hung from the ceiling. They outlined an area, a placard explained, the size of the room where lawyers, spiritual advisers, and family members wait to visit inmates at California's San Quentin prison. Inside this space, two rows of empty chairs faced each other. Stenciled on the posters were instructions taken from the prison's handbook for visitors. One poster warned, for example, that visitors' hands must be visible at all times, another that bras containing wires would set off the metal detector.

Beyond this space, along one wall of the gallery, were mounted cafeteria trays, the kind with partitions. Most of the trays were empty, inscribed with the names of executed prisoners, the dates of their death, and the words, "Declined last meal." A few trays held renditions of some portion of a requested last meal—an ear of corn, a banana, a hamburger. Against the opposite wall, four video monitors played tape loops of interviews with relatives of condemned prisoners or their victims' families. Speakers concealed around the room emitted two other persistent sounds, a ticking clock and a beating heart. Every once in a while the heartbeat would speed up briefly, then stop.

"So what did you think of it?" my husband asked when I'd finished this description.

"Interesting," I shrugged, "but is it art?"

My offhand gibe concealed the bothersome questions that had beset me all the way home. These questions weren't about the aesthetic merits of the show. True, I found somewhat overblown the artist's description of his work as "very dense." (For real density, you need to visit the Texas Prison Museum in the old drugstore on the town square, where you can see not only Old Sparky, the retired electric chair, but such *objets d'art* as photographs of Bonnie and Clyde's bullet-riddled bodies, crude weapons fashioned by ingenious prisoners from toothbrushes and spoons, and the changing fashion in convict clothing.) As for the question of artistic genre, it hardly behooved someone attending her first "installation" to challenge the typology.

Nor was I troubled by the moral issues the exhibit raised. If you live in Huntsville, a town routinely and accurately labeled by the press "the execution capital of the nation," you've already heard and wrestled with every legal, sociological, and theological argument both for and against the death penalty. That—and our profound uneasiness with our town's media persona—probably explained why so few of the hundred or so people filling the auditorium that afternoon were residents of Huntsville.

It was what had gone on in the second room of the exhibit that remained a disconcerting enigma. In the museum's auditorium the artist had designed what he described as a "social sculpture." The printed program had listed it as "A Community Conversation." Why "community?" That was where, I discovered, the whole experience began unraveling for me.

How and under what conditions does an aggregate of individuals merit the name *community?* What has the word come to stand for in our collective imagination? Clearly, in any number of contexts, *community* has taken on a certain coloration that distinguishes it from its dark doppelganger, *society*, which in recent decades has come to mean some distant and impersonal power, one that exerts an almost exclusively negative influence on our lives. Society now serves as a convenient catchall culprit for our every affliction. Membership in society, like affiliation with a political party, we somehow assume to be optional for human beings.

Community, on the other hand, is essential. We decry society's "demands," but we seek the "support" community offers. Society is impersonal, cold, and oppressive; community is redolent of maternal snugness, warmth, and goodwill. If one is "in community," one floats in the warm, amniotic fluid of caring and sharing. Conversely, belonging to no community strikes us as about the most miserable fate that can befall a person.

This shift in vocabulary has had, in fact, some beneficial practical effects. For one thing, it refocuses our attention closer to home, puts our imaginations to work on local problems like neighborhood crime and school-bond elections. But semantic shifts can also disguise intractable problems, allowing us to pretend we have dealt with a difficulty when in reality we have merely renamed it. Whatever the brochure had called it, I was certain that what happened in the museum auditorium that afternoon had *not* been a conversation, nor did its participants constitute a community.

The Cast

What took place in the museum under the banner of conversation might more accurately have been called a drama. Visualize, if you will, the stars of the cast: four panelists who sit on a low stage up front. They are assisted, in classical fashion, by the chorus, made up largely of two groups wearing T-shirts, one group in purple, the other in black. The shirts are emblazoned with the names of two separate coalitions against the death penalty. From time to time, lone speakers will emerge from the audience in the not-so-classical tradition of guerrilla theater.

But this opening act belongs to the panelists. The first, a white-haired woman who served in the Texas legislature for five years and once ran for governor, tells us she came to be an death-penalty abolitionist by education and family tradition. Still, she says, "I continue to test this position against every horrendous murder that takes place in this state, including most recently the despicable dragging death of James Byrd in Jasper last year." But not even James Byrd's murderers should be executed for their crime, she concludes, because "the ability to be transformed is the ultimate identifying mark of humanity," and execution forecloses the possibility of such transformation. Clearly resonating with these sentiments, the audience hums like a well-tempered tuning fork.

The next panelist, Huntsville's district attorney, provides the first complication for the dramatic action. A handsome man with dark longish hair and a beard, he is the panel's sole proponent of the death penalty. He too mentions his early education and family tradition. Surprisingly, he was schooled in the pacifism of the Church of the Brethren. That he felt compelled to break so decisively with such a background suggests, he says, how deeply his personal experiences at the bar have affected his beliefs.

At this, the audience stirs restlessly. As if to mitigate their distrust, the attorney adds that he still keeps up a personal correspondence with one of the men he sent to death row fourteen years ago. The audience, unimpressed, maintains a stony silence.

Moving forward a couple inches in his chair, the lawyer recalls his last capital murder case, prosecuted two years earlier. A twenty-three-year-old mother had been raped and killed, her sixteen-month-old baby buried alive beside her. "A little baby," he repeats, "still running on its tiptoes. A child that couldn't have given evidence and was no threat at all to him." There are some acts, he concludes, so monstrous, their violence so gratuitous, that they put their perpetrators "beyond the pale of human society."

The sea of silence stirs uneasily, but does not warm.

Sensing that, at this point, he may as well go for broke, the attorney continues. "As for whether the death penalty deters criminals, I believe it does." As proof, he cites a leader of the infamous Texas Syndicate, a powerful narcotics ring, who recently offered to plea-bargain rather than face execution. "He told me he could face a lifetime in prison but not the death penalty. But you see? Without the threat of that sentence, I'd have had nothing to bargain with." The D.A. closes by affirming that individuals are ultimately responsible for their own actions and that society has a right to protect itself.

Murmurs of dismay ripple through the audience. Maybe he should have said "community" instead of "society." At any rate, a steady stream of people, led by black and purple T-shirts, begins to eddy from the auditorium in protest.

Suddenly, down near the front, a large woman in a gauze dress, her black topknot slipping askew, charges forward and splashes something liquid onto the dais.

The people in the doorway freeze, the audience gasps. "What's that?" someone shouts.

"That, sir," the woman cries, her voice trembling with rage, "is your blood."

I am still puzzling over this—shouldn't it be a *prisoner's* blood?—when the artist, trying not to sound like a scolding schoolmarm, stands up to ask that we all "try to sit still and listen." Obviously, his "social sculpture," Pygmalion-like, is getting out of hand.

The next panelist quickly regains our attention, binding us in her oratorical spell. Casting an appraising sidelong glance at the district attorney, she begins by echoing the previous two speakers' theme of personal experience. And her experience upstages theirs, for she has, she tells us, coming down hard on each syllable, spent "nine years, five months, and twenty-four days in a Texas prison for a murder I did *not* commit." (Throughout her remarks, whenever she refers to her sentence, she always spells out its exact length, driving home rhetoric like ten-penny nails.)

"And if," she adds, "the charge had been capital murder, I would have been sent to death row and possibly be pushing up daisies by now. Fortunately," she fixes the district attorney with another baleful look, "I survived to help the prosecutors discover the *real* culprit."

Here she takes us on an instructive tour of the appeals process wherein we learn that an appellate court is not allowed to consider the plaintiff's guilt or innocence, only whether there has been an infraction of correct judicial procedure. "Guilt or innocence is irrelevant," she says, pronouncing each Latinate syllable of the final word separately and distinctly. "And as for the death penalty *preventing* crime, if I had been executed, the real murderer would never have been found. I was the one, who, from a jail cell, discovered the suppressed evidence that had been sitting in the D.A.'s desk drawer for the past *nine years!*"

The audience cheers, claps, whistles. Even the district attorney shakes his head as if to commiserate with her long pursuit of justice.

Given her passion and eloquence, the woman is a tough act to follow, but the last panelist, despite his unfamiliar New Hampshire accent and subdued demeanor, soon has us in the palm of his hand. Stationed at the end of the table, he turns slightly so as to put himself at right angles and a little removed from his fellow panelists.

His voice is low and consciously controlled. "I too am part of a community," he begins, "one defined by experience—the experience of having a family member murdered."

He recounts his story thus: One June day in 1988 he was called to the hospital emergency room in his small town. There he found his father on a gurney, his chest "blown to hamburger" by an intruder's shotgun. A few minutes later, the body was sent to the morgue, "no longer my father, but just a piece of evidence." After he had called his six siblings with the news, "I was left alone to wonder how I was going to get the blood washed off my mother's walls at home."

His story stills the audience the way arctic cold slows the movement of air. We hold our breath for the denouement.

"I don't oppose the death penalty because I care about murderers, but because I care about their victims, including the families they leave behind," he tells us. "If I could trade the life of my father for the life of his murderer, I'd do it in a minute." He reckons a life for a life to be true justice, and a trade he would gladly make if he only knew how. "But I will never get my father back by killing his murderer. I don't need vengeance," he says. "I need healing."

The audience, silent and wary till that final phrase, now murmurs its sympathetic approval.

But the man quickly continues, as if fearing that we mistake his meaning. "The isolation imposed on victims' families hinders that healing. Neither side in the death-penalty debate wants to talk to us. Advocates of the death penalty want to exploit our grief as an argument for execution. They don't understand that killing the murderer compounds the pain; it only creates another grieving family."

A smattering of applause ripples through the audience.

But abolitionists, he adds, too often find victims' families an embarrassment to their cause. "It's as if there's only so much sympathy to go around. Any compassion for us means less for people on death row." Abolitionists, he says, also resent those family members who support execution. "They think these people are only out for revenge. But most of them are motivated by deep moral convictions. They're not hate-mongers, not for the most part. They just want to spare others the pain they're living with; they want to make sure that what happened to them doesn't happen to someone else."

He rolls a pencil between his fingers for a long moment, then rakes his gaze across the audience. "I don't know that I can ever forgive my father's murderer, but I do know if the state were to take his life, that would forever preclude that possibility."

Intermission

As we trickle into the foyer for the scheduled break, each of us scans the crowd for someone we know, eager to discharge the static electricity we've accumulated during the past hour. The black and purple T-shirts clump together, making the rest of us seem aimless and unconnected.

Before I return to the auditorium, I take another turn through the posters and cafeteria trays in the main gallery, recalling a conversation I had with the artist a couple of weeks ago while he was installing his show. We sat in the museum foyer, empty then, across from a display of quilts made by local women.

Richard Kamler is a slight man with a shining bald head, his white chin whiskers divided symmetrically into two points, giving him the air of a sixty-year-old elf. I asked if this were his first trip to Huntsville.

"Oh no," he shook his head. "I've been here several times during the past couple of years while I was working on this piece, interviewing different people."

He mentioned the man who manages the Texas Department of Criminal Justice, as well as the warden at the Walls, the original state prison that houses the execution chamber, only a few blocks away from where we sit. "And professors in the criminal justice department at the university," he added.

"Was everyone cooperative?"

"Yes. Very helpful. Well," he paused, "almost all. I wanted to film inside the former residence of the prison director, that big brick mansion across from the Walls, but they didn't encourage that."

"What about prisoners?"

"Yes. Of course, they wouldn't let me take a videocam in there, but I got audio tapes."

"What about guards?"

"Guards?" He peered at me over his reading glasses. "No. I'm afraid I don't have any contacts among the guards."

Act Two

Back in the auditorium now, "Community Conversation: Part II" is cranking up, and I hurry back to my seat. As disjunctive as the panelists' presentations have been, they all gave me something to ponder, and I'm eager to hear what will doubtless be the question-and-answer part of the program. The moderator, a professor from Michigan, asks for input from the audience. And this is when the already precarious coherence of the artist's carefully contrived "social sculpture" really begins to crumble.

No sooner does the moderator pause for breath than the woman who earlier threw make-believe blood onto the platform jumps to her feet. "I am a doctor," she announces, "and I have spent my life working among the poor in Mexico." The death penalty, she tells us, is part of a conspiracy by the state of Texas to subjugate and colonize Central America. Her outline of this plot is interspersed with tidbits of her family history: her daughter is also a doctor, as is her father—who, however, was abusive and patriarchal.

The moderator, rattling his notes, gets to his feet.

"You people are wrong," she cries to the audience. "You need to do more than just abolish the death penalty. You should shut down all the prisons!"

People stir in their seats. The moderator nods uncomfortably in her direction. An invisible isolation booth seems to form around her, sealing her in a kind of unspoken solitary confinement. A number of people are waving hands while others, not waiting to be recognized, shout demands that the district attorney explain how he can justify serving a justice system that favors the rich and powerful.

The attorney glances accusingly at the moderator. "I think most people prefer an imperfect system to none at all," he says.

Another woman gets to her feet. "What we need is more economic development, more education. That's the only way to get rid of violence."

"Only poor people go to jail," someone near her adds. "The rich get off."

"All depends on who you are whether you go to jail or not," yet another voice calls out.

"And who you kill," someone else chimes in.

The moderator from Michigan rocks forward on his toes, appearing stunned. Fortunately, one of the panelists, the woman who spent time in prison, grabs the reins of this runaway fracas. "What it really depends on is your county's district attorney," she says with the authority of one who knows, turning toward the lawyer on her left.

The D.A. takes the ball and runs with it. "Absolutely," he agrees, leaning his elbows on the table and hunching toward the audience. "This office has a great deal of power. It's the district attorney who decides whether to bring charges and what those charges will be." He sits back. "But you know who determines what constitutes a capital crime? The state legislature. It's your representatives who decide if Texas even has a death penalty." He aims a finger at the audience. "So it's the voters who really have the power. And the responsibility."

His challenge is ignored. Instead, someone shouts, "How come Houston has four times as many inmates on death row as Dallas?"

A woman gets to her feet. "As a lawyer from that city, I can tell you in one word. Economics. The county figured it was just too expensive to prosecute capital cases. It costs three times as much to prosecute and execute a criminal as it does to keep him in prison for forty years."

To judge by the exclamations of surprise, this information comes as news to most of the audience, but before the issue can be pursued further, a thin man with a mustache near the back of the auditorium stands up.

"I'm here today," the man says a bit nervously, "both because my sister was murdered and because the state executed the woman who killed her."

A murmur rustles through the audience. This is Ron Carlson, someone whispers, whose sister was killed by Karla Faye Tucker, the first woman executed in Texas for a hundred years. "I have two other people here with me," he says, gesturing toward a middle-aged couple next to him. "Their son is scheduled for execution next week." The pair look down at their laps.

"Six months after my sister was murdered," he continues, "my father suffered the same fate. Yet his murderer escaped the death penalty by plea bargaining. Where's the fairness in that?"

His voice shatters, and for a moment silence falls over this conglomeration of people hemmed up together in the auditorium. But whether they are pondering the inequities of the criminal justice system or gauging the extraordinary odds of having two family members murdered in the same year, I can't tell. I'm not even sure which has caught *my* attention.

In any case, the silence lasts no more than a moment. Then a woman wearing a purple turban to match her T-shirt stands and delivers a well-scripted speech about the Thirteenth Amendment. It did not, she claims, as we all probably believe, abolish slavery. "Oh yes, we still have slavery in this country.

And why? Because the Thirteenth Amendment exempted prisoners from the provisions against forced labor. It was planned that way—to fill the labor demands of giant corporations!"

A hubbub, part protest, part confusion, follows this speech. The scene in the auditorium is beginning to resemble a painting by Hieronymus Bosch, macabre and self-devouring.

The panelist from New Hampshire tries to swing our attention back to Ron Carlson and the plight of victim families. "We rely on victims to justify the death penalty," he says. "We tell the families 'Look what we're doing for you! Killing the murderer to make you feel better.' But the death penalty is a cheap substitute for what victims' families need. It allows us to abandon them and their pain."

I want to hear him say more about this, but his point fails to grab the crowd's roving attention. Instead, their focus swings to a thin man with a two-foot-long gray ponytail, just getting to his feet. "I once came within seventy-two hours of execution," he says in a gravelly voice. He pauses briefly for the crowd to take this in. "So you can understand when I say I'm not exactly comfortable in this town." The crowd murmurs its comradely comprehension. "In fact," he chuckles confidentially, "I had to have a few drinks just to get here."

"We're with you, brother," someone calls out.

The man sticks his fingertips in his jeans' pockets. "I just want to say, you know, this room is full of family." He takes his hands from his pockets and hugs his elbows, as if not knowing how to go on. He frowns, concentrating. "And also that voting is the answer. Thank you. Thank you very much." And, sinking into his seat, he waves to us all as people break into applause.

The void is immediately filled by a tall African American woman. She's not a Texan, she tells us, but came here twenty years ago as a student from Chicago to interview three hundred prisoners as part of her graduate research. "I now work in the Restorative Justice Program, and this is the part you're going to find hard to believe. My boss is the man you all have been dumping on." She points to the district attorney. "He knows my position on capital punishment, and though we don't agree on that point, he always listens to me with respect. We should be glad to have him serving in the office he holds."

Suddenly, the woman who doesn't believe in prisons jumps up and shouts at her, "Shame on you! You're a Judas. Shame on you!"

There is a collective gasp from the audience, followed by a fretful stirring. Our concentration is shredded by the constant volleys of stories, accusations, pleas—none of which we have time to absorb.

The Michigan moderator, intuiting that everyone has had enough, stands, thanks us all for coming, announces there are refreshments laid out now in the foyer, and dismisses us with the relief of a harried schoolteacher at the end of a particularly rowdy day in the classroom.

Out in the foyer, I glance at the delicacies and drink set up on a long table. Rarely has food seemed so unappealing. I head for the parking lot instead, feeling the way Alice must have, exiting the Mad Hatter's tea party.

Many of the stories told here had come from the deepest levels of human experiences. Yet none had been honored as they deserved. What, I wondered, had caused roughly a hundred people, most of whom obviously shared the same opinions about capital punishment, to pay so little attention to these stories?

Why do people with the best intentions often have the worst manners and show the least interest in what others have to say? Why does the language of advocacy so often polarize rather than clarify?

Eventually, all these questions, like moons around a more massive planet, settled into orbits around a core enigma—one that, I have come to believe, pertains to community. A cause, we think, unites people. Common goals create community. But under certain conditions (the event at the museum being a case in point), a cause—whether the right to bear arms or defeat of the death penalty—becomes instead a device for defining personal identity. Carving out one's position, claiming moral territory, takes precedence over making your cause common. Like James and John, those sons of thunder who wanted to call down fire on a Samaritan village, we are often more interested in destroying our enemies than in consolidating friendly forces.

This is not to say that town meetings and city councils, even church boards, are not frequently cantankerous and divisive. So are families, for that matter. But it takes more than similar views on issues to make a community. Some glue that makes us stick together even when we differ. Ties of place or blood or work, for example. Everyone in the auditorium came and went away free of such ties, thanking our lucky stars we'd never have to meet again. Such haphazard and transient couplings don't produce a community.

Perhaps in the artist's mind, shutting people up in a large room for a couple of hours with a volatile topic was a form of art, "subversive," defiantly unscripted: a "happening." Nevertheless, that afternoon's "Community Conversation" had not been artful. No care had been taken to fit the pieces together. Indeed, the "conversation" was profoundly careless. Even worse, it was unholy. Real suffering, both present and represented there, had been trivialized and desecrated by our casual and shifting attention. The result was an anti-conversation carried on by an anti-community.

Epilogue

The same week Richard Kamler's installation opened at the museum, the Texas Department of Criminal Justice began transferring the 461 prisoners on death row to a unit in another county. The citizens of Huntsville weren't sorry to see them go; in fact, they would just as soon the executions took place in the neighboring county as well, instead of the condemned prisoners being brought back to the Walls to receive the lethal injection. Not all of our citizens would admit they're ashamed of our town's reputation; they'd merely say they don't like the worldwide publicity the executions focus on us. Either way, it comes to the same thing: we care what other people say or think about Huntsville, the same way families feel responsible for, proud of, or shamed by their members. This is another necessary aspect of community.

I said that no one in Huntsville protested transferring death row to another county, but there was one telling exception: the community of execution itself, which included both the death-row inmates and the seventy men who guarded them. Cloistered together for years, preparing for death, prisoners and guards had annealed in a furnace of waiting.

In the new prison, death-row cells are equipped not with bars but with solid steel doors, leaving their occupants in virtual solitary confinement. Their new jailers have had no training in dealing with condemned men, a situation that puts both prisoners and guards at risk.

As time for the move approached, the old death-row guards became distraught about their charges' uncertain future. In response, the spiritual adviser to this strange monastery, a chaplain who has served on death row for many years, reserved the local theater. He invited the seventy veteran guards to a showing of *The Green Mile*, the movie in which Tom Hanks plays the superintendent of a Depression-era death row. Afterwards, they ate dinner together and talked it over. And that, I'll bet, was a real community conversation.

REYNOLDS PRICE

LETTER TO A MAN IN THE FIRE

In 1994, Reynolds Price published a memoir, A Whole New Life, *in which he recounted his prolonged struggle with spinal cancer and the miraculous healing that allowed him, though his legs remained paralyzed, to return to productive life. In 1997, Price received a letter from a stranger: a young man in his mid-thirties who had been forced to withdraw from medical school by the recurrence of a cancer that would soon take his life. What follows is part of Price's reply.*

Dear Jim,

It hardly seems appropriate to thank you for letting me know the hard facts of the cancer which has interrupted your medical training. A malignancy in the colon with a spread to the liver and pancreas sounds more daunting to me than the threat of my own tumor years ago. Mine was confined to the spinal cord. As you know, it managed to paralyze both my legs; but with heroic care from others, its threat was turned and has been absent for long years now. Still, hard as your news is, I feel some thanks that the even harder questions you ask have pressed on me a need to think my way again, if only in the most personal manner, into the bottomless mystery of suffering.

I understand that you've contacted me because you know, from my own cancer memoir, that I've survived, though with paralyzed legs from the tumor that gave every sign of killing me when it was discovered in 1984. And you know as well how strongly I believe—from several kinds of evidence—that the means of my survival worked outward from a sense of God's awareness of my ordeal and his willingness to watch and to brace me, generally in deep silence, in my own fierce hope to live.

Beyond that one credential—and a lifetime of watching the world fairly closely and reading widely, and the fact that you've contacted me—you must know from the start that I have no further potent claim to make on your time or credulity. I'm no trained theologian, no regular churchgoer, no mathematical cosmologist, no theoretical physicist, and no statistician with an eye for your chances or anyone else's. What I do claim to be is a watchful human in his seventh decade who harbored a similar killing invader deep in his body a few years ago and who thinks he was saved by a caring, though enigmatic, God.

In the face of those limits, you've asked me two ancient and sizable questions which, given the facts of your present trials, I'll attempt to look at, however partially. You know that they're questions I've stared in the teeth on more than one occasion since the agonized death of my father from lung cancer when I was twenty-one and he was a young fifty-four years old, with nearly four decades of smoking behind him. While you don't state your bafflements outright, it seems to me that you've implied your questions in these sentences from your letter—

• • •

I want to believe in a God who cares . . . because I may meet him sooner than I had expected. I think I am at the point where I can accept the existence of a God (otherwise I can't explain the origin of the universe), but I can't yet believe he cares about us.

What I hear you asking, in the slimmest summary, is this—

1. Was our universe created by an intelligent power; and if so, is the Creator conscious of its creatures and benignly concerned for their lives?
2. If the answer to both halves of that question is Yes, how can a gifted young human being be tormented and perhaps killed early?

I've already asserted a troubled Yes to the first of your mysteries. And the Yes is firm enough in its groundings to make me wonder how any close observer can believe otherwise. What's *troubled* in the Yes is my inability to prove the truth of my claim to others. Nonetheless, what I assert with no serious doubt is that our one universe anyhow was created and is maintained by a single divine intelligence who still exists and continues to oversee his primeval handiwork. I'll refer to that God, as the Jewish-Christian-Islamic tradition does, with masculine pronouns; and I hew to that tradition, with all the problems it brings, not in male pride but because I suspect that there's more than a chance that God's revelation of his nature as *male* could offer a chink of light on the question of who God is.

Beyond that assertion of private faith, I can offer no other person any evidence more convincing than the patterns that

I think I've detected in my own history, in certain private intensities which I'll describe, and in the final fact that— repeating the words of an old philosophy professor of mine— "A belief in God, and in the immortality of the soul, has tended to be the opinion of a vast majority of the human race." His claim has always seemed reasonable to me, and the majority opinion of Homo sapiens throughout our known history is worth, at a minimum, initial respect. Yet I'm more than aware that such an assertion of belief from me, or any other human being in whatever time or place, may be of no more value than a paranoid's conviction that the CIA has planted a listening device in his molars.

My belief in a Creator derives largely from detailed and overpowering personal intuition, an unshakable hunch, and a set of demonstrations that go far back in my consciousness— well before I began to comprehend the details of the world of deeply held but unoppressive Christian faith in which my parents had been formed, and in which they raised me. What' I've called *demonstrations* have come in a very few experiences of my own, beginning when I was six years old.

Starting on a warm afternoon in the summer of 1939, when I was wandering alone in the pine woods by our suburban house in piedmont North Carolina, I've experienced moments of sustained calm awareness that subsequent questioning has never discounted. Those moments, which recurred at unpredictable and widely spaced intervals till some thirteen years ago, still seem to me undeniable manifestations of the Creator's benign, or patiently watchful, interest in particular stretches of my life, though perhaps not all of it. And each of the moments—never lasting for more than seconds but seeming, in retrospect, hours long—has taken the form of sudden and entirely unsought breakings-in upon my consciousness of a demonstration that all of visible and invisible nature (myself included) is a single reality, a single thought from a central mind.

To be more descriptive, in those moments or openings— which are far from exotic in humankind (Wordsworth's accounts, in *The Prelude* and other poems, of similar findings in his youth are the classic description, as I learned years after my own began)—I've heard what amounts to a densely complex yet piercingly direct harmony that appears to come from the heart of whatever reality made us and watches our lives.

There've been no shows of light, no gleaming illusory messengers, almost no words; and the music that underlies each moment is silent but felt in every cell like a grander pulse beneath my own. Always simultaneously, I've been assured that this reality is launched on a history that's immensely longer than any life span I can hope to have and that it's designed to end in some form of transformation and eternal entry into the presence of that central mind, God.

If I were not nervous, in the prescribed modern fashion, I'd call such experiences revelations. I'll repeat that they've come exceedingly rarely, no more than four times in my entire life; and only twice have they taken a visual or audible form—the moment when Jesus washed my cancer wound and the moment, weeks later, when my legs were plainly failing. Alone in a dark bed, I asked how much more pain I must suffer; and a voice answered *More.*

Still, the experiences were as real as any car wreck. They've proved overwhelming in their unanswerability, and their power has meant that I've literally never had to make the touted "leap of faith" into sudden belief. Belief came toward me early, as it's come to many others. To say so is no boast. Many men, women, and children have been far more richly gifted than I with such grace; and it's worth remarking that belief confers no necessary bliss on its recipient. When I was a college student, I asked Elizabeth Bowen, the novelist, about the religion of her friend T. S. Eliot; and my question implied that his adult embrace of Anglo-Catholicism had been a retreat. Bowen took the question seriously but then said that belief was often a more difficult course than many others.

Till now, I don't claim unusual difficulties. The usual lions have appeared in the road, the usual boulders crash on through the roof, I go on lapsing into old and new faults. But since those childhood openings, there's been no sustained time in my life when—in the aftermath of all absurdities and disasters—I couldn't repeat what Tertullian said, in effect, in the second century—*Credo quia absurdum est*, "I believe *because* it's absurd." And that affirmation is made, not in the blind embrace of an empty irrational hope of love-from-the-sky but in full possession of what I take to be ample proof.

The scarcity of what I've called personal openings is one of the reasons I've taken them seriously. If they'd come with any frequency, I'd suspect myself of brain damage or unconscious fraud—or a sanctity that is patently unavailable to me. But I'm further persuaded by the fact that my occasional references in memoirs to such private moments have elicited dozens of letters from apparently lucid strangers who attest to similar experiences and who then confide that I'm the first person to whom they've mentioned their curious luck. I've come to suspect that, far from being the exclusive experience of saints and mystics, many more perfectly normal human beings than we can easily imagine share such dawnings and keep them secret in some desire to avoid the appearance of lunacy.

A remarkable writer, who's eighty-seven years old, has recently confirmed my suspicion and sent me this description of one such opening she herself has experienced—

> . . . such inner events are much more common than people dare to admit. They carry their own authentication, I think, in the atmosphere of complete simplicity and great depth that surrounds them. Mine came, like yours, at a time of medical stress, during some exhausting tests before an operation. I can't exactly say "it came" though; it was rather that I went out to meet it. . . . This time I went out along the Galilee hills and came to a crowd gathered around a man, and I stood on the outskirts intending to listen. But he looked over the crowd at me and then said, "What do you want?" I said, "Could you send someone to come with me and help me stand up after the tests, because I can't manage alone?" He thought for a minute and then said, "How would it be if I came?"

Few events I've heard of elsewhere are as plain or as convincing as that. The very words in which my correspondent describes her encounter have a clarity and a last-moment grasp which rivals, in contemporary diction, that ultimate dawn meeting of the fishing disciples with their risen Lord at the end of the Gospel of John. From the shore he directs their boat and their net toward a big school of fish; but when they land the catch, they discover that he has already roasted a breakfast of fish and bread.

Impressive as my own openings were, and remain for me, their witness to a still-existing Creator was supported powerfully and far more steadily by my early luck in having haplessly generous parents, kind and guileless as the best of children, who guided my early intimations into a quiet variety of sane attention to ultimate concerns. So from childhood till now that attentive worship has largely been private, not institutional, and has mostly been grounded in the figure of Jesus, son of God and man.

My worship has also been informed and braced by my reading, primarily in Hebrew and Christian scriptures and in ancient and modern theology. I'll try to make clear, as I proceed, that most of those theologians were either physicists or artists—novelists, poets, painters, composers. Only occasionally have I studied professional thinkers about the mysteries of life, having seldom found one who spoke to my own concerns. A lifetime's friendships, enmities, loves, and solitudes, and four decades of teaching have also contributed their weight; and the effort to bring the heft of those findings into daily life and work has been continuous, though often more than regrettably sporadic.

Even more powerfully, I've been supported by the manifest conviction of the world's supreme artists—the classic Buddhist and Hindu scriptures, and sacred music; the cathedrals of medieval Europe; and the painting, poetry, and music of burdened but staunch believers such as Dante, Michelangelo, Donne, Milton, Bach, Handel, and W. H. Auden. (Though Auden is a far more recent name to place in such august company—he died in 1973—I'm convinced that his voluminous poetry and critical prose have earned him a place in such surroundings. I had the luck to know him and study with him in graduate school in England in the mid-1950s. There—in his late forties, before age and physical decay marooned him in a painful solitude—his outrageous but always humane intelligence and wit were powerful carriers of his unblinking scrutiny of God and the world and the brilliance and shy warmth of his best poems, secular or sacred, are still firm guarantors of his findings and claims.)

I don't know of the occurrence in your life of any such events or meetings, so I have no sense of whether you've had external hints of the existence and attention of a transcendent reality. I've known many men and women who claim to have had none, even in troubled straits. And since I've claimed that my own early acceptance of the fact of God derives from such events, you'd be more than fair to ask what I might say to anyone who's experienced no such clues—or has got negative intimations of meaninglessness or even malice at the heart of things.

In the absence of some such confirmation of meaning, what can a still-searching man or woman do? I'm aware of how empty, even demented, my claim may sound, especially to anyone in present and unrelieved trouble. But since you've asked me your questions, my single assertion—and the body of my life's written work—is the substance of what I have to offer. If you go on to ask what a searcher may do to make an earnest start—especially a searcher as well-informed as you—I'm afraid I could offer little more than a proposal which you may feel you've already exhausted: the shamefaced suggestion that you go on waiting as long as you can at the one main door, requesting entry from whatever power may lie beyond it.

Prayer is not a language in which I'm proficient. I've read the prayers of saints and martyrs, the reflections on prayer of Teresa of Avila, John of the Cross, and their very few peers; and I've admired their powers of invention and stillness. But my own prayers, though frequent in hard times, have mostly been either repetitions of ancient models (the Lord's Prayer, the Apostles' Creed, the Jesus prayer, the Hail Mary) or brief private requests, generated in word and aim by the weight of a given moment in my present life or the lives of those near me.

And it's been my finding, and the finding of many famous doubters, that the simplest prayer reiterated in the face of silence—*Stand by me here* or *Guide me on* or *Face this creature you've brought to life and show him that this is at least your will*—may slowly or suddenly pry a chink of reliable light, a half-open window, a glimpse of a maybe passable road. Sudden floods of assurance have come, unsought, to certain reluctant men and women— Paul of Tarsus, for instance, or the Emperor Constantine or Simone Weil at that crucial moment in 1938 when she felt that Christ was present in her room: "A presence more personal, more certain, and more real than that of a human being." Both the silent and the seismic responses to such assurance have been enacted numerous times in our history. But it's well to note, at every point, that there's no guarantee that any prayer— modest or grand—will receive a remotely detectable answer but you surely know that.

Behind my own convictions, of course—and implicit in my claim to have had personal demonstrations of God's existence when many of my friends have had none—lie private questions, one of which is common. I come from a part of America— the site of the blood-and-guilt-drenched old slave-owning

Confederacy—in which Calvinist notions arrive in our mother's milk, notions of our helpless election by God to an eternal salvation or damnation. That dreadful conclusion of John Calvin's seems confirmed by a good deal that's happened in my particular world and by much that I've undergone and witnessed in my own mind and body, so I'm compelled to say that I'm profoundly uncertain of whether or not the Creator notices and *loves* every creature as much as another. I mean *love* in all its best human senses, unable to fathom God's own definition.

And no one who's had my early brushes with the devastating logic of Calvin's doctrine of predestination could deny that even Jesus' assurance that the very hairs of our heads are numbered can be taken to mean that God *knows* the detailed sum of our qualities and actions without necessarily approving us or loving us. It's worth noticing also that Jesus' assertions about God are made to particular historical audiences—the Jews and Gentiles of first-century Palestine who chose to stop and hear him. His teaching may not always have been intended for the remainder of humankind, in all ages.

It has seemed to me for years that there may well be many human beings of whom the Creator takes sporadic notice, if any. Few believers known to me have survived to midlife without the sense of occasional, or frequent, desertions by God or absences of his interest or—hardest of all—his intentional silences. It was no accident that I felt compelled as a relatively buoyant undergraduate to write a long paper on the influence of Saint John of the Cross's descriptions of the Dark night of the Soul on the poetry of T. S. Eliot. (Eliot, that most affluent and meticulously dressed of all the half-blind trekkers through the wastes of God's desertion, was very much alive as I wrote. Far the most honored English poet since Tennyson, he looked still, in photographs from the 1950s, like a nearly starved heron miles short of an oasis.)

Even the most generous-hearted saints have reported such parched treks through the silent deserts of melancholia, disease, and the hatred of their enemies; and even at the age of twenty, I sensed that danger for me if I went on living as my sense of a writer's life appeared to demand—a long silent watch on the world, then decades of solitary reporting. A single bleak statistic speaks to such absences of hope and foresight; some twenty percent of Americans who seek medical help with clinical depression will eventually kill themselves in despair. And a psychiatrist, who is herself a bipolar manic-depressive, claimed recently on CNN that, early in the new century, such self-violence will be the second leading cause of adult death in the United States.

I should add quickly, though, that I have no sense whatever that God chooses to notice individuals who look especially "noticeable" by our standards of personal worth or social standing. The stinking wretch on the frozen pavement, the abandoned orphan in a Romanian warehouse of unwanted children, may be of more concern to God than I and all my social peers. Certainly the steady notice of God is likely to cause eventual suffering, as the lives of virtually all saints show. Think only of Joan of Arc chained to the stake but alive in the flames, crying "Jesus, Jesus"; of Francis of Assisi pierced through hands and feet with the bleeding wounds of his Lord; of Bernadette of Lourdes consumed by her own hungry tumor that ate her, young, with no trace of mercy.

Of course if we assume with Calvin that some human lives are chosen by the Creator, from all eternity, to be damned and destroyed, then God—or God the Father—must be seen as a menacing force, a force so far past the comprehension of even the most fervent mystic or the bravest theologian as to make our secular contemplation all but pointless. And with that same presumption of Calvin's (and before him, of the even more formidable Augustine), it would seem that the choices which predestine our behavior and our final destination have been made, for unrecoverable reasons that at least hint of conscious cruelty on God's part, far beyond the realms of human comprehension.

Thus any questions that an individual may ultimately ask about the meaning of his or her destiny will be idle gaming in a very long night—long by the infinitesimal standards of humankind. And while I can see that such a predisposing God is deducible from certain speeches in Hebrew scripture, certain words of Jesus, from outright claims in Paul's epistles (most vividly in his letter to the Ephesians, which may not be by Paul but has always had canonical standing in Christian scripture), and from the occasional real-life spectacle of a man or woman who seems undeniably cursed, I nonetheless recall quite plainly the many instants through multiple years in which I've soberly contemplated acts or words I knew to be dead-wrong or -right and have then deliberately chosen wrong or right in crystal clarity of will and aim.

So my inveterate conviction of personal freedom compels me—as it does most men and women, I suspect—to reject any hidebound belief in pre-election and predestination. Some of our choices seem to flow spontaneously from the facts and needs of a given moment; other choices feel inevitable, even fated; and we appear to have imperfect control over that difference. I feel convinced, however, that no one soul is damned from the start by a dice-throwing God. It seems more likely to me that all are, in some inscrutable way, saved forever. To indicate that such statements are no mere personal whim, I could go on, for instance, to point out also how drastically an outright Saved or Damned notion of Fate—a faith that even no Greek dramatist quite claims—collides with those assurances from Jesus and occasional earlier prophets that we are the children of a loving and merciful parental God (though I'll glance later at other speeches in which Jesus portrays an angry avenging final Judge).

Nonetheless, I'm prepared to ask if one of the most damaging weaknesses of modern Christianity and of some branches of Judaism doesn't arise as a direct result of our passionate need to believe both in our individual freedom and our innate worth—our deep-rooted conviction that we deserve and have amply earned the particular close attention of God. That resulting weakness is most visible in the insistence by centuries of clergy and generations of hungry souls that God, the Maker and Keeper of billions of galaxies of stars and planets seething in their violence, is literally our personal father as well—and a father, we're told, who is even more attentive and caring than the best of earthly fathers.

We're constantly asked to trust in the soothing voices which tell us that the stoker of the furnace of the most immense suns, the delicate fashioner (through the instrument of evolution) of the hummingbird's wings, the infant's lungs, the white shark's jaws, and the AIDS virus is likewise the

architect and builder of one's own fragile body—the very fingers with which I write these blundering words. And not only
is he my Maker and yours, he is steadily attuned to our needs
and fears and has the final purpose of bringing us toward him
in a union of everlasting bliss. Or so we're taught in the churches
and some of the synagogues known to me and in most of the
enduring prose and poetry of the Christian tradition.

To be sure, in one astonishingly ultimate and apparently
unique moment, Jesus addresses God as *abba*, the Aramaic
informal word for *father*. It is one of the rare moments when we
can be sure that we are hearing what scholars call the *ipsissima
verba* of Jesus, the convincing word and voice in which he
spoke on a given occasion (as we are similarly convinced when
he often introduces, rather than concludes, his most solemn
remarks with the words *Amen amen*, Hebrew words which the
King James version translates as *Verily, verily*). Surely any father
whom the adult Jesus can address as *abba* will hear all his
prayers and answer them with good—with bread not stones,
fish not serpents.

Elsewhere in the Gospels, Jesus extends that promise to all
his hearers and perhaps to the remainder of humanity—God
may be every human's benign father. Despite the distinguished
credentials which such promises bear, however, they've always
been as doubtful as they are welcome among realistically wary
believers. No theological learning is required, after all, to stand
in the ashes of one's private hopes or beside the literal ashes of
an innocent loved one—a five-year-old son, say, who has died
before our eyes in the torment of leukemia—and to wonder,
from that point in human time and place, just where *abba* is
now to be found. What precisely is *abba*'s address at the scalding

moment? What line will now reach him and will he reply? In an unbroken note of the most serious eloquence, from the known beginnings of sacred poetry, the cry of humankind has begged to know how the hand that made us has likewise struck us down or has let some other force destroy us.

I can only glance here at the Christian mystery of the Trinity—a belief in the existence of one God consisting of three persons: Father, Son, and Holy Spirit. I attempt to lighten that crucial obscurity for the students in my class in Milton's poetry by suggesting to them that, young as they are, they already comprise several distinct yet united persons—they may be, for instance, simultaneously and completely Child, Lover, Student, Mother, or Father. (Milton's private views on the Trinity were mildly heretical, though the fact is all but invisible in *Paradise Lost.*)

Belief in the Trinity is of such a dangerous complexity that many contemporary believers have ironed it out to their own comfort, a comfort that comes close to faith in several gods. Many Christians are unaware of a grievous misunderstanding when they attempt to see the Son of God and the Holy Spirit as our sources of boundless mercy while the Father becomes the distant and eventually negligible principle of law and justice. But Christian scripture and a close attention to human experience provide little defense for a dodge that tries to imagine the Father's punishing you through your child's illness while the Son and the Holy Spirit attend to the child's healing—or its safe transport to Heaven, if the Father's anger rejects all prayers.

At this hard point, again I hear your final question—does God care about us? . . . For what it's worth, my own conviction,

from here in my midsixties, is that a created universe which
has evolved the staggering richness of life that we observe on
this one planet can scarcely permit that phenomenon to die in
eventual cold silence like a candle forgotten in a room deserted
by all other life—not unless the components of that flame and
its fuel will transform into ongoing and enduring forms of
being and consciousness.

Even the law of entropy can't deny that the energy which
is steadily dispersed into space may have a destiny grander, or
more interesting, than darkness and frigid silence—and I
claim that just as the news is announced that the visible galaxies are apparently flinging outward, and apart from one another,
toward the perhaps nonexistent walls of the universe at a far
faster rate than we'd known. If I and the major part of the
human race are wrong in that hope for a conscious endurance,
then the worst that faces us is surely oblivion—purest black
rest like that afforded by the best anesthesia, with which
you're likely familiar. No dreams, no fears, no expectations, no
waking, no sense whatever of self or another.

It may be entirely a matter of the outlook I've been pro-
grammed to take ever since the conjunction of my sanguine
and welcoming parents. It may flow from some lucky gift in
my earliest days among often afflicted but finally laughing kin;
but if forced to speculate, I'd have to say that the mind in the
ultimate pith of things is benign, that it tells itself our long
slow story from a comprehensible taste for *stories*; and only a
mad mind hopes that stories end in crushed lives and strangled
cries. My bred-in-the-bone conviction about you is that you're
bound toward a goodness you can't avoid and that the amount
of calendar time which lies between you and that destination

is literally meaningless to God, though surely of the greatest importance to you.

Apt comfortless sayings, as you must know, are often brought out when a short life is threatened—*The good die young* or *Whom God loves, he soon reclaims*. A quick look at history will, at a minimum, confirm that God sets little if any importance on the length of a human life. Think only of Flannery O'Connor dying at thirty-nine, Raphael and van Gogh at thirty-seven, Mozart at thirty-five, Simone Weil at thirty-four, Schubert at thirty-one, Emily Brontë at thirty, and Keats at twenty-five.

Yet what human being, facing his own death or that of a loved one, was ever awarded the smallest share of that unplumbed equanimity with which God monitors time from eternity? In my own threatened days, I sometimes glimpsed the chance of calm surrender but never the smiling peace that turns its back on a count of the moments and years doled out to this one or that—the cut-down child, the doddering tyrant. And my hunger for more, and still more, competent working time is unabated.

Whatever you get from God or your own mind or these few pages, be assured at the end here that—once again—all I've said derives from no more than the faith and expectation of a single creature and the lucky disclosures he thinks he's glimpsed in a life already longer than either of his own parents had. If you think I'm mumbling in soft-brained error, I might not deny you. I may be gravely misled in any new notion I've offered.

I know I believe that God loves his creation, whatever his kind of *love* means for you and me. Again, some version of that belief lies near the center of all major creeds. From the range of emotions that might inspire you or me, or another rational human, to create a universe, love seems the one most likely to cause such a mammoth and long-lasting enterprise. The only other imaginable inspiration would seem to be a ravenous brutality or a cold curiosity of unthinkable proportions; and however burdened we and our world may be with intermittent darkness and worse, I suspect that very few human creatures would confess to believing that we're mad and managed by a psychopath of universal proportions.

So surely God works and watches, in some sense—no doubt many senses—from love or from some barely imaginable intensification of the ideal lover's feeling for the beloved—an emotion which Augustine defines in the words *Volo ut sis*, "I will you to be" or "I want you to be who you are." I don't claim certainty for much else I've said. But that claim feels like firm ground to me. And it would take more strength than I've got to deny Eliot's still assertion at the end of the *Four Quartets* that

> . . . all shall be well and
> All manner of thing shall be well
> When the tongues of flame are in-folded
> Into the crowned knot of fire
> And the fire and the rose are one. . . .

or Bach's findings at that final moment in the B Minor Mass when somber but glorious horns begin to bloom and then flood the abyss beneath the choir's "Give us peace" or Dante's hard-earned vision at the end of his *Comedy* that the "scattered leaves of all the universe" are gathered inward and bound together in one volume by love, that love which is both the binding and the fuel of all life and all movement—"The love that moves the sun and the other stars." In any case, I'd want you to know that I haven't dealt idly with the questions you ask nor do I, again, share easily the news of your trial.

Now that you've made this first contact, sad news from you would be a harsh discouragement. News of your intact perseverance would be most welcome. If my answer to what you so baldly ask amounts to no more than a stumbling guess, then know that this one long surmise comes from as deep in my mind and nature as I know how to go. Whatever a far-off fellow creature can offer by way of the earnest company of prayer and thought, I offer gladly.

All hope from
Reynolds

EARTHLY FATHERS

He wasn't our real father. He was Daddy Robert. The one who had a last name different from ours. *Charles Robert Sawyer.*

Daddy Robert—the father who looked different from us. Whose face wasn't like ours. His was round—ours were long. And he wasn't skinny, as we were. He was tall, but stocky and strong. When my older brother, Tommy, and I asked him to flex his muscles for us, he usually demurred. But when he complied, his biceps became like boulders. Tommy and I each wrapped our tightest grip around an arm, and, in one swoop, he lifted us both off the ground.

Daddy Robert didn't talk to us the way our mother did. And he didn't touch us the way Momma did. He was hard to Momma's soft, no to Momma's yes. He smoked Kools, in the green package, not Momma's red Winstons. And he blew the smoke out through his nose, like a dragon, not just out of his mouth the way Momma did.

He wasn't the father in our baby photos—the father who held us, jiggled us, gave us nicknames to go with the first traits we showed. He hadn't been there then.

Yet Daddy Robert *was* our father. He'd been with us from the time *we* could remember. He was the father we knew—the one we touched, saw, tasted, smelled. The one we examined as he napped on Saturday afternoons—his stomach rising and falling, his twisty gold watchband stretched around his thick, hairy wrist, his black-framed glasses tucked neatly between his ears and brown hair. Everything rising and falling, rising and falling.

He was the father whose few waking words amused us, scared us, taught us to pay attention, doubled us over in laughter as no one else could. Whose work—along with our mother's—gave us allowance, school clothes, even cars when we graduated. Whose every expression, tender or loud, loving or profane, increased his mystery to us.

He rarely divulged his own youth to us. But he took us to the elementary school field to hit pop flies to us, so we could break in our gloves before our first year of Little League. He punted high ones to us at the old high-school football field—the one where his knee had been hurt, years before—so we could practice catching and see how it felt to be out there. He was the father who seemed to love us, but who at times seemed apart from us and alone.

Our real father was Daddy Ronnie. *Ronnie Witten Burk.*

The father who had died before we knew him. The one who'd swept Momma off her feet in college. A tall, lanky senior who walked into the lobby of her dorm and recognized the blonde freshman, even though it was a blind date. Her back was turned to him, yet somehow he knew this was Patricia Meadows. He checked his cool, strode up behind her, and said, "Hi, Patty Pigtails." And that was that.

He was the father who, as a first-year coach in the small town of West, Texas, had set his sights on becoming head track coach at Rice. Who had tossed Tommy, less than a year old, high into the air and made him laugh. Who had looked at me as an infant and said to Momma, "He's our special one, isn't he?"

Daddy Ronnie—the one who'd gotten polio because he never got vaccinated. Who thought about us as he lay in an iron lung, knowing he was going to die. Whose gravestone we put flowers on whenever we visited our grandparents in the faraway town of Brady.

Ronnie Burk. The father who lived in heaven. Who lived in our minds, in our sudden, surprising griefs, in gold-and-black picture frames hidden away in dresser drawers. Whose face was friendly and handsome in the photograph that hung in the hallway of our grandparents' home. Whose eyes gazed out contentedly from under dark brows in that photo—looking somewhere toward an infinite horizon, so many years above our heads.

That was Daddy Ronnie. Not Daddy Robert.

And that was why we weren't perfect, we thought. Because Daddy Ronnie had died.

It was why we were sad sometimes when people talked about him. And awkward when people mentioned him around Daddy Robert. It was why Tommy and I fought constantly, with each other and with Buzzy, our younger half brother who came along later. It was why I was caught between my two brothers, wishing for peace half the time, warring against Buzzy the other half. It was why we sometimes heard yelling matches behind closed doors. It was why things weren't perfect.

It's why I can still be mean today, I think, for no particular reason, and to no one particular—except, sadly, to those I love most. It's why I tend to rock on my heels when I'm talking with someone. Why I don't know what to do with my hands at social gatherings. Why I don't make decisions easily, or even know—*truly* know—what I want.

It's why I possess the ghostly traits of one father, idiosyncrasies I never witnessed—compulsively making lists, wagging a foot while reclining, greeting people with magnanimity. Being curious and inquiring with acquaintances, yet vaguely distant. Friendly and hail-fellow-well-met on some days, moody and retreating on others.

It's why I have the familiar traits of the earthly father I *did* witness—the way I jest when I'm ill at ease, deflect compliments, tease with unearned familiarity—a familiarity meant to usher in an informal bond, but one that actually establishes distance.

It's why I have the brooding thoughts of one father, the practical worries of the other. The gracious humor of one, the earthy, bawdy perspective of the other. The pretension to otherworldly nobility of one, the lip-biting stoicism of the other.

Maybe it's why. Or maybe it's not.

But Daddy Robert *was* perfect, we thought. Because he *was* our father.

I looked at his picture next to Momma's on the wall in their bedroom and saw a perfect man—handsome, muscular, youthful. How was he any less perfect than Daddy Ronnie? Both had dark hair—not like Momma, whose hair was blonde. Both were tall and strong, in contrast to Momma's softness and tenderness. Both were larger than life to us, larger even than our imaginations allowed. The way all fathers are.

Daddy Robert—our father with us. *Robert Sawyer.* The insurance man, not the coach. The city man, not the farm boy.

The father who went dove hunting one Saturday each year, not the father who wanted to go fishing every weekend. The Deke, not the Sig Ep. The University of Texas dropout, not the North Texas State grad. The powerful running back, not the lanky split end. The one who'd twisted his knee on a high-school football field and was never the same. Not the one who went to college on a track scholarship.

He was Daddy Robert—the second one, not the first one.

Daddy Robert wasn't the one who might have raised us on a farm in keeping with family tradition. Who might have taught us to fish in a stock tank, grow vegetables, milk cows, kill rattlesnakes. Who might have disciplined us with stern authority. Who might have.

Instead, Daddy Robert was the one who came home at night from his job in Dallas. He brought home bags of Sonic burgers or Pizza Hut boxes on weeknights when Momma stayed late at the high school for her students' play practices. He mowed the lawn and washed the car on weekends. He spanked Tommy for getting bad grades in conduct. He got irritated at us, threw footballs to us in the front yard, fried an occasional dinner, laughed with Momma, got in arguments with her, stayed up late on Christmas Eve setting up our toys. He scared us into laughter when we turned off all the lights in the house and had to find him, and he'd pop up out of nowhere shining a flashlight underneath his face, having covered it with Momma's pantyhose. He scared us for real at times.

At times he pounded his fist on the kitchen table when one of us spilled something. At times he let out a string of curse words whenever something went awry. He couldn't hide his frustration whenever we did something wrong that we didn't know was wrong. And he couldn't hide his contempt whenever we did something wrong and we knew it.

Daddy Ronnie—our father in heaven. Tommy and I were reminded of him every day at school, as we sang "My Country 'Tis of Thee." When we came to the line that says, "Land where our fathers died," we each started crying in our respective classrooms. Every day we were taken to the principal's office separately, and our mother was phoned at the high school.

We never talked about our sadness to each other, much less offered an explanation to anyone else. But we each knew why the other cried. We cried because *he* had died. And even though we'd never known him, we knew his dying was sad.

Tommy was fifteen months old, I eight weeks, when Daddy Ronnie died. Our grandmother, Nanny, was a nurse, and she'd given each of us our polio shots—Momma, Tommy, me. But, evidently, Daddy Ronnie waited around too long, and never took his. He got sick, caught pneumonia from the complications, and died—all within two weeks.

"Why didn't he take the vaccine?"

My mother hesitates. She musters a gracious smile for me. She always does when we speak of those days.

"I don't know, honey. I think he was probably working out at the time, trying to stay in shape. He was careful about his training. He never wanted to put anything in his body that might interrupt that."

But, polio?

.   .   .

When you're younger, you accept that kind of answer. I accepted it as a child—not because it made sense, but because it gave me something more of him. Something more to imagine about him, to lock onto. One more myth that sculpted another feature in him—dedication? pride? neglect?

Grief does odd things to people. When Daddy Ronnie died, and Tommy and I were still babies, Momma decided to go back to college to finish her degree.

Patricia Meadows Burk.

She knew she had to support us somehow. So she moved us back in with her parents, Nanny and Granddaddy, and reenrolled at North Texas State College, where she'd met Daddy Ronnie. The college was in Denton, on the far side of Dallas from my grandparents' home in Waxahachie. The drive was a three-hour round trip at minimum. Momma decided to room at the college during the week, and drive home on weekends to be with us.

A year later, Tommy and I stood holding Nanny's hands on a curb near the campus, waiting to greet Momma. It was a Saturday morning in the fall. We watched as a parade of uniformed college students passed by us on the street. Finally, we caught a glimpse of our mother. From around the corner chugged a long, wide homecoming float. Momma was standing on it and waving, wearing a crown on her head.

"Did we recognize you?"

The briefest of moments passes. Again, she smiles.

"Nanny pointed me out to you. Tommy was old enough to recognize me, and he waved."

Her eyes are wet.

"But you were still too young. Nanny took your hand and waved it."

She lets herself cry.

She'd cried back then, too, she says. Even as she waved to everyone in the crowd.

She just hadn't known what to do, she said.

I remember a portrait of her wearing a crown. It was a tinted photograph of faint yellow and blue, to match her blonde hair and blue-green eyes. It hung somewhere in Nanny and Grand-daddy's home, and we saw it every day. Whether the crown in that photo was the same one we saw in the parade, I don't know. It easily could have been another. Granddaddy had always told my mother, "Tricia, walk in like you own the place." She took him at his word.

Yet it would have been difficult for my mother to be arro-gant. Nanny wouldn't abide any favoritism in her family. For a lifelong Republican (an odd loyalty for a dirt-poor farm girl from red-clay Georgia), she was strictly democratic toward her children. Granddaddy at least gave lip service to this, and still does.

"I love you, Daddy," one of his children says.

"I love all my children," he answers slyly.

But Uncle Dennis, Momma's younger brother, tells me, "Tricia always had Daddy wrapped around her finger."

I never would have guessed it. In fact, I'd have thought the opposite. I'd known my mother to have a flaw of melancholy. She cried at night when she read to Tommy and me—books with heart-wrenching passages, such as *Black Beauty* and

Charlotte's Web. We learned to cry along with her, even if we hadn't been listening.

Yet her melancholy made her a good listener, and a consistent giver to others. She seemed to want to shore up others' courage in places where hers couldn't be. In some ways, she was supremely confident of the ground beneath her feet—in other ways, frightfully aware of the fragility of life.

She lay on the narrow bed in my grandparents' small guest bedroom. She'd lain there almost continually for a month.

The air was still. The afternoon sun bore through the blinds, making dust particles glow like circling vultures.

Someone entered the room.

"Tricia."

She was unable to move.

"Tricia."

It was her father.

"Oh," she said.

He pulled up a chair.

"What, Daddy.

He leaned forward, his hands folded.

"You have to get up, Tricia."

She said nothing.

"You've got to get up and do something."

She knew this. But what was there to do?

"What do you think I should I do, Daddy?"

"What do you want to do?"

"I don't know."

She didn't.

"Have you thought about it at all?"

She had imagined only a few things.

"I thought about becoming a stewardess."

Her father dropped his head.

"That's not for you, Tricia."

She turned her head to the wall. Gazed at the big square of sunlight. It had barely moved since she last saw it.

"Why don't you go back and finish school?" he said.

She didn't answer. She was thinking about her sons.

"Your mother and I can help you. I think you need to finish your education, Tricia. Nobody can take that away from you."

We were the sons. Tommy—*Thomas Witten Burk.* And Scotty—*Ronnie Scott Burk.*

Everybody said Tommy looked just like Daddy Ronnie—from the slight, downward curve of his nose to the pronounced dimple in his chin. We checked this out for ourselves in our baby albums. Black-and-white photos, with Momma's handwriting at the bottom of each, pasted onto black pages. There was a picture of Tommy lying in his crib, looking up, his tiny nose jagged even then. *That* does *look like Daddy Ronnie.* A picture of him wearing Daddy Ronnie's hunting hat. A picture of him in diapers, trying to walk in Daddy Ronnie's work boots. Then, a picture of Daddy Ronnie holding Tommy in one arm—father and son staring comically at each other.

"He would toss you in the air," Granddaddy told Tommy, "and you would *laugh* and *laugh.*"

When Tommy got big enough, Nanny bought him some jeans. She cuffed the pants using white material with a red polka-dot pattern. That Friday, when Momma came home from Denton and saw Tommy wearing those pants, she burst into tears. She had the same reaction later, when she walked in one weekend and heard Tommy call Nanny "Momma."

That's the day, my mother tells me, when she began racing home even faster. She regularly topped one hundred and ten. Every week, she was stopped by one of the highway patrolmen on U.S. 77. She didn't care. She became known among them as the "wicked widow of Waxahachie." Yet those men always let her go without giving her a ticket. They'd all heard her story, at one time or another, and they believed her as she told it. Her first baby had become a little boy, she said, and she hadn't been looking.

On Saturdays, we all watched a TV program hosted by a dark-haired emcee. Every time Tommy saw this man, he pointed to the screen excitedly and said, "Daddy." He thought it was our father. Our father—somewhere out there, away from us, but somehow still near.

In later years, my big brother always claimed he remembered Daddy Ronnie. But I was never sure if he did. Whenever he made this claim to me, he looked more dreamy than convincing. I always thought it was merely the dream of our father that appealed to Tommy—that our first father was alive somewhere, even if it was in heaven.

There's a pair of elementary-school pictures of Tommy and me that, in my mind, typified us. My brother's sandy brown hair is slightly grown out from a crew cut. He's got a cowlick on one side of his forehead that would stay with him throughout his life. His head is turned slightly to one side, and you can't tell from his expression if he's being sly or just shy. Either would have been true. More tellingly, there's a round, slightly misshapen, blood-colored scab between his upper lip and his right nostril. How Tommy managed to get a scrape in that unlikely location may have been clear at the time, but it escapes us all now.

As for me, I'm looking straight at the camera. Careful to turn neither to the right nor left. Just doing my job, teacher—staying out of trouble, making good grades, using my extra time after assignments to draw pictures. My hair is combed neatly, my face well scrubbed, my forehead shiny. I'm even wearing a button-down collar. My singular expression, a smile.

Smiley Burk. The name given to me by Grandjesse, Daddy Ronnie's father. Always a smile for everyone, he said.

And the sweet one, everybody said. Not that Tommy wasn't sweet, too; he just never seemed to care about coming across that way. Everyone loved him regardless. He wasn't mean, they realized—he just wanted something, all the time. Even if it meant picking fights with me.

"He was all over you," my relatives tell me. "Just hanging on you, all the time. I mean *all* the time."

But even then, I was Smiley Burk. Always a smile. Until, like my brother, I wanted something. The problem was, no one ever knew what I wanted. (How could they, when I didn't?) I would smile along happily through the day, and from one day to the next. Then, out of the blue, something would snap.

One day Granddaddy and Nanny saw it coming. But, apparently, there was nothing they could do to stop it. They were about to drive us somewhere, and had placed me in the back seat of their Volkswagen. When they returned with Tommy, I'd kicked a hole through the back of the passenger seat.

Smiley Burk.

"Nobody knows to this day what possessed you to do that, Scotty," Granddaddy chuckles.

An odd mixture of things, perhaps. Like those days when heavy raindrops fall, even though the sun is still shining.

My mother has said on rare occasions that she had only two blind dates in her life and she married both of them.

When Daddy Robert became our father, we began to learn what fathers do. He dressed smartly and neatly, and he was conscientious about our appearance. On Sunday mornings, he tried not to puff smoke in our faces as he raked Momma's steel comb across our tender heads. I stood as still as possible, in my khaki pants, white shirt, bow tie, and the loafers Daddy Robert had shined. He topped everything off by opening a bottle of cologne and peppering my face with his palm, saying, "Here, let's put some smell-good on you." When he'd finished, and I walked stiffly out of the bathroom, he whistled the Texaco tune behind me, "You can trust your car to the man who wears the star—" and Momma had to stifle her laughter.

Then he drove Tommy and me to Sunday school, handed us each a nickel or a dime for the collection plate, and dropped us off.

We placed our coins in the round, wooden plate that got passed around the table in class. But one day, as we were walking into the big church building, Tommy stopped me.

"Don't give them your nickel," he said knowingly. "Don't put it in the plate anymore. Just keep it."

"Why?"

"All they do is buy chairs with it."

I looked down at the tarnished coin in my palm. They used this to buy chairs? I thought this money went to God. That, somehow, it got all the way to heaven. That's where everything good was. How could they taint this God-money by using it here—*on chairs?*

I had a hard time imagining God when we were at church. He was everywhere, our teachers said, yet he was invisible.

But I had actually seen a picture of God. It was in a book at the doctor's office. God was a little boy, like my brother and me—with brown, curly hair, and a little round purple hat that sat on the back of his head. He was with his father, in a workshop. After that, I supposed, he grew up to be God.

Yet that's how I continued to imagine him—in his purple hat, up on a cloud somewhere that was just big enough for him to play on. And every once in a while, God crawled over to the edge of cloud—being very careful, so he wouldn't fall off—and he looked down at us all, and loved us.

HERMITS AND HARLOTS:
AN EXPLORATION OF IMAGES

(From *Harvard Divinity Bulletin*)

I owe the opportunity to speak to you today to Paul Dudley, who over two hundred years ago established this anniversary lecture "for the confirmation, illustration, and improvement of the great Articles of the Christian religion properly so called or the revelation which Jesus Christ the Son of God was pleased to make, first by himself and afterwards by his holy Apostles to his Church and the world for their Salvation."

What Dudley expected his speakers to talk about in lectures on "revealed religion" I am not entirely sure—probably neither hermits nor harlots. But by extending the definition of "holy apostles" to include hermits and by taking his reference to "the world" to include harlots, I would like today to examine with you some texts from the deserts of Egypt in the fourth century. Let us hope that the fact of hearing words from these texts about "the revelation which Jesus Christ the Son of God was pleased to make" will indeed satisfy the founder of these lectures as it becomes "for our salvation" for us.

To illustrate the kind of importance I think lies in the monastic literature that comes from the desert, may I begin in the twentieth century rather than the fourth, with the last stanza of W. H. Auden's poem "In Memory of W. B. Yeats," who died in January 1939, just before the outbreak of World War II, in a time as grievous as both the fourth century and our own:

> In the desert of the heart
> Let the healing fountain start,
> In the prison of his days
> Teach the free man how to praise.

The "desert of the heart" and the "healing fountains" are I think at the basis of much of the literature of early monasticism. To illustrate this I have chosen to talk about both in relation to friends of mine. I do not find it possible to write or talk deeply about those whom I do not love, so you must excuse me for choosing my friends as the subject of today's discourse. These are, to refer to my title, both hermits and harlots.

Who were these hermits? Those who lived in the *eremus*, the desert. In the fourth century in Egypt there was a flowering of Christian monasticism in the desert that was never equaled and that provided a basic reference point for all later Christian monks. The records of these people are in the form of short stories about them, collections of their sayings, some of their letters, and the travel diaries of those who went to visit them. A few of them were scholars and educated, a very few were priests; most of them were laypeople of the fellahin, or peasant, class, grown up and experienced, not children who had chosen to become monks. Their stories vary from the tale of Arsenius, a friend of the emperor, a wealthy, well-educated man from Italy and a never-ending source of wonder to his simpler brothers, to those of Moses the Black, a Nubian from the south who had been a robber, and Apollo, a lively but uncouth shepherd who had been a murderer.

The records of these people show they inhabited a world of spiritual daring and adventure, in which all kinds of experiments in living at the limits of existence, human and divine, took place with energy and delight. They became the focus for a pious and thriving tourist route and many of the records of them come from recollections of their visitors. Later theologians like Evagrius and John Cassian structured their remembrances of the desert into formal theological accounts of this way of life, but the original stories are both less sophisticated and more lively. It is with these that I am concerned.

Who were the harlots? The word was used from its Old English root to describe men who roamed around, both actually and sexually, until in the sixteenth century it began to be applied, like the word "shrew," which had a similar history, to women who were roving in their sexual adventures. I am using the word in its modern sense, the equivalent of a woman who is a prostitute. This is not to imply that there were not men as well as women connected with the desert of whom stories of sexual indiscipline were told; in fact, in its widest sense most of the monks fell into that class. None of the desert fathers were born saints; they were adults with experience of life behind them; they had their own background of sin and suffering. But among their stories the most striking of all were about women harlots who became hermits.

There were plenty of prostitutes in the ancient world—both high-class call girls, the courtesans of nobles and emperors and temple prostitutes, and women on the streets. They were often highly educated and sometimes rich. They were independent women who, like widows, were free from the control of husbands or fathers; they could amass and dispose of property and of their persons, and sometimes this led them to choose the ascetic life of the desert. In the desert they were received by monks neither with lust nor condemnation, but welcomed with wonder and admiration. These examples of dramatic and public sin turning to heartfelt and private repentance, from the city to the desert, were not primarily told as stories about sexual lust seen through abstemious eyes; they were not so peripheral. Etymologically, the essence of being a monk is to be *monos*, one, alone sexually, not with a partner; the essence of the prostitute is to have many physical partners. In these stories these extremes are linked in a dramatic fashion in individuals, catching the imagination and stirring the heart. As Emile Malle put it in *The Gothic Image:* "Beauty consuming itself like incense burned before God in solitude, far from the eyes of men became the most stirring image of penance conceivable. The generosity of expiation, the gift of tears, were to the Christian a perpetual subject of meditation."

This center of repentance is, in fact, the key to the lives of all the desert monks, and their essence. And as with repentance in any age, the true explanation of it is not psychological, but theological. What moved Arsenius so that "he had a hollow in his chest channeled out by the tears that fell from his eyes all his life" was not a gloomy reflection upon his own acts of sin in the past, but a heartrending understanding of the love of Christ our God always before him. "It was said of him that on Saturday evenings preparing for the glory of Sunday, he would turn his back on the sun and stretch out his hands in prayer towards the heavens, till once again the sun shone on his face."

As I have said, the conversion of prostitutes, their turning from selling sexual love to a life of receiving the gift of love, was especially striking to the monks of the fourth century. Perhaps the earliest and simplest version of such stories in this literature is the account of the conversion of Paësia, as follows:

The parents of a young girl died and she was left an orphan. She was called Paësia. She decided to make her house a hospice for the use of the fathers of Scetis. But in the course of time her resources were exhausted and she began to be in want. Some wicked men came to see her and turned her aside from her aim. She began to live an evil life to the point of becoming a prostitute. The fathers, learning this, were deeply grieved and they called John the Dwarf and said to him: "We have learned that this sister is living an evil life. While she could she gave us charity, so now it is our turn to offer her charity and to go to her assistance. Go to see her then and according to the wisdom that God has given you, put things right for her."

So Abba John went to see her and said to the old doorkeeper, "Tell your mistress I am here." But she sent him away saying, "From the start you ate her goods and see how poor she is now." Abba John said, "Tell her I have something that will be very helpful to her." The doorkeeper's children mocked him, saying, "What have you to give her that you want to meet her?" He replied, "How do you know what I am going to give her?" The old woman went up and spoke to her mistress about him. Paësia said to her, "Those monks are always going about and finding pearls." Then she got ready and said to the doorkeeper, "Please bring him to me."

As he was coming up, she got ready for him and lay down on the bed. Abba John entered and sat beside her. Looking into her eyes, he said to her, "What have you got against Jesus that you behave like this?" When she heard this, she became completely still. Then Abba John bent his head and began to weep copiously. She asked him, "Abba, why are you crying?" He raised his head, then lowered it again, weeping, and said to her, "I see Satan playing in your face; how should I not weep?" Hearing this, she said to him, "Abba, is it possible to repent?" He replied, "Yes." She said, "Take me wherever you wish." "Let us go," he said, and she got up and went with him.

Paësia is described as an orphan who had given hospitality to the monks of Scetis and was therefore well known to them; she undertook a life of prostitution because she became poor, and the implication is that she had beggared herself through charity toward them. Their motive in visiting her was neither desire nor rebuke, but loving-kindness. It was their tears of care for her that touched her heart. She died in the desert on the way there, and John commented, "One single hour of repentance has brought her more than the penitence of many who persevere without showing such fervor in repentance."

There is a similar story of a brother whose natural sister became a prostitute in the city. He went to see her and was bringing her back, repenting, to the desert, but like Paësia, she died before they reached it. The moral drawn was the same, that "one hour of repentance is enough."

Such stories were well known and much used as edifying
tales for monks. Preeminent among them was a group of four
longer stories, each written in Greek but translated into Latin
and circulating as a group in the *Vitae Patrum*, that popular reading matter for monasteries and convents of the West and also a
source of examples for preachers throughout the Middle Ages.
The story from the Gospels of the composite figure Mary Magdalene as a converted prostitute and great contemplative was of
course even more popular and better known, but the other four
illustrate the theme as well. The first is the story of Mary of
Egypt; the second, the tale of Thaïs; the third, that of Maria,
the niece of Abraham; and the fourth, the history of Pelagia.

Mary of Egypt has been the heroine, from the fifth century
onward, of a story of dramatic repentance. Elaborated and
extended, it still forms a central theme of the liturgy of the
Eastern Orthodox Church for the fifth Sunday of Lent, the
Sunday of St. Mary of Egypt, in which the prostitute in need
of redemption is seen as the sinful soul of everyman, unable to
repent and asking only for the mercy of God: "Thee we have
as a pattern of repentance, all-holy Mary. Pray to Christ that
in the season of the fast this gift may be conferred on us, to
raise thee in our hymns with faith and love."

Mary chose to live from childhood in Alexandria as a prostitute. It was said that she enjoyed her trade so much that she
did not take money for it, but lived by spinning. Going to the
harbor one day, she took a ship for Jerusalem with a party of
pilgrims, each of whom she seduced during the voyage. In
Jerusalem she continued to find new lovers until one day she
came with a crowd of pilgrims to the Holy Sepulcher, where
the relic of the cross was offered for veneration. Wishing to

enter, she found herself held back by an invisible force, some-thing that shocked her into awareness of herself for the first time. Turning to an icon of the Mother of God, she promised repentance if the Virgin would first pray for her to be allowed to venerate the cross. She found she could do this and then went at once over the river Jordan and lived there in solitude for many years. There was no period for counseling, advice, sacraments, preparation, or even instruction; one genuine moment of truth was received by Mary of Egypt completely, and she acted upon what she knew.

Not that it was easy. Her own account of the suffering she had to go through alone makes sobering reading. There is the moment of assent to God, but from it follow all the works of love and degrees of agonizing change. After many years, she was discovered one day by the good monk Zosimas. Mary told him her story, and received from him communion. Finally when she died, she was buried by him, with the help of a lion from the desert. Such a story is clearly packed with intricate symbols— her approach to the cross; a detail of three loaves of bread, which Mary took with her into the desert; her action of passing over the waters of the Jordan; her appearance by moonlight, walking on the waters; the lion who came out of the desert at her death. All are replete with Christian significance that would not be lost upon those who heard or read the story. But really central to its message is the contrast of the good, self-satisfied monk Zosima, who really thought there was no one in the world more holy than he after a lifetime of prayer and effort, and the penitent sinner who had nothing but stillness before the work of God. The story is about the amazing fact that the free gift of redemption is not for the specialists alone, but for all.

Was this story true? Certainly there were prostitutes in both Alexandria and Jerusalem, some of whom may well have retired to the desert as ascetics. There may have been an actual person at the center of this story in spite of the fact that at times the story of Mary of Egypt was confused with apocryphal legends about the later life of Mary Magdalene. Honorius of Autun, for instance, said of Mary Magdalene:

It is told that after she, with the other disciples, saw the Lord ascend into heaven, she received the Holy Spirit with the others. Afterwards, because of her love for Him, she did not wish to see any other man, but coming into the desert she lived for many years in a cave. When a certain wandering priest came to her and inquired who she was, she answered that she was Mary the Sinner and that he had been sent to bury her body. With these words she departed from this world, which she had long despised, entering into glory, and with angels singing a hymn she ascended to the Lord.

This somewhat garbled memory of the story of Mary of Egypt here attributed to St. Mary Magdalene was denounced by the medieval author of *The Life of St. Mary Magdalene;* he included some very lively information about the later career of his heroine and her brother Lazarus and sister Martha in southern France, but he denied that this piece of legend belonged to her: "It is very false and borrowed by creators of fables from the deeds of the Egyptian penitent."

The point of both stories is, of course, the same: the prostitute, the lover of many men, is turned by love of Christ to the solitude of the desert and is there absorbed by the ardors of prayer and penance that overflow for the healing of the world. When later writers wanted to uncover the dynamics of repentance, they chose this story; it has always had a vivid appeal to preachers and liturgical worshipers, as well as to dramatists and poets, as in Jonathan Heath-Stubbs's poem "Maria Aegyptica":

> Thrust back by hands from the sanctuary door
>   Mary of Egypt, that hot whore,
> Fell on the threshold. Priests, candles, acolytes,
>   Shivered in flame upon her failing sight
>   And when at last she died,
> With burning tender eyes, hair like dark flame,
>   The golden lion came;
> And with his terrible claws scooped out a tomb,
>   Gently in the loose soil,
> And gave that dry burnt corpse to the earth's womb.

When Humbert of Rome wrote a pattern sermon book for preachers in the thirteenth century, he included a sermon that could be preached to fallen women. Just how he expected his friars to meet these ladies is not clear, and it may be that the sermon was included only for the sake of completeness. The penitent sinners whom he used to illustrate the hope held out for prostitutes were Mary Magdalene, Mary of Egypt, and Pelagia. All three, he said, found the sins of the flesh hard to relinquish; they enjoyed what they did, they were used to doing it, and they were notorious for it. With many biblical examples, Humbert went on to show that they turned to three genuine ways of repentance: they wept much, they went away into solitude, and they suffered greatly in their penances. At death they were taken into very great glory. To expand that point, Humbert refers to another repentant harlot, Thaïs, for whom Paul the Simple saw a marvelous bed prepared in heaven. Where sin abounded, concluded Humbert, grace did much more abound. Here two more of the harlots of Egypt were introduced for the edification of the thirteenth century: Pelagia and Thaïs.

Pelagia was an actress in Antioch, and therefore belonged to the class of immoral persons such as jesters, mimics, jongleurs, clowns, and musicians who used their bodies to give pleasure for payment. Her story, told by James the Deacon, began when she passed through the streets of the city one day with her companions, dressed in pearls, singing and laughing, in a cloud of sweet perfumes, accompanied by music, delighting all the senses. She was seen by a group of bishops, all of whom hid their faces in horror except for the Bishop Nonnus, a monk from the desert, who "did long and most intently regard her and after she had passed by still he gazed and his eyes went after her."

The account continues: "Turning his head, he looked at the bishops sitting around him. 'Did not,' he said, 'her great beauty delight you?' " The story then showed Nonnus weeping when he was alone because in his own life he had not cared to prepare his soul to please God half as carefully as Pelagia had cared to prepare her body to please men. Pelagia, meanwhile, aware of and moved by his interest in her, heard him preaching and wrote him a letter asking him to prepare her for baptism. Nonnus received and baptized Pelagia and later helped her to run away disguised as a man to become a hermit in Palestine. There is a theme of tender love between the two that reached its conclusion when the Deacon James, who wrote the story, went to Jerusalem and was asked by Nonnus to visit the "hermit

Pelagius," of whom so many wonders were told. James realized when he arrived that this was Pelagia, and gave her greetings from Nonnus; when he made a second visit she had died, loved and admired as a hermit and only known as woman when prepared for burial.

It is a story of great charm told with a moving simplicity, in which the beauty of a woman revealed the glory of God to a monk and stood as judgment on the whole life of a timid, self-righteous episcopate. It is also another story in which love and wonder, rather than revulsion and condemnation, moved a soul toward Christ; and it is also a love story, of deep care for the integrity of each by the other. Perhaps writers did not retell it so often because it is already told superbly well; or perhaps the idea of the monk and bishop gazing in wonder at a lovely actress on the road was felt to be too dangerous in a more prurient age. At any rate, there are few repetitions of the story of Pelagia in popular literature in the Middle Ages.

More popular was the savage tale of Thaïs, the shortest and the least appealing of this group of *sanctae meretrices*. Thaïs was a prostitute in Alexandria who attracted great trade and caused violence and even murder among her jealous lovers. Like Mary and Pelagia, she was wealthy. Paphnutius, one of the tougher and more unbending monks of the desert, heard of this, disguised himself, and went to challenge her. Unlike Zosima and Nonnus, he used stern words of rebuke to her, and she repented and followed him into the desert, first burning all her ill-gotten gains. Immured in a cell in a convent with no outlet, she passed three years alone in her own filth, praying only, "O thou who didst create me, have mercy upon me." Paphnutius visited St. Anthony and his disciple Paul, and there was told of a vision in which a rich bed prepared in heaven for a saint was revealed and known to be for Thaïs. Paphnutius opened her cell to assure her that her repentance had been accepted in heaven; she died within a few days.

This story formed the basis for one of the plays of Hrotswitha, a canoness of the abbey of Gandersheim, in the tenth century. Hrotswitha admired the comedies of Terence and set herself to write plays that would praise the chastity of Christian women. In her play *Paphnutius,* she used the story with great skill and sensitivity. It belongs to a group of plays that she sent to the court of Otto II after her first plays had been welcomed there, and it may be that a certain desire to impress the literati of the court induced her to place in the first act a long discussion of the liberal arts in the mouth of the unlikely figure of Paphnutius. In the rest of the play, however, Hrotswitha retells the story keeping close to the source, making a vivid and dramatic scene out of the burning of Thaïs's goods, handling the dialogue before she is shut into her cell with great insight into her shrinking yet courageous words. In spite of elaborations, the point of the story remained what it had always been: the patient love of God toward the needy. It is significant that when this story was included in the Latin collection of sayings of the desert fathers, it was not placed in the section "Lust," as an example of Thaïs's conversion from sin, but in the section "Patience"; it is the long-suffering and infinite patience of God that is underlined, not the surface shortcomings of humans.

Hrotswitha included among her plays another on the same theme, a dramatic presentation of the story of Maria, the niece of the desert father Abraham. The story forms the end of the life of Abba Abraham the hermit, who received into his hermitage when he was old his young orphaned niece Maria. He taught the seven-year-old heiress how to sing the Psalms and how to fast and keep vigil, and disposed of her inheritance so that she might never be tempted by worldly goods. After many years of companionship in prayer, with Abraham and his friend and disciple Ephriam, who wrote the account of Abraham's life, Maria was seduced by a visiting cleric and in despair ran away and became a prostitute in the city. Her uncle heard where she was and how she was employed and, disguised as a soldier, went to find her. Entering the brothel, he approached Maria in her room as a lover and then revealed himself to her, begging her to return and learn repentance with the support of her uncle and Ephriam, who, he affirmed, both loved her. There was no judgment, no condemnation of any sexual sin, only assurance that all that was wrong was to despair. The story emphasizes that there is a way out of every sin and that is, simply, to chose life and love instead of self-accusation and guilt.

Maria was moved to tears by the kindness of the old man and said, "Go before, and I will follow your goodness and kiss the traces of your footsteps; for you have so grieved for me that you would come and draw me out of this cesspit." In the desert, Maria lived a life of repentance and her tears and prayers became a source of healing to those who heard her. The story ends with a moving passage by Ephriam, written after the death of both Abraham and Maria, an example of the response of the average to the lives of the stars:

Alas for me, for those two have fallen asleep and gone their way to the Lord, in whom they believed; their minds were never occupied with worldly business, but only with the love of God. And I, unprepared and unfit, remain here, and lo, winter has overtaken me and the winds of infinity find me naked and poor and without any covering of good deeds.

These stories of sin and repentance remained popular especially in the monastic circles for which they were written. It is perhaps worth asking how they can be read today. The difficulty is this: we read the Bible and indeed all texts with a narrow concern for what we call fact, which is quite alien to this literature. In the world of the early church, accustomed to reading the scriptures with the inner eye of faith, no text, and especially no spiritual text, would be of interest simply for its surface meaning; that would be too thin by far. The key to the meaning of these tales is underlined by the use made in them of scripture. For example, in the story of Abraham and his niece Maria, Ephriam breaks off his narrative at a crucial point, indeed at the climax, to give what seems at first a rather obscure reference to Genesis: "Come now, beloved brethren, and let us marvel at this second Abraham. The first Abraham went forth to do battle with the kings and smote them and brought back his nephew Lot; but this second Abraham went forth to do battle with the Evil One and having vanquished him brought home again his niece in greater triumph."

The obvious parallels of the two Abrahams and their nephew and niece are not the whole, nor even the center, of this comparison. A glance at commentaries on this passage from Genesis 14 shows how it was read habitually by the faithful: Abraham, "the mystical figure of Christ, the seed of

Abraham," went to rescue Lot, who had been captured by "four kings with five," that is, "the four elements of the worlds are signified with the five senses by which man is taken captive"; "Abraham went forth to that battle with the Cross of Christ and in the name of Jesus, that strong sign, that banner of faith, and brought back the captive with triumph." In other words, these stories of the harlots of Egypt were presented and read as stories about the one theme of perennial interest in every age: the redemption of souls by Christ. His *kenosis* is paralleled in the monks who go to save the women, who are themselves images of the captive human being, redeemed solely by the mercy of God. The drama of their great bondage is built up in order to stress the even greater wonder of their salvation and freedom and their consequent great love. The sinner becomes the contemplative not out of merit or effort, but by the touch of God; all that is needed is to be at the point of need where such mercy can be received. And behind this theme is the image of Israel as the unfaithful bride of Yahweh, fallen humankind as the unfaithful bride of Christ.

The appeal of these stories is perennial, but it has perhaps been blurred by the kind of literal interest taken in them by later writers. For instance, when Anatole France published his deadly indictment of asceticism in 1890, he chose Thaïs as his base. Operas, stories, poems, even a cartoon strip, have chosen this starkest of the stories, which was meant to illustrate the drama of the soul, the dilemma of redemption, and have used it simply to sneer at asceticism by looking only at the surface sense.

To read these stories as they were meant to be read is to enter into a realm of permanent and universal ideas rather than to stay with specific events that are transitory by nature. To understand them, one must adopt their point of view. Once this is done, legend becomes, in a sense they themselves would have approved of, truer than history. The readers were meant to absorb these stories as they would scripture, to understand more about Christ and more about themselves.

To summarize my own reading of these stories, I would like to conclude with four points. First, they present the soul and Christ in the fundamental configuration of salvation for all. They are about the refocusing of desire toward God. The soul, feminine in gender in most languages, is given form as a woman to show the idea of the soul as fallen, as dispersed, as going after other gods, taking the short-term view of pleasure and fulfillment and finding them fundamentally unsatisfying.

Second, a parallel is being drawn between the self-righteous, good in their own strength, and the sinner aware only of need for God. The one praised is the one who has learned how to receive love as a gift. The monks are as much harlots as the women. This underlines the fact that both prayer and repentance begin in heaven; they are not specialist skills that we have to begin for ourselves and learn. Perhaps one of the least regarded of all biblical phrases is "Behold I make all things new," which must include all ways of prayer and of life. This seems to have been emphasized recently in the fact that there is now an alternative to the Gospel reading for Ash Wednesday, the beginning of the penitential period of Lent, so that instead of words about what we should do in order not to show off when fasting, we are presented with the image of the woman who was a sinner weeping at the feet of Jesus. These stories show that everyone is a sinner before the Savior, a creature before the Creator. Perhaps it is also not unrelated to the fact that it is not Mary the all-pure Mother of God who stands before the Risen Christ as the new Eve in the new garden of the resurrection; it is Mary Magdalene the sinner who hears the word "Mary" and, turning herself, says, "Rabboni."

Third, there is no outright contempt here for the beauty of created things. The detailed care of the harlot for her body is not despised, only its focus and intention. It is wasted on men; it is used as a right model for the Christian who should deck his or her soul with equal care and fastidiousness for Christ. One of the most striking facts about the literature of the desert in general is exemplified here: there is no condemnation, no judgment. "They said of Abba Macarius that he would cover the faults that he saw as if he did not see them and those that he heard as if he did not hear them." This aspect of these stories is a reminder, perhaps, of the words of Dostoevsky expanded by Solzhenitsyn in his Nobel address, "One Word of Truth": "Beauty will save the world." The gospel, especially in the desert, is always good news of life and love and beauty.

Fourth, these are no selfish accounts of withdrawal from the world for self-perfection out of fear or shame. Here the forgiveness of one is seen as a cosmic event; it is part of the forgiveness of all. A fountain of mercy is opened and it flows out in tears, that sign of baptism renewed, in the barren desert of one human life, and so it gives new life to all. Today, the unity of all creation is a difficult concept perhaps—in which one fragment of bread is the whole Christ, in which one person before Christ is the whole world there also. The tears of these penitents renew far more than themselves.

One striking example of the fruitfulness of such repentance is the young Augustine, reading in a private garden in Milan toward the end of the greatest empire the world has ever known. He was visited by some friends who described how two colleagues of theirs in the imperial civil service had left the world to live in the desert after hearing of the life of Antony of Egypt, one of the most renowned of the desert fathers. It was the turning point in the conversion of one of the greatest of Christian theologians. "What is the meaning of this story?" Augustine asked himself. "These men have none of our education and yet they stand up and storm the gates of heaven." Unspeakably moved, Augustine left his companions. "I flung myself down," he wrote later, "under a fig tree and gave way to tears."

A man who would not fail to describe himself in his early life as a "harlot" received that touch of mercy through the example of the desert; and the fruit of such tears was clearly for all mankind. Perhaps it is all too simple for us; nothing is required; God asks only the human heart. The message of the gospel in the desert is clear in these stories, and it is that salvation is for all and that it works. Moreover, where one person turns from self-love even by a fraction, a hair's breadth, to receive the love that is Christ, all the world is made fresh and green again:

> In the desert of the heart
> Let the healing fountain start,
> In the prison of his days
> Teach the free man how to praise.

PHILIP YANCEY

LIVING WITH FURIOUS OPPOSITES

(From *Christianity Today*)

> In order to arrive
> at what you are not
> you must go through
> the way in which you are not.
>   T. S. Eliot, *Four Quartets*

As a form of truth in advertising, I feel obligated to explore how faith works in actual daily practice, not just in theory. My own life of faith has included many surprises that no one warned me about. Of course, if the journey did not include a few potholes, dark stretches, and unexpected detours, we would hardly need faith.

I used to think that everything important in my life—marriage, work, close friends, relationship with God—needed to be in order. One malfunctioning area, like one malfunctioning Windows program on my computer, would cause the entire system to crash. I have since learned to pursue God and lean heavily on his grace even when, especially when, one of the other areas is plummeting toward disaster.

As one who writes and speaks publicly about my faith, I have also learned to accept that I am a "clay vessel" whom God may use at a time when I feel unworthy or hypocritical. I can give a speech or preach a sermon that was authentic and alive to me when I composed it, even though as I deliver it, my mind is replaying an argument I just had or nursing an injury I received from a friend. I can write what I believe to be true, even while painfully aware of my own inability to attain what I urge others toward.

Exercising faith in the present means trusting God to work through the encounter before me despite the background clutter of the rest of my life. As the recovery movement has taught us, our very helplessness drives us to God. Addicted persons may discover their weakness to be a gift disguised, for that is what presses them daily toward grace—whereas the rest of us try vainly to deny our need. Anne Lamott, who writes openly about her alcoholism, says she has two favorite prayers: "Thanks, thanks, thanks!" and "Help, help, help!"

I have visited William Cowper's home in the tiny stone village of Olney, England. Cowper wrote some of the church's most popular hymns—"O For a Closer Walk with God," "God Moves in a Mysterious Way His Wonders to Perform," "There Is a Fountain Filled with Blood"—and for a time shared a house with John Newton, the converted slave trader and author of "Amazing Grace." As I toured the sites where Cowper lived, however, I realized how little grace he actually experienced. Tormented by fears that he had committed the unpardonable sin, hounded by rumors of an illicit affair, Cowper suffered a nervous breakdown, attempted suicide several times, and was kept straitjacketed in an insane asylum for his own protection. The last quarter of his life, he avoided church entirely.

In the idealism of youth, I would have pounced upon Cowper as a typical Christian hypocrite, one who wrote about what he could not put into practice. Now, though, as I reflect on the grand words the poet left behind, I see his hymns as perhaps the only marks of clarity in a sadly troubled life. "Redeeming love has been my theme, / And shall be till I die," wrote Cowper. Though he felt little of it personally, he left lasting proof of redeeming love in his treasury of hymns.

God's grace may work that transformation in any of us, using the failures of the present as the very tools to shape us in God's image. As Cowper expressed it:

> Sometimes a light surprises
> The Christian while he sings;
> It is the Lord who rises
> With healing in His wings;
> When comforts are declining,
> He grants the soul again;
> A season of clear shining,
> To cheer it after rain.

Acting Therapy

"My teaching is not my own," Jesus said. "It comes from him who sent me. If anyone chooses to do God's will, he will find out whether my teaching comes from God or whether I speak on my own." Note the sequence: choose to do God's will, and the confidence will later follow. Jesus presents the journey of faith as a personal pilgrimage begun in uncertainty and trust.

Some psychologists practice a school of behavior therapy that encourages the client to "act as if" a state is true, no matter how unreasonable it seems. We change behavior, says this school, not by delving into the past or by trying to align motives with actions, but rather by "acting as if" the change should happen. It's much easier to act your way into feelings than to feel your way into actions.

If you want to preserve your marriage but are not sure you really love your husband, start acting as if you love him: surprise him, show affection, give gifts, be attentive. You may find that feelings of love materialize as you act out the behavior. If you want to forgive your father but find yourself unable, act as if he is forgiven. Say the words, "I forgive you," or "I love you," even though you are not entirely convinced you mean them. Often a change in behavior in one party brings about a remarkable change in the other.

Something similar works in my relationship with God. I wish all obedience sprang from an instinctive desire to please God—alas, it does not. For me, the life of faith sometimes consists in *acting as if* the whole thing is true. I assume that God loves me infinitely, that good will conquer evil, that I can triumph in any adversity—though I have no sure confirmation and only rare epiphanies to spur me along the way. I act as if God is a loving Father; I treat my neighbors as if they truly bear God's image; I forgive those who wrong me as if God has forgiven me first.

I must rely on this technique because of the inherent difference between relating to another human and relating to God. I go to the grocery store and run into a neighbor I have not seen for months. Judy just went through a divorce, I think to myself, remembering we have not heard from her lately. Seeing Judy prods me to act. I ask about her life, check on her children, maybe invite her to church. "We must get together with Judy and the kids," I say to my wife later that day, recalling the grocery-store encounter.

With God, the sequence reverses. I never "see" God. I seldom run into visual clues that remind me of God *unless I am looking*. The act of looking, the pursuit itself, makes possible the encounter. For this reason, Christianity has always insisted that trust and obedience come first, and knowledge follows.

Because of that difference, I persevere at spiritual disciplines no matter how I feel. I do this for one main goal, the goal of all spiritual discipline: I want to know God more fully. And in pursuing a relationship with God, we must come on God's terms, not our own. The famed spiritual director Fénelon advised his students that in difficult times, "Prayer may be less easy, the presence of God less evident and less comforting, outward duties may be harder and less acceptable, but the faithfulness which accompanies them is greater, and that is enough for God." We obey first, Jesus said, and then find the source of his teaching.

Old Testament prophets were quite blunt as they set out the preconditions for knowing God, as in this verse from Micah: "And what does the Lord require of you? To act justly and to love mercy and to walk humbly with your God" (6:8, NIV). Along the same line, the New Testament epistles repeatedly tell us that love for God, which means acting in loving ways toward God, nurtures the relationship and leads toward growth. I do not get to know God, then do his will; I get to know him more deeply *by* doing his will. I enter into an active relationship, which means spending time with God, caring about the people he cares about, and following his commands— whether I spontaneously feel like it or not.

"How shall we begin to know You Who are if we do not begin ourselves to be something of what You are?" prayed Thomas Merton. He adds,

> We receive enlightenment only in proportion as we give ourselves more and more completely to God by humble submission and love. We do not first see, then act: we act, then see. And that is why the man who waits to see clearly, before he will believe, never starts on the journey.

How can we obey without certainty, when plagued by doubts? I have concluded that faith *requires* obedience without full knowledge. Like Job, like Abraham, I accept that much lies beyond my finite grasp, and yet I choose to trust God anyhow, humbly accepting my position as a creature whose worth and very life depend upon God's mercy.

The Obedience Habit

Most of us face a lesser trial than what Job and Abraham confronted, but a trial nonetheless. Faith also gets tested when a sense of God's presence fades or when the very ordinariness of life makes us question whether our responses even matter. We wonder, "What can one person do? What difference will my small effort make?"

I once watched a series on public television based on interviews with survivors from World War II. The soldiers recalled how they spent a particular day. One sat in a foxhole all day; once or twice a German tank drove by, and he shot at it. Others played cards and frittered away the time. A few got involved in furious firefights. Mostly, the day passed like any other day for an infantryman on the front. Later, they learned they had just participated in one of the largest, most decisive engagements of the war, the Battle of the Bulge. It did not *feel* decisive to any of them at the time, because none had the big picture of what was happening elsewhere.

Great victories are won when ordinary people execute their assigned tasks, and a faithful person does not debate each day whether he or she is in the mood to follow the sergeant's orders or go to work at a boring job. We exercise faith by responding to the task that lies before us, for we have control only over our actions in the present moment. I sometimes wish the Gospel writers had included details about Jesus' life before he turned to ministry. For most of his adult life, he worked as a village carpenter. Did he ever question the value of the time he was spending on planing wood or fixing a broken chair?

Ignatius of Loyola, founder of the Jesuits, found that nearly all of his followers went through periods of futility. Their faith began to waver; they questioned their worth; they felt useless. Ignatius set down a series of tests to help identify the cause of spiritual despair. In every case, regardless of cause, Ignatius prescribed the same cure: "In times of desolation, we must never make a change but stand firm and constant in the resolutions and determination in which we were the day before the desolation or in the time of the preceding consolation." He advised fighting spiritual battles with the very weapons hardest to wield at that particular time: more prayer and meditation, more self-examination, more repentance. Obedience, and only obedience, offers a way out.

A person reared in a Christian home who absorbs the faith along with other family values from trusted parents will one day face a crisis that puts loyalty to the test. She may have had religious experiences, may have felt something of the closeness of God. Without warning, that sense vanishes. She feels nothing, except doubts over all that has gone before. Faith loses all support of feeling, and she wonders if she has been living under an illusion. At such a moment, it may feel very foolish to hold on to faith regardless. Yet, as Ignatius counsels, now is the time to "stand firm." Faith can survive periods of darkness, but only if we cling to it in the midst of the darkness.

More often than I would care to admit, doubts gnaw away at me. I wonder about apparent conflicts in the Bible, about suffering and injustice, about the huge gap between the ideals and reality of the Christian life. At such times, I plod on, "acting as if" it is true, relying on the habit of belief, praying for the assurance that eventually comes yet never shields me against the doubts' return.

Truth in the Extremes

As Andrew Greeley said, "If one wishes to eliminate uncertainty, tension, confusion, and disorder from one's life, there is no point in getting mixed up either with Yahweh or with Jesus of Nazareth." I grew up expecting the opposite: that a relationship with God would bring order, certainty, and a calm rationality to life. Instead, I have discovered that living in faith involves much dynamic tension.

Throughout church history, Christian leaders have shown an impulse to pin everything down, to reduce behavior and doctrine to absolutes that could be answered on a true/false test. Strangely, I do not find this tendency in the Bible. Far from it. I find instead the mystery and uncertainty that characterize any relationship, especially a relationship between a perfect God and fallible human beings.

In a memorable phrase that became the virtual cornerstone of his theology, G. K. Chesterton said, "Christianity got over the difficulty of combining furious opposites by keeping them both and keeping them both furious." Most heresies come from espousing one opposite at the expense of the other.

Uncomfortable with paradox, Christians tend to tilt in one direction or the other, usually with disastrous consequences. Read the theologians of the first few centuries as they try to fathom Jesus, the center of our faith, who was somehow fully God and fully man. Read the theologians of the Reformation as they discover the majestic implications of God's sovereignty, then strive to keep their followers from settling into a resigned fatalism. Read the theologians of today as they debate the intricacies of written revelation: a Bible that expresses God's words to us that is nonetheless authored by individuals of widely varying intelligence, personality, and writing style.

The first shall be last; find your life by losing it; work out your salvation with fear and trembling, for it is God who works in you; he who stoops lowest climbs highest; where sin abounds grace abounds more—all these profound principles of life appear in the New Testament and none easily reduces to logical consistency. "Truth is not in the middle, and not in one extreme, but in both extremes," nineteenth-century British pastor Charles Simeon remarked. With some reluctance, I have come to agree.

Inside every person on earth, we believe, the image of God can be found. Yet inside each person there lives also a beast. Any religious or political system that does not account for both extremes—furious opposites, in Chesterton's phrase—will sorely fail (surprisingly, the utopians' failures bring down more catastrophe than the cynics'). As a rabbi put it, "A man should carry two stones in his pocket. On one should be inscribed, 'I am but dust and ashes.' On the other, 'For my sake was the world created.' And he should use each stone as he needs it."

Life Really Is Difficult

The dynamic tension inside each one of us works itself out in daily life, exposing what truly lies inside our hearts. Scott Peck's book *The Road Less Traveled* spent more time on the *New York Times* best-seller list than any book in history, and I believe the secret of its success unfolds from the very first sentence: "Life is difficult." Peck raised a thoughtful protest against the how-to, problem-solving books that normally occupy such lists—and especially occupy the Christian best-seller lists.

When a woman gives birth to a profoundly retarded child, no how-to book will remove the pain. Poverty and injustice do not go away, despite our best programs. Kids in the most affluent suburbs shoot their classmates at school. Marriage problems don't get solved. Death snares us all eventually. And any faith that does not account for complexities such as these cannot last. Quite simply, being human is hazardous to health. Unlike angels, human beings get cancer, lose their jobs, and go hungry. We need a faith that somehow allows the possibility of joy in the midst of suffering and realism in the midst of praise.

I used to believe that Christianity solved problems and made life easier. Increasingly, I believe that my faith complicates life, in ways it should be complicated. As a Christian, I cannot *not* care about the environment, about homelessness and poverty, about racism and religious persecution, about injustice and violence. God does not give me that option.

The late Quaker philosopher Elton Trueblood recognized this. He wrote, "In many areas, the gospel, instead of taking away people's burdens, actually adds to them." He cited John Woolman, a successful Quaker merchant who lived a comfortable life until God convicted him of the offense of slavery. Woolman gave up his prosperous business, used his money to purchase slaves' freedom, wore undyed suits to avoid using dye produced by slave labor, traveled on foot because slaves were not permitted to ride in carriages, and refused to eat sugar, rum, molasses, and other products tainted by slave labor. Largely because of this "quiet revolutionary," by 1787 not a single American Quaker owned a slave. Trueblood continued:

> Occasionally we talk of our Christianity as something that solves problems, and there is a sense in which it does. Long before it does so, however, it increases both the number and the intensity of the problems. Even our intellectual questions are increased by the acceptance of a

strong religious faith. If a man wishes to avoid the disturbing effect of paradoxes, the best advice is for him to leave
the Christian faith alone.

At the heart of the gospel lies the paradox of the yoke.
Jesus offers us comfort—"Come to me, all you who are weary
and burdened, and I will give you rest"—but the comfort consists in taking on a new burden, his own burden. "Take my
yoke upon you and learn from me, for I am gentle and humble
in heart, and you will find rest for your souls. For my yoke is
easy and my burden is light" (Matt. 11:29–30).

Jesus offers a peace that involves new turmoil, a rest that
involves new tasks. The "peace of God, which transcends all
understanding" promised in the New Testament is a peace in
the midst of warfare, a calmness in the midst of fear, a confidence in the midst of doubt. Living as resident aliens in a
strange land, citizens of a secret kingdom, what other kind of
peace should we expect? In this world, restlessness, and not
contentment, is a sign of health. The Bible uses the word "pondering" to describe how a person carries this kind of tension.
When Jesus' mother Mary encountered things she could not
rationally resolve, she held them inside her soul, "pondering"
them, carrying the tension rather than trying to eliminate it.

My father-in-law, a lifelong Bible teacher with strong
Calvinist roots, found his faith troubled in his final years. A
degenerative nerve disease confined him to bed, impeding him
from most of the activities that gave him pleasure. His thirty-
nine-year-old daughter battled a severe form of diabetes.
Financial pressures mounted. During the most severe crisis, he
composed a Christmas letter and mailed it to others in the

family. Many things that he had once taught he now felt uneasy about. What could he believe with certainty? He came up with these three things: "Life is difficult. God is merciful. Heaven is sure." These things he could count on. When his daughter died of diabetic complications the very next week, he clung to those truths ever more fiercely.

Mr. Hopeful's Advice

Paul mentions three Christian virtues—faith, hope, love—at the end of 1 Corinthians 13, his great chapter on love, and each one expresses a paradox.

Love involves caring about people most of us would prefer not to care about. In Paul's words, love is patient, does not envy, is not self-seeking, is not easily angered, keeps no record of wrongs; it always protects, always trusts, always hopes, always perseveres. Such a program may seem reasonable on another planet run by different rules, but not on our planet, where people act with injustice, meanness, and vengeance. By nature we keep records, right wrongs, and demand our rights; love does not.

Hope gives us the power to look beyond circumstances that otherwise appear hopeless. Hope keeps hostages alive when they have no rational proof that anyone cares about their plight; it entices farmers to plant seeds in spring after three straight years of drought. "Hope that is seen is no hope at all," Paul told the Romans. He mentions some of the good things that might come out of difficulties: "Suffering produces perseverance; perseverance, character; and character, hope" (5:3–5). He lists hope at the end, instead of where I would normally expect it, at the beginning, as the fuel that keeps a person going. But, no, hope emerges *from* the struggle, a byproduct of faithfulness.

As for faith, it will always mean believing in what cannot be proven, committing to that of which we can never be sure. A person who lives in faith must proceed on incomplete evidence, trusting in advance what will only make sense in reverse. As Dennis Covington has written, "Mystery is not the absence of meaning, but the presence of more meaning than we can comprehend."

For several centuries, *The Pilgrim's Progress* sold more copies annually than any book except the Bible. Rereading it recently, I was struck by how John Bunyan's version of the Christian life differs from what I read in most Christian books today. Every few pages, the pilgrim makes some stupid mistake and nearly loses his life. He takes wrong turns and detours. His only companion sinks in the Slough of Despond. The pilgrim yields to worldly temptations. He flirts with suicide and decides again and again to abandon the quest. At one such moment, Mr. Hopeful assures him, "Be of good cheer, my brother, for I feel the bottom, and it is sound." Acting in courageous faith, the pilgrim continues his journey and in the end arrives at his destination, the Celestial City.

The Pilgrim's Progress proved a reliable guidebook for millions of Christians over the years. Cheery, problem-solving books offer a much more attractive road map today, but I cannot help wondering what we have lost along the way.

BIOGRAPHICAL NOTES

JOSEPH BOTTUM is books and arts editor of *The Weekly Standard*. His essays and reviews appear regularly in *First Things*, *The Wall Street Journal*, and other periodicals. He is the editor of a forthcoming collection of primary documents on Pius XII's pontificate.

STEPHEN L. CARTER is William Nelson Cromwell Professor of Law at Yale University Law School. His essay in this volume was published in book form in *God's Name in Vain: The Wrongs and Rights of Religion in Politics*. Among his earlier books are *Integrity*, *Civility*, and *The Culture of Disbelief: How American Law and Politics Trivialize Religious Devotion*. He is at work on his first novel.

DENNIS COVINGTON'S *Sand Mountain: Snake Handling and Redemption in Southern Appalachia* was a finalist for the 1995 National Book Award for nonfiction. He is also the author of two novels, *Lizard* and *Lasso the Moon*, and—with his wife, novelist Vicki Covington—the memoir *Cleaving: The Story of a Marriage*.

CATHERINE H. CROUCH is a postdoctoral fellow in applied physics at Harvard University. For her essay in this volume she received a prize from the John Templeton Foundation.

DEBORAH SMITH DOUGLAS, trained in literature and law, is a laywoman in the Episcopal Church. She conducts retreats and writes on spiritual matters. With her husband, David, she has recently completed a guide to historic Christian sites in Britain.

EDWARD E. ERICSON, JR., is professor of English at Calvin College. He is the author of two books on Aleksandr Solzhenitsyn and a study of Mikhail Bulgakov's novel, *The Master and Margarita*. His abridged, one-volume edition of Solzhenitsyn's *Gulag Archipelago* will be reissued next year by HarperCollins with a new introduction.

ERIK H. ERIKSON was one of the foremost psychoanalytic theorists of the twentieth century. Perhaps best known for his account of stages in the adult life cycle, he was the author of such influential books as *Childhood and Society*, *Young Man Luther*, and *Gandhi's Truth*.

ELIZABETH FOX-GENOVESE teaches literature, history, and women's studies at Emory University. Among her books are *Feminism Is Not the Story of My Life* and, most recently, *Reconstructing History: The Emergence of a New Historical Society*, which she edited with Elisabeth Lasch-Quinn.

DAVID HANSEN is pastor of Kenwood Baptist Church in Cincinnati, Ohio. He is the author of *The Art of Pastoring*, *A Little Handbook on Having a Soul*, and *Long Wandering Prayer: An Invitation to Walk with God*.

SARAH E. HINLICKY is a student at Princeton Theological Seminary.

ALAN JACOBS is professor of English at Wheaton College. He is the author of *A Visit to Vanity Fair: Moral Essays on the Present Age*, just published, and *What Became of Wystan: Change and Continuity in Auden's Poetry*. In addition he has three books forthcoming, the first of which, *The Hermeneutics of Love: A Theology of Reading*, will appear in the spring of 2002. He can be heard regularly on the *Mars Hill Audio Journal*.

PRESTON JONES teaches American history at Logos Academy in Dallas, Texas. He is a reviewer for the *National Post* (Toronto, Canada) and publishes in a wide variety of other periodicals and journals, both popular and scholarly.

JOSEPH T. LIENHARD, S.J., is professor of theology at Fordham University. He is the author of many studies in patristics, including *St. Joseph in Early Christianity: Devotion and Theology* and *"Contra Marcelleum": Marcellus of Ancyra and Fourth-Century Theology*.

ROGER LUNDIN is Clyde S. Kilby Professor of English at Wheaton College. Among his books are the prizewinning biography *Emily Dickinson and the Art of Belief* and *The Culture of Interpretation: Christian Faith and the Postmodern World*. He is the editor of *Disciplining Hermeneutics: Interpretation in Christian Perspective*.

ALICE MCDERMOTT'S novel *Charming Billy* won the 1998 National Book Award for Fiction. She is the author of three other novels: *That Night, At Weddings and Wakes,* and *The Bigamist's Daughter.*

GILBERT MEILAENDER holds the Phyllis and Richard Duesenberg Chair in Christian Ethics at Valparaiso University. Among his many books are *Bioethics: A Primer for Christians* and, most recently, *Things That Count: Essays Moral and Theological.*

RICHARD JOHN NEUHAUS is editor-in-chief of *First Things* and head of the Institute for Religion and Public Life. He is the editor of *The Second One Thousand Years: Ten People Who Defined a Millennium,* a collection of essays originally published in *First Things,* two of which appeared in *Best Christian Writing* 2000. A longer version of his essay in this year's volume was published in *The Eternal Pity: Reflections on Dying,* a book edited by Neuhaus.

VIRGINIA STEM OWENS is a novelist, essayist, and poet. She directed the Milton Center at Kansas Newman College, a training ground for writers, before moving to Texas to take care of her aging parents.

REYNOLDS PRICE is the author of more than 30 books—novels, stories, poems, essays, translations, memoirs—and has won most of the awards available to an American writer. Two of his books offer his own translations of Scripture: *A Palpable God: Thirty Stories Translated from the Bible with an Essay on the Origins and Life and Narrative* and *Three Gospels.* His 1994 memoir, *A Whole New Life,* recounts a miraculous healing from cancer. A letter from a young man who read that book, himself diagnosed with cancer, prompted Price to write *A Letter to a Man in* *the Fire: Does God Exist and Does He Care?* For more than 40 years he has taught at Duke University, where he is James B. Duke Professor of English.

SCOTT SAWYER is a writer and editor whose essays and reviews have appeared in *Christianity and the Arts*, the *Mars Hill Review*, and many other publications. *Earthly Fathers: A Memoir* is his first book.

BENEDICTA WARD, of the Sisters of the Love of God, is reader in the history of Christian spirituality at the University of Oxford. She is the author of a number of books on early monasticism and the Middle Ages. Her essay in this volume was given at Harvard Divinity School as the Dudleian Lecture in Revealed Religion.

PHILIP YANCEY is the author of many books, including *The Jesus I Never Knew*, for which he won the 1996 Gold Medallion Christian Book of the Year Award, *What's So Amazing About Grace?*, and, most recently, *Reaching for the Invisible God*.

READER'S DIRECTORY

For more information about or subscriptions to the periodicals represented in The Best Christian Writing 2001, *please contact:*

Books & Culture
465 Gundersen Drive
Carol Stream, IL 60188

Christian Century
104 S. Michigan Avenue
Chicago, IL 60603–5901

Christianity Today
465 Gundersen Drive
Carol Stream, IL 60188

Commonweal
475 Riverside Drive, Room 405
New York, NY 10115

CRISIS
1814 1/2 N Street, NW
Washington, DC 20036

DoubleTake
55 Davis Square
Somerville, MA 02144

First Things
The Institute on Religion and
    Public Life
156 Fifth Avenue, Suite 400
New York, NY 10010

Harvard Divinity Bulletin
45 Francis Avenue
Cambridge, MA 02138

Image
3307 Third Avenue West
Seattle, WA 98119

Leadership
465 Gundersen Drive
Carol Stream, IL 60188

Pro Ecclesia
Box 327
Delhi, NY 13753

re:generation quarterly
P.O. Box 3000
Denville, NJ 07834–9369

The Responsive Community
2130 H Street, NW, Suite 714
Washington, DC 20052

Weavings
1908 Grand Avenue
P.O. Box 189
Nashville, TN 37202–0189

"The Only Honest Man" by Alan Jacobs. First published in *Books & Culture*, May/June 2000. Copyright 2000 by Alan Jacobs. Reprinted by permission of Alan Jacobs.

"History, Discernment, and the Christian Life" by Preston Jones. First delivered as a Logos Institute lecture in September 2000 at Logos Academy in Dallas, Texas. First published, in slightly different form, in *Christianity Today*, April 2, 2001, under the title "How to Serve Time." Copyright 2000 by Preston Jones. Reprinted by permission of Preston Jones.

"Origen and the Crisis of the Old Testament in the Early Church" by Joseph T. Lienhard. First published in *Pro Ecclesia*, Summer 2000. Copyright 2000 by Joseph T. Lienhard. Reprinted by permission of Joseph T. Lienhard.

"Living by *Lear*" by Roger Lundin. First published on beliefnet.com. Copyright 2000 by Roger Lundin. Reprinted by permission of Roger Lundin.

"Confessions of a Reluctant Catholic" by Alice McDermott. First published in *Commonweal*, February 11, 2000. Copyright 2000 by Alice McDermott. Reprinted by permission of Alice McDermott.

"Divine Summons" by Gilbert Meilaender. First published in *The Christian Century*, November 1, 2000. Copyright 2000 by Gilbert Meilaender. Reprinted by permission of Gilbert Meilaender.

"Born Toward Dying" by Richard John Neuhaus. First published in *First Things*, February 2000. Copyright 2000 by

Richard John Neuhaus. Reprinted by permission of Richard John Neuhaus.

"Death and Texas" by Virginia Stem Owens. First published in *Books & Culture*, November/December 2000. Copyright 2000 by Virginia Stem Owens. Reprinted by permission of Virginia Stem Owens.

"Letter to a Man in the Fire" by Reynolds Price. From *Letter to a Man in the Fire*, Reynolds Price, published by Scribner in 1999. Copyright 1999 by Reynolds Price. Reprinted by permission of Reynolds Price.

"Earthly Fathers" by Scott Sawyer. First published in book form as part of *Earthly Fathers* by Zondervan in 2001. Copyright 2001 by Scott Sawyer. Reprinted by permission of Scott Sawyer.

"Hermits and Harlots" by Benedicta Ward. First published in the *Harvard Divinity Bulletin*, Fall 2000. Copyright 2000 by the President and Fellows of Harvard College. Reprinted by permission of the *Harvard Divinity Bulletin*.

"Living with Furious Opposites" by Philip Yancey. First published in magazine form in *Christianity Today*, September 4, 2000. Adapted from *Reaching for the Invisible God*, by Philip Yancey, published by Zondervan in 2000. Copyright 2000 by Philip Yancey. Reprinted by permission of Philip Yancey.